Family Farming

A New Economic Vision

MARTY STRANGE

University of Nebraska Press, Lincoln and London

Institute for Food and Development Policy, San Francisco

Acknowledgments for the use of
previously published material appear on page xi.

Copyright © 1988 by
the Institute for Food and Development Policy
All rights reserved
Manufactured in the United States of America

The paper in this book meets the minimum require-
ments of American National Standard for Information
Sciences—Permanence of Paper for Printed Library
Materials, ANSI Z39.48–1984.

Library of Congress Cataloging-in-Publication Data
Strange, Marty.
Family farming: a new economic vision / Marty Strange.
p.   cm.
Bibliography: p.
Includes index.
ISBN 0-8032-4156-9 (alk. paper)
1. Family farms–United States. 2. Agriculture–
Economic aspects–United States. 3. Agricultural
innovations–United States. 4. Agriculture and
state–United States. I. Title.
HD 1476.U5S86 1988   338.1′6–dc19   87-27012   CIP

To my parents, Albert H. Strange, Sr. and Agnes Tisdel Strange

Contents

Preface

In the early 1970s I was on my way to law school at an East Coast university after having spent three years working in various antipoverty programs in Nebraska. I stopped in Walthill, Nebraska, intending to spend a few months in gainful employment at yet one more community-action program before enrolling. Within a few weeks, President Nixon had unveiled a budget that called for the elimination of the nation's War on Poverty, and of the local agency that employed me.

It was not a personal crisis for me because the money wouldn't run out until I was tucked away in school, but I was stunned by the local response. The governing board of the community-action program convened and drew up a news release announcing its regret at the president's decision and its intent to ignore his message. The War on Poverty wasn't about to end in northeast Nebraska, even if the federal commitment to it did. They would carry on, they said, with or without Mr. Nixon.

Their survival strategy involved separating their local organization into two parts. One part would continue to provide services to poor people in northeast Nebraska—meals to the elderly, preschool programs for children, and other social services. It would be funded by federal grants and contracts still available for social services.

The other part would be leaner and more political. It would take on public policy issues, especially agricultural policy issues, that struck at the root causes of rural poverty in northeast Nebraska. It would do research, advocate positions, and organize support. It would be financed by private sources—individuals, churches, private foundations—shedding its relationship with the federal government and its vulnerability to federal budget cuts. Don Ralston, then the deputy director of the agency, and I were asked to organize this "other" part.

I might have said, "No, thank you, I've got other plans," but I didn't. I was intrigued by this rural resistance, especially since the leaders among the all-volunteer governing board were farmers. Their independent, don't-push-me-around attitude was appealing. I knew how stubborn farmers could be, because I'd spent a good part of the previous three years in other parts of Nebraska battling with them over such things as housing and food stamps for migrant and seasonal farm workers. I'd come to doubt the agrarian, progressive image of farmers that I'd brought with me from Massachusetts. But here were farmers who fit that image battling the arrogance of Washington politicians about to turn their backs on the poor. I decided that American agriculture was a bundle of paradoxes, and that within family farming there must be a fierce war of values that was more important to learn about than anything they would teach me in law school. So I called the Coast and told them I wasn't coming.

As it turned out, the antipoverty agency carried on without Mr. Nixon, but with federal funds. A year after his notice to terminate the War on Poverty, Mr. Nixon was battling unsuccessfully to escape his own political termination, the War on Poverty in northeast Nebraska was in full force, and we had launched the other part—the Center for Rural Affairs—to reckon with social and economic justice issues within American agriculture.

This book is my unfinished report on our progress in understanding these issues. I am especially grateful to the Center board and staff for the lessons they've taught me, which make up the bulk of this work. In many ways it is really their work, interpreted by me. Particular credit is due to Center staff people whose analysis I've borrowed heavily from, especially Dennis Demmel, Ron Krupicka, Rob Aiken, Sarah Fast, Richard Ness, Eugene Severens, Chuck Hassebrook, Annette Higby, and Nancy Thompson. Lynn Spivak, whose pioneering research into changes taking place in pork production really gave the Center credibility to build on, deserves thanks for laying the foundation for this book. Special thanks are due to Chuck Hassebrook, who has done more to set things right in American agriculture than anyone I know, and with whom

I've discussed every issue raised here many times, and benefited from each discussion.

In another way, this book has been made possible only by Don Ralston, my colleague and co-director at the Center since 1973. His steadiness at the helm allows me to work on extended projects like this book without feeling guilty about time taken from other Center projects. Janet Nielsen, the Center's administrative assistant who has kept things running smoothly for many years, is another important reason why projects like this can be undertaken.

Of course, no group offers much that is new unless it is the product of disagreements that are thrashed out honestly. The Center has spawned many such internal disagreements, from which I've learned a good deal. Where those disagreements remain unresolved, I've spoken my own piece in these pages rather than duck some crucial issues. In that final, essential way, the book is mine. I'm particularly indebted to Vince Rossiter, Bob Warrick, Ken Mesner, Bob Steffen, Pat Rogers, David Hansen, Allen Heine, and Lois Schank for the chance to hear the arguments, and for remaining friends with me and each other.

The manuscript was reviewed in whole or in part by Harold F. Breimyer, Ted Kooser, Charles Francis, Gabriel Hegyes, V. James Rhodes, Vernon W. Ruttan, Phillip Raup, Ron Krupicka, Chuck Hassebrook, Ruth Tonachel, Eugene Severens, and Jim Browne. They ferreted out most of the mistakes and I found a few more. Those we might have missed, or those that I might not have acknowledged as mistakes at all, are mine to hear about.

I also want to acknowledge and thank North Point Press for permission to use material from "The Economic Structure of a Sustainable Agriculture," a chapter I wrote for publication in *Meeting the Expectations of the Land,* copyright © 1984 by the Land Institute, Inc.

And a warm thank you to Gary and Delores Young and John and Theresa Fleming for letting me describe their farms in some detail, and for being the kind of people they are.

Finally, thanks to Frances Moore Lappé, cofounder of the Institute for Food and Development Policy. She urged me to write the book and was patient with the pace of a writer whose first duty is not to writing, but to social action. She deserves special thanks for the very careful way she edited the text for clarity. If anyone could turn a sow's ear into a silk purse, it would be Frankie. Of course, the sow has something to say about it, and if this work still resembles a sow's ear more than a silk purse, it's my fault, not hers.

Introduction

Most Americans don't think much about farming. It's what goes on where not much else is going on. That's not necessarily an unkind impression. In fact, farming is a collage of blurry but generally favorable images, whether they be the bucolic image of stern, self-disciplined, hard working, and austere life-styles, or the romantic image of fresh air and sunshine, simple pleasures, and straightforward ways. In a jaded, complex world, we're attracted to the common sense and basic values these images convey.

But increasingly, farming also has a troublesome image. We hear more about farmers going broke, rural communities dying, the high cost of government farm programs, and the farm chemicals in the food we eat and the water we drink. These dark images trouble us not only because they conflict with our more comfortable images of farming, but because we don't understand them.

At the heart of all these images is a powerful cultural institution we call the family farm. Perhaps no part of our cultural life is more widely approved of in America. It is praised for its virtues and pitied for its problems. Defending it has long been the common rhetorical fare of politicians and opinion makers. You can't get a farm bill through Congress without invoking the cause of the family farm.

But in fact, the family farm is an institution eroding from within, struggling somewhere between decline and death to hang on to the things it stands for. A long-term transformation is under way in American agriculture from small-scale, broad-based family farming to large-scale, industrial farming. This transformation is complex, incremental, and pervasive. It occurs subtly, within family farms as they grow, as well as from the outside as corporate and other types of investor-owned farms develop. The changes involve methods of food production, ownership of land, and the health of rural communities. But most important, this transformation is unnecessary and, to many of us, undesirable.

A number of trends underlie this transformation. One is the trend toward bigness and concentration. Over half the food in America is produced on about 4 percent of the farms, and economists project that further concentration of production can be expected. Another trend is toward specialization, as more farms produce a narrower range of crops or livestock and invest larger sums of money in more expensive, less versatile buildings and equipment.

Implicit in these trends is another: the separation of people from the land, of ownership from work. More people who work the land have little or no hope of owning it, and possibly no desire to do so. On the other hand, those who own land often have no desire or need to farm for a living. Thus, many who actually farm have little long-term interest in conserving the land for future generations.

These trends have fragmented agriculture into a potpourri of farm types. Where once the word "farm" sufficed there are now "small farms," "hobby farms," "family farms," "corporate farms," and even "superfarms," and none has a clear definition. In terms of our images of traditional agriculture, some of these actually sound incongruous. If ever there were an oxymoron, it is the term "corporate farm." So, where the economic character of agriculture once seemed clear, it now seems jumbled. The simple term "farmer," which has a common meaning and suggests a real person, has largely been replaced in official circles by the more impersonal and less definitive term "farm operator."

As agriculture changes, so do its problems. Farms are larger and more complex—technologically, financially, and managerially. The small group of superfarms that now dominate food production operate on thinner margins of error than have farms of the past. They have more money at stake, more debt, heavier cash-flow requirements. Locked financially into certain production techniques, they also have fewer options about how to farm. They are rigid, less resilient than the vaunted family farms of old. The idea of tightening your belt and hunkering down during hard times just doesn't fit many modern farms any more than it fits most major corporations.

The risk of making mistakes that are devastating to the farm are therefore greater, and so is the risk to society that a few very large farms will all make the same mistake, jeopardizing the cost of food and the quality of the environment. Vulnerability is the watch-word of modern farming operations.

Agriculture as a whole thus compares less and less favorably with our traditional image of the family farm. At least emotionally, this bothers a good many of us. We were comfortable with the family farm. Still, these changes, like others in our fast-changing world, seem to be a product of natural economic selection. And since they are remote to our daily lives, we don't get too worked up about them.

This book is written by someone who knows those feelings well. I have had to study both farming and agricultural economics as an outsider. I've never been a farmer, and growing up in rural west-ern Massachusetts, I could count the number of farm families I knew on the fingers of one hand. Mostly they came from the hill towns whose children attended the consolidated high school in my hometown. And despite a degree in agricultural economics, I don't consider myself a farm economist, either.

Nonetheless, the future of family farming has been near the center of my life since 1973. Since then, I have served as codirector of the Center for Rural Affairs, a Nebraska nonprofit organiza-tion. This book shares some of what I've learned during those years.

It is unabashed in its advocacy for family farming. A system of small-scale, widely dispersed farms, owned and operated by in-dependent proprietors who are permitted to enjoy the fruits of their efforts, is best for our society in these times. I don't think family farming is best for all societies in all times, but given our cul-tural values and natural endowments, I think it is best for us.

My perspective is admittedly a little provincial. It focuses on the Midwest and its institutions. But that is the region where both the image and the reality of family farming are strongest, and where the future of family farming hangs in the balance of decisions we are now making about farm policy.

Though sympathetic, my view of family farming is not uncrit-ical. Because I acquired my affection for family farming rather than inherited it, I have never felt the need to apologize for its short-comings. They are many.

No tradition is more glorious in its acclamation of egalitarian values than the agrarian tradition, yet none tolerates and even admires the accumulation of wealth more. No tradition proclaims more loudly the value of neighborhood and community, yet few have tolerated and rewarded predatory behavior more. Most disappointingly, no system of agriculture brags more that it respects the soil, yet none has respected it less. We've done more damage to the topsoil of the Midwest in a hundred years of family farming than the communal cultures of the Native Americans did in a millennium, or the ancient civilizations of the Middle East did in their span. We have been richly endowed, and we have squandered it.

But the fact that family farming has fostered some disappointing behavior and cloaked it in self-righteousness is no excuse to abandon it. So what if the performance falls short of expectations? The remedy is not to forsake the expectations, but to make the performance equal to them. Farmers should be held accountable for the way they treat the soil, and their predatory behavior should be restrained. But to reach these conclusions requires that we love family farming enough to resist its dark side. This book is for people who do, or who would like to.

* * *

The first three chapters place the family-farming issue into a cultural and historical context. The farm crisis of the 1980s should be seen as part of a dramatic transformation in the institutional character of agriculture. This crisis is essentially financial—a product of misplaced values, both economic and cultural. As a result, where earlier crises resulted largely in farm consolidation, with fewer family farmers operating more land and using more technology, this crisis is causing more fundamental changes in the way farms are owned and operated.

To get a grip on this change, it is important to contrast as sharply as possible the traditional family-farming system from the emerging system of agriculture that many call industrial agribusiness. I overdraw this difference in Chapter 2, creating a caricature of both farming systems, in order to make the point that many farmers who consider themselves family farmers have bought into the values of industrial agribusiness.

This fact has important political implications. Those who have bought into industrial values are the farmers with the most political power. They dominate farm policy and work their will on the system as a whole, producing public policies that reward expansion and economic cannibalism, even when it is economically unwise. When from time to time government intervenes to insulate farmers from the natural consequence—attrition—it merely reinforces these competitive values. Agriculture loves competition but abhors failure. Those whose personal behavior is most destructive of family farming are therefore frequently rewarded most by policies allegedly designed to save the family farm. Helping people to understand the political significance of that irony is the most important objective of this book.

This dilemma is revealed most clearly in the land issue. Who will own land, how will they pay for it, and who will decide its use are the most basic questions in farm policy, yet they are rarely publicly discussed. They are as vital today as they were two hundred years ago. Land has long been the resource that places limits on economic opportunity in agriculture. As such, it is not only a valuable natural resource, but a financial asset as well. Land is no longer needed simply as a place to use one's labor, but is also coveted as a place on which to deploy one's technology and capital. In such an environment, those who are better financed will often prevail over those who are more skilled at farming. In Chapter 3 I outline the importance of this issue as the crux of the future of family farming.

The next two chapters address two prevailing myths that prejudice farm-policy discussions. The first myth is that American agriculture is now dominated by two kinds of farms. Very small farms dominate in numbers, but, the argument goes, they really aren't farms at all because they depend on nonfarm income. For this same reason they aren't really an agricultural policy issue, either. On the other hand, very large farms dominate in production, and while they are farms, they aren't really *family* farms, and don't need any help even if they are. The middle-sized farms between them are at the center of the family farm issue. They are too small to compete with the big farms, but too big to be mere hobbies. What to do with them is a problem. But since they are disappearing at a reasonably rapid rate, anyway, maybe the best thing is to do nothing.

Chapter 4 challenges this by now conventional analysis of the structure of agriculture, which suffers from a static, one-dimensional way of measuring farms by their volume of sales. With a multidimensional approach, a completely different picture emerges in which small, commercial farms are an important and resilient part of the food-production system. This perspective demands a fresh analysis of policy implications, especially with respect to the need to balance the competitive relationship between various kinds of farms.

Chapter 5 dismantles the second myth, that efficiency improves as farm size increases. The bigger-is-better notion is deeply ingrained in agricultural economics and it underlies most of American farm policy. But it is not well founded. I discuss the analytical weaknesses that lead to this false conclusion and offer some hard evidence to contradict it. Most important, I believe farms above a very moderate size may become increasingly inefficient, suggesting that the public has something to lose by encouraging farms to expand.

If Chapters 4 and 5 argue that how we look at agriculture determines what we see, Chapters 6 and 7 argue that what we see determines what we do. Believing that bigger is better, many farmers have decided to expand their farms, and the result for many has been disastrous. The financial crisis of the 1980s has affected big farms more than has been widely recognized. Out of the promise of greater efficiency has emerged a big, troubled farming system, increasingly inefficient and unstable, top-heavy with highly specialized superfarms and unable to right itself without massive public support. As more farms pursue the myth that bigger is better, the general public can expect more instability in American agriculture and more public expenditures to steady it.

To add insult to injury, public policies actually encourage these private mistakes by offering a wide array of subsidies, incentives, and protections for farmers who invest in capital-intensive expansions. In Chapter 7 I discuss how commodity programs, tax policies, and credit policies have been especially effective in persuading farmers to chase the myth that bigger is better. As a result of these mistaken policies, farmers who can't or don't want to expand are put at a disadvantage as wealthier farmers and nonfarmers use these public policies to tighten their grip on available farmland. The result is attrition among existing farmers and diminished opportunity for beginning farmers.

These misguided policies are partly thwarted by the underlying economic merit of smaller farming operations. They are resilient and difficult to crush. They crop up like bindweed in July, weaving their way through the nooks and crannies left by the destructive forces of large-scale farms, finding market niches, resourceful production methods, and better ways of doing things. They do not always prosper, but they persist, despite public policies that would wish them away. Their tenacity sometimes earns them the wrath of the experts whose analysis they defy. They're an irritant. But in fact, much of the hope for restoring family farming as the centerpiece of American agriculture lies in elevating these resourceful farmers as role models.

There are alternatives to current approaches both in public policy and in private behavior, but there are also some traps to be avoided. The most treacherous of these traps lies within the tangled relationship between technology, commodity prices, and land prices. It seems simple enough to try to help family farmers by raising the prices of the commodities they sell. This approach has appealed to many farmers and farm activists for generations.

But as technology has dramatically increased the amount of land farmers can manage and the volume of commodities they can produce, it has also driven commodity prices down and increased competition for land. Unless technology is restrained, efforts to raise commodity prices by fiat will only intensify the demand for land on which to use technologies, driving land prices yet higher. This will be grand for anyone who now owns land, but it will only raise rents for tenants and increase the cost of acquiring land for the next generation of farmers. Most likely, it will result in the establishment of a wealthy landowning elite whose ancestors were farmers, but who no longer need to bother themselves with farming for a living. These complex relationships and the many political dilemmas they create are discussed in Chapter 8.

Ultimately, farmers who recognize that there is little room for them in industrial agribusiness will demand, and shape, a better technology. In doing so, they will be getting back control of their own farms. This is the subject of Chapter 9.

This change in direction requires confronting American agriculture's (and American society's) deterministic attitude toward technology, the view that if it can be done profitably, it will be done and must be allowed. Of course, we are becoming increasingly cautious about the secondary effects of some technologies, but we have not even begun to place restraints on the use of dangerous farm technologies. To the contrary, a twisted loyalty to the family farm has prevented us from imposing the kinds of controls we ought to on farm chemicals, livestock feed additives, and soil-erosive practices.

The great irony is that the technologies that are most environmentally destructive are also those that best accommodate industrial farming systems and therefore most threaten the future of family farming. Many alternative technologies exist or can be developed, but the goals of agricultural research have to be changed in order for this to occur.

The values that currently drive the development of farm technology reflect part of the internal conflict within family farming. On the one hand, family farming adores competition and commercial liberty and elevates self-interest to the the status of inherent virtue. Farm technology today reflects these values. But on the other hand, family farming also proclaims the importance of interdependence, community, and mutuality of interests. In a real way, the battle over the future of family farming depends on the outcome of this internal conflict in its own value base.

WITHIN FAMILY FARMING

These conflicts within family farming must be faced by family farmers and their advocates. This book is intended to delineate the dimensions of the challenge and to offer a new economic vision for the future of family farming.

The public perceives these internal conflicts dimly. We are used to thinking of farmers as a homogeneous interest group with common needs and common interests. We fail to see the important distinctions among farmers, or to appreciate that political differences among them are well founded on differences in their situation and in their personal values. Disagreements among farmers and the proliferation of farm groups therefore confuse us. Politicians are frequently heard to lament that "farmers can't agree on what is best for agriculture." That is true, but it is not necessarily lamentable.

Farmers can't agree both because their interests are genuinely different and because often they have defined their interests individually in terms of their own well-being rather than in terms of the well-being of family farming. Too frequently they have preferred to support policies that favor their individual farms rather than the values they proclaim for family farming. In order to support family farming, their own interests may have to be subjugated to the interests of a system of agriculture that nurtures stable farming communities.

Every farmer, for example, wants the opportunity to own that first piece of land, but few are satisfied with that first piece alone. The individual's right to property is in tension with the abstract right of others to an opportunity. As property rights concentrate, opportunity rights diminish. The more we try to protect the property rights of farmers, especially those who are aggressive competitors, the less we will be able to ensure that those who lack property will have the opportunity to apply their skills to farming. Property rights, like all other rights, are empty rights if most people have no meaningful chance to exercise them.

Public policy should balance these interests, making it possible for each generation of farmers to pay for land by farming it, but restraining the tendency to want more than is necessary to make a good living on the land. If we want a dynamic agriculture that rewards hard work and craftsmanship, we cannot protect the right to accumulate the one physical resource all farmers need—land.

The rights of property also carry with them the obligations of good land use. No part of the social contract governing human behavior should be considered more vital. Stewardship ought to be as much the objective of farm policy as family farming, and if family farmers cannot accommodate their property interests to good land use, they have no claim on public goodwill. Land abuse in the name of family farming is still wrong, and should be curbed by limiting any property right that protects it.

Instead of restraining some of the least admirable traits of farmers, however, the general public and its elected officials have generally been inclined to "help the farmer." In doing so, they have frequently mistaken the immediate interests of the most vocal farmers for the long-term interests of family farming. Restoring family farming requires placing its public value as an economic system above the individual interests of those farmers who have staked their own fate on its continuing decline. We need to see beyond the individual family farm.

This book is not a blueprint for agricultural reform. Specific suggestions are tightly packaged in a special section following the main body of the book. They are rough proposals and are not intended to be comprehensive or detailed. Some important issues are scarcely mentioned: the marketing system, the distance between consumers and farmers, the role of the American farmer in the world food system, the quality of food, and the relationship between agricultural reform and rural community development are but a few examples.

My goal is to assist that stage preceding all good policy action—

asking the right questions. Answers change with time and circumstances, but the important questions are timeless. Instead of a prescription for change, I offer a way of looking at the problem that is grounded in widely shared human values such as community, conservation, equality, opportunity, and mutuality.

Does it really matter? It might not. If the underlying economic problems of industrial farming methods are what I think they are, those methods cannot prevail. But what will we have lost along the way as these economic truths play out their influence?

When I first moved from Massachusetts to Nebraska I was struck by one difference in particular between the two places. In Nebraska, there were still many self-employed people who owned the productive assets that provided their means of sustenance. They were less independent than they liked to think they were, and despite claims to the contrary, they were no harder working or civic-minded than the working-class people I had known in Massachusetts. But they owned their own destiny in a way that most people never will. They had control over resources and a capacity to change things for the better. It is sad to see that capacity atrophy as family farming gives way to more powerful but less durable institutions. It is frustrating to see family farming erode from within as its commercial values overpower its community values.

Nonetheless, family farming remains one of the last vestiges of widespread ownership and control of production by working people in our society. It is flawed and it is crippled, and its decline has been underway a long time, but it is not yet dead. There are durable qualities within family farming.

The discomforting fact that the rest of us have to face is that because we live in a democracy, each of us has a duty to sort out these complex economic and social issues in American agriculture. Wishing that farmers would all get together and do it for us is both unrealistic and irresponsible. We might hope for their leadership; indeed, we might demand it. But at the base of our political system lies the expectation that all of us will help search for answers.

The democratic tradition, like the family farming tradition, has its disappointments, of course. But it is wiser to demand better civic performance from the public than to give up on democracy, just as it is wiser to demand better of family farming than to give up on it. None of the progress we've made in civil rights, environmental protection, and other complex social issues justifies giving up. We have a long way to go in these areas, but we've come a long way, too.

In agriculture we have barely begun the journey. The issues are elusive and complex, and experts seem to dissuade us from every hopeful course. But while apathy and fatalism are always the enemies of good self-government, many people do care and are willing to take the risk of trying. In the past ten years, agriculture has catapulted from the margins of American social-policy debate to the center. It is clear that the need for clear thinking in farm policy and the public demand for it have rarely coincided as they do today. This is a time for both thinking and doing. The farm crisis of the 1980s offers a good starting point.

1.

Farm Crisis Again

American agriculture burst onto the front page and into the top spot on the evening news in the mid-1980s. Protests, demonstrations, confrontations, soft-spoken pleas, and hard-sounding rhetoric filled the air as farmers and their advocates made their case for the family farm. The irony of farmers applying for food stamps, the poignancy of farms that had been in the family for four generations being sold at auction, and the outrage of food producers going broke as millions starved in Africa—all this caught public notice. For the first time in many years, farm prices got more attention than food prices. Not since the Depression had so much ink been devoted to the plight of farmers. Even the *Wall Street Journal* struggled through a five-part series on the changes taking place in agriculture.

Nothing, it seems, so invokes the American sense of injustice like a farm crisis. It's the moneyed interests tearing hard-working farmers from their sweat-enriched farms. It's Tom Joad forced into California refugee camps in *The Grapes of Wrath,* and it's Woodie Guthrie's quiet insistence that "this land is your land"—don't let the big men take it from you. It's the universal black-caped villain tying Nell to the railroad tracks to force her to sign over the deed.

Farm protest movements inevitably come with the crisis. From Shays's Rebellion in 1786 to the Granger movement in the 1870s to the Farm Holiday movement in the 1930s to the American Agriculture Movement's tractorcade in 1977, farm protest has been synonymous with a call for social and economic justice. One of my own earliest memories of social protest (after the lunch-counter sit-ins by blacks in the South) is of farmers dumping milk in the gutter rather than accept an unfair price for it in the 1960s.

So the farm protests of the mid-1980s have a familiar and sympathetic ring to them. Demands have changed little from crisis to crisis: higher prices, lower interest rates, emergency credit, and more crop exports. The protest methods are also familiar: penny auctions, huge rallies with some mighty fine oratory (farm protests have produced some of our best political rhetoric), and a few villains hung in effigy. President Reagan's first budget director, David Stockman, did the honors in effigy this time for callously remarking that farmers deserve what they are getting because they are greedy.

The financial troubles that prompted the protests were all too real. By 1984, ordinarily conservative experts were cautiously estimating that between 40 and 50 percent of our commercial-sized family farms had so much debt that they could not remain solvent for long with current interest rates and commodity prices. Less conservative experts were freely predicting that a fourth to a third of the farmers wouldn't survive two more years under current conditions. As the crisis wore on, fewer and fewer admonitions were heard that these estimates were too pessimistic. The federal government spent over $28 billion on farm programs in 1983 and the figure rose to $30 billion in 1986, but it seemed to do little to break the fall of American agriculture.

If the public or the Congress needed any more convincing that the farm crisis was real, they got the evidence they needed when banks and other lending institutions in the ordinarily solid Midwest began to fail in 1984. In less than three years, 22 Nebraska banks failed. A leading banker in Iowa predicted that up to one-third of that state's banks would not survive the farm crisis. Federal regulators classified 174 agricultural banks as "problem" banks in 1986, about two-thirds more than three years earlier (Gersten 1986). Bankers as much as farmers were lobbying Congress for federal relief for farmers. The cynic's old adage was affirmed: It's not a farm crisis until bankers are in trouble.

Although much public sympathy remains for the farmer among the American public, that sympathy is becoming more reserved, and less easily mobilized into political action. When Congress responded to the crisis in March 1985 with a modest package of emergency debt-relief measures, President Reagan vetoed the bill.

Almost instantly the story of farm distress left the front pages and the evening news.

The public's short attention span concerning the farm crisis is not difficult to understand. For one thing, farmers are hard to know as people, simply because there are too few of them for most Americans to have met one. People who live on farms constitute only about 2.4 percent of the population (U.S. Bureau of the Census jointly with USDA 1983) and only about a third of them are farmers first and foremost (people who depend on farming for their primary income). Hardly anyone in the United States knows a real farmer. Television can let you see farmers going broke, but it can't make you feel the pain of losing a neighbor or watching a friend's life collapse.

During the Great Depression, over one-fourth of the American people were farmers and many more had grown up on farms or knew parents who had been farmers. You could see the migration as much of the population of Oklahoma uprooted itself and moved to California. The crisis of the 1980s is far less visible and much less personal to most Americans.

Farmers today are not only harder to know, but a few of them seem harder to like, too. They are not quite as modest, and seem not quite as virtuous, as farmers used to be. The irony of air-conditioned, four-wheel-drive tractors in "tractorcades" protesting the financial woes of their owners has not escaped the public. Farm advocates have explained that the big tractors are a necessary part of contemporary agriculture, and that their presence in protest rallies merely demonstrates that even the biggest, and presumably most efficient, farmers can't survive current economic conditions.

But still, to many, these farmers are not as much like common people as farmers once were. Widespread stories of multimillion-dollar payments by the federal government to superfarms confirms the suspicion that the Old MacDonald image is not the whole story.

In fact, the term "farmer" seems to mean less than it once did. There are big farmers and small farmers and family farmers and corporate farmers. Even the experts debate the meaning of these terms. What once seemed like simple truth about justice and injustice on the farm is not so simple anymore.

If farmers seem less like common people, perhaps it is because they have separated themselves from the vital struggles of many common people. Just a few decades ago the cause of common people and the cause of farmers was synonymous. But farmers have been associated with none of the great social movements since the Second World War. In efforts to end poverty and racial discrimination, to recognize women's equality, to improve the environment, and to end the threat of war, farmers as a group have had little involvement. Sometimes, as in the effort to reduce pesticide pollution or to improve the living and working conditions of farm workers, farmers have vehemently opposed social justice and the public interest.

Even more discrediting to the farmers' cries for social justice is the fact that they appear to have welcomed the very economic policies that have placed them in such jeopardy. Were they not among the most supportive of President Reagan when he sought reelection in 1984, even as the farm crisis deepened? Did not 70 percent or more of the farmers vote for him in that election when he pledged to reduce the budget deficit by cutting social spending? How could they be surprised and outraged when his first veto in 1985 was of an emergency farm-credit bill that would have added to the deficit? Weren't they being a little hypocritical to think he would cut all social spending *except* agriculture? The public probably believes that farmers are not to be blamed for their economic problems, but that they have no one but themselves to blame for their political problems.

And so, American agriculture is an enigma, both politically and economically. It is productive but troubled. It is desperate, but supports the status quo. It frequently issues calls to "get the government out of agriculture," but regularly fights prolonged battles to protect farm programs with complicated rules, regulations, and subsidies. It is modern and progressive, but stuck in the mud.

Still, the farm crisis and protest whets the public interest and appeals to the public-spiritedness in us all. What's this crisis all about? And what should we do to keep the people of the land on the land? Church people and environmentalists want to know, labor-union leaders want to know, policy makers and journalists want to know. Even farmers want to know.

To seek answers we start with the greatest irony of all: The crisis always begins in the "good" years.

The farm crisis that reached headline proportions in the mid-1980s actually began in 1973 with a series of events that encouraged an incautious optimism about agriculture's future. For the next seven years, despite warning signals, capital investment in farming expanded without interruption.

Both domestic and international events triggered this wave of enthusiasm. First, a world-wide food production shortfall occurred because of a combination of circumstances, ranging from drought in Africa to anchovy kills in the waters off Peru. Reserve stocks of wheat, coarse grains, and rice fell sharply. The capacity of the world to feed itself was being challenged. Popular writers such as Lester R. Brown were talking about a fundamental shift from "chronic excess [agricultural] capacity" to "chronic scarcity and higher prices" (Brown 1974). Climatologists suggested that changes of epic proportions were occurring in weather patterns, that the tropics were moving north and the polar caps south. Central Intelligence Agency experts surveying climatological studies which forecast a shift to a less agriculturally desirable climate publicly advised that "the politics of food will become the central issue of every government" (U.S. Central Intelligence Agency 1976).

Would this need for food be translated into effective demand for American agricultural products? People would want food, but could they pay for it and would they buy it from the United States? These questions were barely asked; the answers were quickly assumed to be "yes." There were, after all, other developments that encouraged optimism.

The formation of the Organization of Petroleum Exporting Countries (OPEC), composed primarily of Third World nations with burgeoning populations to feed, encouraged American farmers in the notion that rising oil prices would translate into grain purchases. "A barrel of oil for a bushel of wheat" summed up their case for trade between the oil-rich Third World, with its near monopoly on oil, and the United States, with its near monopoly on grain exports. Countries like Mexico, Venezuela, and Indonesia, and with some improvement in political relations, most of the Middle East, would be a major source of rising demand for farm products. The term "rapidly developing country" differentiated the energy-rich Third World from the rest of the Third World, which could not pay its way in international trade. And the rapidly developing nations would gladly lend U.S. oil dollars to poorer nations.

At the same time, trade relations with nations having centrally planned economies were improving. President Nixon had gone to China in 1972, promising to open up relations with the world's most populous nation. Even more promising were developments with the Soviet Union. Crop failures or food shortages in the Soviet Union ordinarily meant belt tightening for the Soviet people, but not in 1973. Instead, the Soviets entered the grain market in a big way, and seemed intent on staying.

Japan's economic growth was yet another promising development. Its impressive entry into the U.S. automobile market had given it a very favorable balance of trade with the United States, and it found U.S. agricultural products, especially feed grains, to be one of the best ways to spend its U.S. dollars. Japan was rapidly becoming one of our top customers for corn. By 1981, Japan had become the leading importer of corn in the world, consuming 15 percent of the corn trade. Over three-fourths of its corn purchases were from the United States (Leath, Meyer, and Hill 1982).

There was a world food shortage and an export boom. From 1972 to 1981, our agricultural exports increased in value from $8 billion to over $44 billion (Wisner and Chase 1984). The world seemed to be on its knees begging for food and somehow, curiously, able to pay for it. The devaluation of the dollar in 1972 further helped assure that these eager new food buyers would do their shopping in the world's discount food store, the United States.

The intensity of this demand could not help but be reflected in the price of U.S. farm products. The price of wheat zoomed up 132 percent, from $1.76 to $4.09 per bushel, from 1972 to 1974. Corn was up 92 percent and soybeans 52 percent in the same period. Between 1972 and 1976 the price of cotton more than doubled. Rice doubled in one year, from '72 to '73 (U.S. Department of Agriculture 1984a).

In response, the United States unleashed its agricultural potential, freeing farmers from most of the production constraints which had been adopted to keep farm prices from falling too low. The secretary of agriculture, Earl Butz, became the principal cheerleader of the boom. With a chamber-of-commerce optimism he exhorted farmers to plant every acre. At last, agriculture could make its way in the market place, free of government interference. In the boom years, the chorus sings loud and clear to "get the government out of agriculture."

The result was plain. Between 1973 and 1981, the number of acres planted to crops on American farms increased by 12 percent, from 316 to 353 million. Acres planted to corn, wheat, soybeans, rice, and cotton—the principal export crops—increased by 33 percent, from 179 to 239 million in the same period (U.S. Department of Agriculture 1984a). American farmers were responding to the challenge to feed the world.

They were also making an investment in that challenge. It was a business opportunity that was good for the foreseeable future. And to take full advantage of this opportunity to produce for good, paying customers, all a farmer needed was more land and the equipment to farm it.

Ever-present experts in government, the universities, and the farm trade publications were advising farmers to expand their operations. Now was the time to buy that eighty acres you had had your eye on, or to expand even more to bring "junior" into the operation. Smart farmers were the ones who knew an opportunity when they saw it and were progressive enough to take advantage of it.

"Taking advantage of it" meant borrowing money to buy land and the equipment to farm it. Borrowing has had a bad name among conservative farmers for a long time, and the fear of not being able to pay back a loan has made many reluctant to borrow. But the experts said such attitudes could not be afforded. Farming was no longer a way of life, but a business, and good business is good money management. Borrowing was a necessity.

Borrowing is especially advantageous during periods of high inflation and low interest rates. During the boom years, inflation was raging, turned loose by the very OPEC pricing practices which had given such encouragement to farm exports. At the same time, however, interest rates lingered at relatively low levels. As a result, the real cost of borrowing (the rate of interest minus the rate of inflation) was extremely low, and frequently negative, during the middle and late 1970s. You could borrow today, pay 10 percent interest for a year, and pay back the loan a year later with dollars that were worth 10 percent less because of inflation.

In such a setting, the prudent thing for a wise money manager to do is borrow money and buy any asset that is increasing in value faster than the rate of inflation. And in the 1970s the best buy was farmland. Thus, the export boom and higher farm prices translated quickly into a land boom as buyers bid against each other for the opportunity to participate more fully in the phenomenon of rising exports and rising prices.

Once a land boom is underway, it has a tendency to take on a life of its own. As land values continue to rise, the *expectation* of further increases in its value encourages further investment. Since these expectations result in more investment in land, the price of land does, in fact, increase. A land boom is thus driven by self-fulfilling prophecy more than by economic rationality. It is as much psychological as economic. Land is worth more each year only because we think that it is worth more and that it will be worth even more next year. And since it is the expectation of rising values that leads to rising values, a land boom is a classic demonstration of speculative buying.

Moreover, a land boom is self-financing. As the value of land increases, so does the borrowing power of those who own land. Since their land is "worth" more, they can borrow more against it—especially if they use the borrowed funds to buy yet more land. The practice of borrowing against what one already owns in order to buy more is called leverage. Leveraged buying became the hallmark of excellence in the 1970s. Consultants recommended it, farm magazines touted its virtues, agricultural colleges wrote fine reports demonstrating its wisdom. A progressive farmer was a highly leveraged farmer who knew how to manage money. One farmer bragged on the front page of the *New York Times* that he had borrowed so much to buy so much land that was going up in value so fast that every morning he "woke up $8,000 richer."

Since the price of land bears no relationship to its earning power in a land boom, a farmer cannot earn enough income from farming land to pay for it. At the outset, it was the expectation of increased income from exports that inspired this boom, but once the expectation of rising land prices supplanted the expectation of rising income, those who had to pay for land from the income it produced were not in the best position to participate in what had become a speculative bidding war. Some farmers, of course, are well-off enough financially that they can afford to pay more for land than they can earn by farming it. Most are not. But in a rising land market, anyone seems to be able to play the game.

If some farmers are lured into the land boom, many nonfarmers are as well, because many of them are well equipped to buy land. Anyone with spare cash to invest can take advantage of the boom. In fact, if unused income presents an income-tax problem, buying land might be precisely what your accountant prescribes. During the 1970s, land became both a favored hedge against inflation and a good shelter from Uncle Sam's revenue agents.

Federal income-tax rules allowing borrowers to deduct interest payments from taxable income also encouraged borrowing to buy land. Part of every dollar spent on interest is recovered in tax returns. The higher your tax-bracket rate is, the greater the tax benefit for each dollar of interest deducted. During most of the land boom, a taxpayer in the highest tax bracket (it was 70 percent until 1981 and 50 percent from 1981 until 1986) therefore had an effective interest rate that was only 30 percent of the nominal interest rate. That was a substantial incentive to borrow. At the same time, prior to the 1986 Tax Reform Act, any increase in land value between the time of purchase and resale of land was not considered ordinary taxable income, but capital gain, only 40 percent of which was taxable. Capital-gains tax thus provided additional incentive to use borrowed money to buy farmland.

High-income nonfarmers were a big part of the bidding war for land in the 1970s. I recall a West Coast airline magazine advertisement in the mid-seventies that appealed to investors in midwestern farmland. "When there is more food than people, buy something other than American farmland," it enticed. The sentence doesn't make any sense grammatically, but we all know what it means. Even the English language must give way to the psychology of a land boom.

But a land boom depends on more than borrowers' willingness to borrow. Lenders must also be willing to lend. Ordinarily, one would expect lenders to dampen the speculative enthusiasm because they must carefully assess a productive asset's underlying value—its earning power—before accepting it as collateral for a loan. But lenders were caught up in the land euphoria as well. They lent money aggressively in the 1970s, for both farmland and farm machinery.

Lenders did not focus on the cash flow of the farm—whether the income from it would be sufficient to make the mortgage payment to the lender, but on the net worth of the borrower—whether the value of the land would cover the loan, should the borrower default. So optimistic was the Federal Land Bank, a system of farmer-owned cooperative banks that finance land purchases, that it offered to lend money for up to 95 percent of the value of land, expecting that it would continue to rise in value well above the amount of the loan. As farmers and others borrowed against farmland in order to buy still more, debt against land rose as fast as its value. The value of American farmland more than quadrupled, from $176 billion in 1970 to $715 billion in 1981, but the debt borrowed against it rose almost as fast, from $29 billion to $96 billion.

Land prices were rising so fast during this period that the annual increase in the value of farmland was greater, even after adjustments for inflation, than net farm income nearly every year from 1973 to 1981. It was worth more to own farmland than it was to farm it. It is axiomatic in an era of inflated land values: If you have to pay for land by farming it, you cannot afford it; if you can afford land, it is because you do not need the income from it for your living.

Along the way, certain warning signals, both economic and political, were ignored. As early as 1976 the expected increase in income from exports was not boosting the cash flow of farmers enough to pay for higher land prices (Fiechter 1985). But hindsight is twenty-twenty. Few experts were issuing warnings in 1976. If they did, they were condemned as antigrowth. Except for a little scorn thrown in their direction, they were widely and enthusiastically ignored.

As cash flow fell short of cash requirements, conditions worsened and the farm protest of 1977–78 gave rise to the American Agriculture Movement. Farm production had already outstripped foreign demand so much by 1977 that the falling prices of key export crops, especially wheat, corn, and cotton, were creating significant cash-flow problems for heavily indebted farmers. These farmers drove their high-powered, highly leveraged tractors all the way to Washington, D.C., for an impressive demonstration. (The tractors probably made as deep an impression when they were voluntarily used to clean up Washington streets after an unexpected snowstorm as they did during a demonstration when they tore up the grass mall that runs from the Capitol to the Lincoln Memorial. Washington cabbies still marvel at those tractors.)

No overall change in federal policy toward agriculture came out of the protest. Instead, the government responded with a temporary program to pay farmers not to plant a portion of their fields, and an expanded program of federal credit. The latter was exactly what wasn't needed.

Nevertheless, for a few more years, the illusion of rising land values persisted, propped up by continuing unrealistic expectations and by government programs that kept some land out of production and supported the price of commodities. The price support programs work by first lending money to farmers for the commodities, and then accepting the commodities in full satisfaction for the loan, whether the commodities are worth as much as the government has lent to the farmer or not. Under such programs, commodity prices would be supported, but the commodities themselves would tend to accumulate in the hands of the government. From 1973, when the world appeared to be faced with chronic food scarcity, until 1982, when the boom gave way to the bust, corn in storage increased from 484 to 3,120 million bushels. Wheat stocks bloated from 340 to 1,515 million bushels, soybeans from under 60 to over 344 million bushels (U.S. Department of Agriculture 1984a). In those storage bins sat the accumulated burden of America's most egregious land boom.

THE VICTIMS OF THE BOOM

Before turning to the bust and all of its dreadful consequences, it is worth noting that the boom is dreadful, too. The behavior of a few does much damage to many in a boom like the land boom of the 1970s. There are victims of the boom, just as there are victims of the bust.

The victims of the 1970s land boom included most would-be or beginning farmers who had neither substantial inherited wealth nor parents of means. They could not acquire the land necessary to start farming because they could not pay for it by farming it and didn't have any other means of buying it. Some rented land for cash payments at inflated prices. Luckier ones found a beneficent landlord willing to rent for a share of the crop instead of cash. Most never got to farm at all or didn't last long if they did. Little was said of them during the boom, because they only represented lost opportunity in a sea of enthusiasm and rising expectations.

Some established farmers were victims too, especially those who rented significant portions of their land from landlords who raised rents as land prices climbed. These farmers saw more and more of their income slip away as rent. Frequently they were unable to dissuade the landlord from selling the land to an expanding farmer or to an outside investor. An angry letter published in a midwestern newspaper in the spring of 1985, as state legislators from across the region were flying off to Washington, D.C., to plead for federal aid for distressed farmers, expressed the feelings of such boom victims succinctly and bitterly: "Our greedy neighbors who forced us off our family farm 10 years ago by bidding up the land and rent prices are now in financial trouble. There was no trip to Washington by the state senators or crisis declared by the news media for us" (Barten 1985).

Besides those who could not play the game, there were those who would not. Some diversified farmers, for example, refused to switch from hay, pasture, and small grains to please landlords who insisted they plant high-value export crops. Others who simply felt strongly about conservation refused to convert highly erodible land to row crops for export. Such farmers lost rented land to more aggressive farmers willing to pay more rent and to make such conversions.

There were victims, too, among those farmers whose requests for credit were too modest for their lenders' tastes. They wanted only enough money to make small improvements in a hog barn, or to remodel a dairy barn. "No," the lender might have said, "you're not being progressive enough. I won't lend you twenty thousand to remodel that hog barn, but I will lend you two hundred thousand to build a new one that will produce twice as many hogs." If the farmer refused the offer, he was a victim because he was unable to borrow the funds necessary to carry out moderate plans in a time of extreme behavior. If he accepted the offer, he probably became a victim of the collapse in hog prices that removed a third of all hog producers from 1980 to 1982.

And the victims of the boom were not limited to farmers. Some lenders refused to play as well, because they wisely lacked confidence in the boom. They declined requests for loans for farm expansion that other lenders would willingly make, and lost steady customers as a result to those more aggressive institutions. Many country banks lost regular business to the farm credit system during the 1970s. It is harder to feel sympathy for bankers, but some were victims of the boom as well.

Victims of the boom tend to be silent victims, or perhaps their cries cannot be heard over the din of cheers from those who have outbid them for land and opportunity. They may be forced out of farming, or they may be forced to pay more to farm than they can afford. Some simply never get to farm. You can't play poker if you can't make ante. And if you can't make much more than ante, you can't play poker long.

The pacesetters in this poker game can be a relatively small number of land buyers—well-established, wealthy farmers or high-income nonfarmers. Their motive for buying land has less to do with their need for a production asset from which to generate an income than their attraction to an investment that will continue to appreciate in value. They are speculators. But since there is only one land market, everyone has to match the pace set by the most aggressive bidder for available land. An ambitious few, with the money to pay cash or willing and able to borrow expansively in order to acquire more land, set the price that any other buyer must match.

Among these other participants in the boom bidding war are the son or daughter who buys land from a retiring parent, or the second child whose opportunity to farm depends on borrowing against the family's modest landholdings in order to buy enough additional land to start on, or the small farmer who doubles the farm by buying only another 160 acres. These people, whose lives and livelihoods hang on the thin margin of error present in these decisions, must match or exceed the price of the land speculator, whose calculus is less vital, and whose margin of error may be much larger. Most boom buyers, even at the peak of the land boom, were probably closer in character to the former than to the latter. Most could not afford to run with the speculators. A few years later, most wished they had not.

THE BUST

Like the boom, the bust that inevitably follows is triggered more by developments that affect attitudes and opinions than by the underlying economic health of agriculture.

In late 1979, the Federal Reserve System decided to fight runaway inflation with a tight money policy. The success of this policy was considerable; so was its impact on farmers. Interest rates rose and inflation fell. *Real* interest rates therefore increased to 8 or 10 percent, as high as any in recent history. Suddenly, the wisdom of having borrowed in an inflationary economy was doubtful.

At the same time, growth in exports screeched to a halt. For political reasons, some loudly blamed the 1979 embargo of grain sales to the Soviet Union after its intervention in Afghanistan, but that puny measure was far outdone by other factors, and has been discounted even by the Reagan administration as a prime factor in the collapse of exports.

Rising interest rates in the United States that made the dollar an attractive currency for foreign investors were a prime factor. The dollar promptly rose in value against other currency, increasing the cost of U.S. exports to those nations. Naturally, they bought less. Moreover, the rapidly developing nations, whose oil-fueled future earlier had appeared so bright, discovered a new reality as oil supplies built up, prices slipped, and the OPEC cartel's influence receded. Suddenly, nations like Mexico, once a bright, new star in the constellation of food-importing nations, was a deeply indebted nation no longer able to meet its current obligations, let alone take on new ones. Non-oil-exporting developing nations also soon found themselves buffeted by higher interest rates and lenders' demands to bring their accounts current.

To make matters even worse, evidence mounted that many of the world's food producers besides the United States had mounted drives to capture export markets. Nations that had historically been net food importers suddenly were in the export market for one or another of the crops we customarily exported with virtually no competition. Brazil, whose soybean industry was developed largely with Japanese finance after a mid-seventies U.S. embargo of beans to Japan, was suddenly exporting soybeans. Western Europe, long one of our best customers for farm products, but whose policy has been to protect its farmers and encourage self-sufficiency, became a net exporter of wheat for the first time. China, incredibly to many, increased its own grain production so much that it became the world's leading grain producer, reduced its own imports by a third, and actually exported more corn than it imported (Wisner and Chase 1984).

While U.S. farm exports declined in value by 21 percent in two years from the 1980–81 record high, they were still double the nominal value they had been at the beginning of the boom in 1973. More important, however, exports of other nations were increasing as U.S. exports slowly declined. The U.S. share of world sales was shrinking dramatically. The prospect that we were permanently losing customers was chilling.

Meantime, as farm products began to accumulate in U.S. storage facilities, prices were falling to the level at which the government would support them with crop loans. By 1986 prices of corn had fallen below the government loan rate to as low as one dollar per bushel in some areas of Iowa. Adjusted for inflation, that is about one-sixth of the corn price peak in the mid-1970s. Farmers were producing crops for the robustly growing export market of the 1970s, not for the stagnant export market of the 1980s.

To make matters much worse, a growing portion of farm debt had been issued under variable interest rates during the latter part of the boom to protect lenders from the rising cost of providing capital. The effect of these variable interest rates was to tie farmers to the tail of a tiger. As rates escalated, farmers found themselves paying more interest on loans made during the boom, even as their incomes fell.

The problem was particularly severe for customers of the largest land lender, the federally chartered farm credit system. The system gets its capital by issuing bonds on a regular basis. The interest rate it charges its farm customers is based on a composite of the interest rates it is paying on all its outstanding bonds. When interest rates are going up, as they were in the early 1980s, the system's rates are a little lower than the prevailing rate, because some of its older bonds reflect the lower rates of the past. All well and good for farmers. But when interest rates began to fall in the mid-1980s, as the farm crisis deepened, the opposite was true. In order to meet the interest obligation on its older bonds, the system had to charge higher than the prevailing rates. Moreover, as financially troubled farmers defaulted on loans, the system had to raise the variable interest rates even more on other customers to cover losses. Some loans issued at an 8.5 percent interest rate were being charged a rate of 15 percent only a few years later.

Faced with falling commodity prices and rising costs, especially higher interest payments, farmers were prompted to borrow even more. They now needed the money just to cover their current operating costs. Even those who had not expanded found themselves forced, by the behavior of those who had, to borrow more against the value of their land. This was the cruelest fate of all, for the strategy was doomed.

Having made investments in land and equipment with long- and intermediate-term mortgages, that land and equipment had to be used to produce the income to pay for itself. To pay for itself? The fact and fantasy of the boom began to take hold: we hadn't expected to have to pay for these investments from farm income. We had expected them in part to pay for themselves by inflation and real capital gain in their value. Underlying that expectation had been the assumption that export income would continue to increase at a substantial rate. That's what started this whole thing.

If the premise is false, so must be the conclusion. If exports are not growing fast enough, if prices are sagging, if costs of farming are increasing, especially because of higher interest rates, thus reducing the amount that can be used to meet land payments, then it must be true that land will not continue to rise in value. If land will not continue to rise in value, then it must be paid for out of the income you can get from farming it. If you have to pay for it by farming it, you've already paid too much for it. Land is already overpriced. As in the fable of the emperor's new clothes, it is as if someone stood up and shouted, "The emperor has no clothes!"

The psychology of the bust is like the psychology of the boom. It is fed by expectations that are self-fulfilling. Land goes down in value because land buyers believe that it will continue to go down in value. If anything, the expectations during a bust are even more extreme and irrational. There is an old saying among farmers that sums it up quite well: When land is going up, it's worth $50 an acre more than the last price you heard; when land is going down, it's worth $100 less than the last price you heard. From 1972 to 1981, the value of farmland had increased from an average of $219 to $823 per acre. By early 1986, it had fallen to $596. Adjusted for inflation since 1972, it had fallen all the way back to $232 (U.S. Department of Agriculture 1986).

Nearly all the real capital gain in land from 1972 through 1981 had been squeezed out of the land market by 1986. Some balance had been reestablished. You could almost pay for land by farming it, but only if you could start farming fresh, without the burdensome debt load incurred by most farmers in the 1970s.

In the bust, of course, the victims are legion. And they are very visible. They are going through foreclosures and bankruptcy, they are in the headlines and in the streets. Their complaint is that they were deceived by policy makers who urged them to expand, that they were wrongly induced to borrow money by lenders who overstated the value of their assets as collateral for loans that were too big. They are the innocent victims of fiscal and monetary policies designed to curb inflation and raise interest rates. Their export markets have been stolen from them by a strong dollar and pro- tectionist policies in foreign nations. Their land values are falling and their lender is now insisting that the cash flow from the farm be great enough to assure repayment of loans that were not made on the basis of cash flow at all, but on the basis of the inflated value of the assets that secured them. The rules have been changed. They are victims of events and behavior beyond their control.

They are right, of course, but not quite so righteous as many would like to believe. The victims easily see the damage of the bust. They do not see so easily that the boom years in which many par- ticipated too willingly were just as wrong, just as unjust, as the bust years. Their false pride has been turned into defeat. You can con- clude that farmers are not as virtuous as their reputation makes them out to be, but the larger truth is that they are just human. Who among us would have acted differently?

This crisis must be seen as more than an economic morality play, however. It was caused by and, in turn, furthered some profound changes that are taking place in American agriculture. Out of the boom of the 1970s and the bust of the 1980s is emerging a new, more industrial agriculture that has been budding in America for generations as a replacement for family farming. It is a brave new world of farming which claims to be more rational and less ro- mantic than the old world. It is a world full of new ways, new tech- nologies, and new demands. Its most pressing demand, naturally, is that the old ways and technologies must go.

These changes had been underway for many years, though at a much slower pace. The crisis merely brought them to full flow- ering. They involve the most basic social and economic dimen- sions of farming in America. Perhaps most important, they are changes that suggest there will be many more crises ahead. It is im- portant that we see the farm crisis as part of a transformation in American agriculture, and not just as another episode in farm dis- tress.

That the new agriculture is better than the old is taken for granted by its proponents. The old agriculture, with its nostalgic loyalty to the small and moderate-sized, owner-operated farm, is simply out of date, they say. It cannot survive the changes in recent years which mandate that farms be large and well financed and so- phisticated. Sentimentality alone cannot endure against these compelling forces. Ultimately, more than a few hundred thousand family farms will fail to survive the current troubles. The family farming system itself, they predict, will prove to have been the victim of the farm crisis of the 1980s.

To some extent, these arguments rest as much on the expectations of their makers as they do on solid analytical ground. That the new agriculture is at the threshold is evident; that it is better than the old, or the only alternative to it, may be only as self-evident as the land boom was self-fulfilling. Let's examine the process of industrializing American agriculture.

2.

Industrializing American Agriculture

For years, farm organizations, politicians, and even academics have sounded the alarm: Industrial corporations are taking over American agriculture and destroying the family farm. Other farm organizations, other politicians, and other academics counter impatiently that the number of major corporations in farming is actually small—they control little land, and are engaged primarily in specialty crops, not the basic commodities in which family farmers continue to prevail.

Much of this debate has turned on tedious analytical issues. How many corporations engaged in farming are presumably family farm corporations because they have fewer than ten shareholders? Is the proper measurement of corporate farming the number of acres owned by corporations or the market share of crops they produce?

Increasingly, however, the debate has turned from the issue of whether or not a corporate future for American agriculture exists, to whether or not such a future is inevitable or desirable. Beneath that issue lie two fundamental beliefs held by the opposing sides, neither subject to negotiation: that family farms are good while corporate farms are evil; and that corporate farms are more efficient, else why would they pose a threat to family farms?

Unfortunately, this debate has diverted attention from subtler changes under way. To be sure, corporate farming is a factor. But the appeal that farming has for corporations and the extent to which they have become a factor in the farm economy is a reflection of changes occurring from *within* the traditional, family farm system. The corporate farm is not so much a threat from without as a revelation of what the family farm is becoming, a view of the future for the dominant family farms in America. As comedian Lenny Bruce observed, you need the pervert to tell you when you are going wrong. American agriculture—including the traditional family farm—is becoming industrialized. What, then, is industrial farming?

FAMILY FARMING VERSUS INDUSTRIAL AGRIBUSINESS

Like pornography and patriotism, the term "family farm" eludes definition. But it does have a commonly understood cultural meaning, particularly when it is used to describe a system of agriculture rather than to categorize individual farms. Though we might argue into the night over whether a particular farm is a family farm, we might more easily agree on the characteristics of a family farming system.

What makes any social system functional is shared values and goals, collectively and individually expressed in the behavior of its members. The glue that holds the system together is a consensus about how things ought to be, not necessarily how they are. Widely held expectations about what family farms are supposed to be, and not necessarily universal conformance with those expectations on the part of every farm, gives the term "family farm" its meaning. Individual farms may vary from one or more of the common characteristics of the system taken as a whole, but the system tends to produce farms that bear most of the common characteristics. The system is designed to produce such farms—they are expected of it. To the extent it does, the system is working. To the extent it does not, something is wrong, or the system is changing.

Family farming is thus an abstraction of common experiences and expectations, not a definitive class of farms. Don't ask whether a farm is a family farm—ask whether it conforms to the expectations of family farming, and to what extent it deviates from them.

Family Farming

The family farming system is one in which the farms are or tend to be:

Owner-operated. In a family farming system, it is the goal of most farm operators to own the assets with which they farm—the land, especially. The rights and responsibilities of ownership are vested as a property right in the farmer. It is not important that every farm be owner operated, or that every owner-operator own all the land in the farm. But it is important that this dream be widely held and that the system provide some reasonable prospect of realization for many, or most. To the extent that owner-operatorship is abandoned as a goal, or the system deprives most farmers of a chance of becoming more than tenants, the system is not working.

Entrepreneurial. The capacity to make management decisions is vested in the farmer. To retain such entrepreneurship, the farms must be internally financed from the resources of the farm family, including its own labor. Debt financing is a necessary tool for many to build equity in the farm, but the goal is to retire the debt and burn the mortgage—to pay for the farm—preferably within the lifetime of the heads of household. Ideally, the system should enable the farmer to pay for the farm from the farming income alone, so that the rewards of ownership are a product of the work and entrepreneurship of the owner.

Dispersed. Ownership is widespread and there are many farms somewhat similar in size in a family farming system. This does not mean, however, that all farms are identical in size and character. Some farms might well be larger than others, perhaps two or three times larger. However, genuine dispersion implies that the larger than average the farm, the less normal it is, and more important, it implies that the large farms do not control a major portion of the production. In a family farming system, large farms are not a class of farms for comparative analysis with more modest-sized farms; instead, they are an aberration. How big is the typical farm in a family farming system? It is about as big as its neighbors. Growth occurs, but gradually, and among nearly all surviving farms at the same time, and at about the same rate. Farms that are too big to be farmed by the family itself without hiring substantial amounts of labor have grown too big. By the same token, farms are not so small that their role in providing family livelihood is only incidental.

Diversified. The farms in a family farming system must employ their human, natural, and financial resources in optimal combination. Diversified cropping patterns ensure year-round use of labor, full use of land of varying quality, and reduced dependence on a single market for income. Diversification is an economic precaution against price risks as well as a means of producing internally many of the farm's inputs; for example, soil nutrients from manure and crop rotations.

At equal advantage in open markets. Though the nature and design of the marketing system in a family farming agriculture may vary, all farms must have equal access to markets. None receive a better price or any other advantage in selling products or in purchasing inputs. Naturally, economic factors will place some at a comparative disadvantage—the family farming system does not ensure that you can grow oranges in Alaska, or even that farms twenty miles from the grain elevator won't have greater marketing expense than those two miles away. But these economic factors are independent of the size of the farm or the structure of its ownership.

Family centered. In a family farming system, farms rely on family labor and management skills. The family lives its life in harmony with its workplace. There is no division between home and work. Children grow up learning to farm by apprenticeship. Formal education is not eschewed; in fact, it is valued as a means of increasing the human skills on the farm. But the practical aspects of farm management and decision making, of work and reward, and of problem solving are learned by doing. Most important, responsibility is shared by all family members old enough to assume any. It is learned not as an abstraction, but as a product of shared expectations among family members. Children do work that is useful and important to the family, and they are held accountable for failing to live up to their end of the bargain. Economically speaking, they are an asset to the farm, not a burden to the family.

Technologically progressive. Family farming is innovative, using technology to reduce costs and lighten the load on human beings, but its objective in employing new technology is to enhance the work of the family, not to eliminate work for people. There is, of course, an internal contradiction here. New technology that enhances one family's labor tends to displace another's in the long run, but it is not this consequence which motivates adoption of the technology. Instead, such a consequence is viewed with alarm, if indeed it is understood at all. The point to stress is this: in a family farming system, the farms strive to match capital investments with the labor resources of the people on the farm. New technology and new capital investments must meet the constraints of the farm.

Striving for production processes in harmony with nature. Family farming has a seasonal, rhythmic quality to it. Production is sequential: planting precedes cultivating, which is followed by harvesting. Breeding, birthing, nurturing. Things are done in batches according to biological requirements. Every year a new crop, and at each season of the year a festival of duties that gives pattern to life. Calving in the spring, haying in early summer, harvesting small grains a little later, farrowing hogs in the fall.

Resource conserving. Family farms conserve resources because the natural, human, and financial resources of the farm are owned by the family—they are conserved for its heirs. The planning horizon of farms in a family farming system is, in principle, infinite. Management mistakes that squander those resources and result in failure are considered ignorant or unethical by the community. At its worst, the family farming system tolerates resource ruin, but only in the short run as a survival strategy during hard times—hard times that sometimes stretch into decades. In fact, the conservation record of family farms may be poor, but it is a cause for shame in the conscience of family farming.

Farming as a way of life. Above all, family farming carries with it a commitment to certain values, entirely independent of the pettiness of economics. The agrarian tradition, of which family farming is a part, calls for people to be neighborly, to care for future generations, to work hard and to believe in the dignity of work, to be frugal, modest, honest, and responsible for and to the community. Family farming may be a business, but it is not just a business. It is a way of life as well. The farms in a family farming system operate in a social milieu which constrains the business behavior of farmers. Perhaps the best test of whether a farm is a family farm is this: Does the farmer feel more pain at the loss of a neighbor than joy at the opportunity to acquire that neighbor's land?

By this point, many readers may have long since lost patience with this idealistic description of family farming. Admittedly, it sounds naïve as a description of the kind of family farming we know today. In fact, the ideal system of agriculture described above has never existed anywhere, certainly not in North America. It was the vision of Jefferson and others, but we have never come close to its realization. It is a cultural myth, even a romantic myth, say its detractors.

But the myth has served a useful purpose, nonetheless. In any society, myth serves the purpose of offering a vision of what should be and providing a standard against which to evaluate where we are headed. That pure family farming never came to be is no reason to abandon it as the policy objective of American agriculture.

The myth of family farming also offers a basis from which to recognize and evaluate other myths. The "other" myth in agriculture is the myth of industrial agribusiness, a myth less romantic and more cynical, but no less compelling. Industrial agribusiness is as fundamentalist, as value laden, and as abstract as family farming. What separates the two, apart from their content, is that while we remain superficially loyal to the myth of family farming, we have become culturally and politically committed to the myth of industrial agribusiness.

Industrial Agribusiness

An industrial agribusiness system produces farms that are:

Industrially organized. The most potent difference between family farming and industrial agribusiness is in the relationship between people and the resources they use to farm. If worker, owner, and manager are rolled into one family unit in family farming, the industrial agribusiness model separates them into distinct roles: some people work for wages, others invest for profit, and yet others manage the affairs of both workers and owners. This difference reflects a fundamental difference in the economic motive for farming. In family farming, land represents an opportunity to employ the labor of the farm family in providing a livelihood for the family. In industrial agribusiness, land is a coveted investment not because it yields a livelihood for the family, but because it is expected to produce a long-term, unearned return. Thus, in industrial agribusiness, only those who need not depend on income from farming can afford to own farmland.

Financed for growth. In industrial agribusiness, farms are firms and they are financed by a combination of debt and equity through investor-owners. Debt is regarded as the best means of financing growth, the principal goal of the industrial farm. As debt is retired and the value of the farm-firm's equity increases, earnings are reinvested and more is borrowed in order to buy still more land and other farm assets. Debt is thus regarded as perpetual—it is not the goal of the industrial agribusiness to pay off the debt. Burning the mortgage, a symbolic ritual recognizing a point of accomplishment and a state of stability in family farming, is unheard of in industrial agribusiness. A debt-free farm is a farm that isn't growing. Debt is a necessary tool of expansion, an instrument of conquest.

Large scale, concentrated. Production is concentrated on a few large farms in industrial agribusiness, farms that continue to expand until they run up against farms of equal size and financial power. There may be many smaller farms in the system, but they are economically—and politically—irrelevant compared with the few large farms who compete on their own terms and with each other for market shares and production assets.

Specialized. To permit large-scale production using the most modern equipment, to simplify and routinize labor requirements, and to pay for high capital investments, industrial agribusinesses tend to specialize in one, or at most, two crops. The more specialized, the greater the proportion of production inputs—chemical fertilization, pest control, feed, and, of course, finance capital in the form of borrowed money for operating expenses—that must be purchased from off-farm sources. Even specialized management services in the form of professional consultants are purchased to meet the needs of specialized, industrial agribusiness farms.

Management centered. Work and family life are separate on the industrial agribusiness farm. Children and spouses have no place, unless the management provides living quarters as part of the remuneration of the workers. The center of these enterprises is not people at all, but an abstraction: management. Management makes decisions, allocates resources, evaluates the qualifications of prospective employees, hires, fires, trains, and supervises workers, accounts for the use of resources, and provides financial reports, including year-end tax statements, to owners.

Capital-intensive. Industrial farms would rather employ capital—land, machinery, and technology—than labor. The people who own industrial agribusinesses realize a profit from investing in capital, not by hiring workers. Unlike family farming, where the capital needs of the farm must be balanced against the employment needs of the family, an industrial agribusiness sees labor only as a paid expense and as a troublesome human factor. Industrial agribusinesses therefore tend to use technology to replace labor, whenever possible, even beyond the point that is economically rational. Better to buy an expensive machine than to hire cheap labor. Machines work without protest until they break down, they receive favored tax treatment, and they are not a political or social factor.

At an advantage in controlled markets. Whereas the family farming system requires free access for all to open markets, industrial agribusinesses thrive by seeking special advantages in controlled markets. Because industrial agribusinesses produce specialized crops in large volume and frequently at low profit margins, they are extremely vulnerable to market fluctuations in the prices of their commodities and the inputs they purchase. To reduce this risk, they prefer contract markets—direct purchases of their commodities by processors bypassing traditional markets. Industrial agribusinesses live by volume discounts, price premiums, and other concessions offered to them purely because of their size and the desire on the part of other buyers and sellers to do business with them. This is termed market power and its existence implies that markets are competitive only in the sense that industrial agribusinesses compete for advantage and privilege over others.

Standardized in their production processes. Production in industrial agribusiness is mechanical, not biological. This is especially true in livestock production. In order to keep all parts of specialized, factory-like facilities busy all the time, all phases of production are underway simultaneously and continuously. People are utilized as employees who specialize in one part or another of the production process, their labor routinized. Animals are treated as machines that operate continuously, not seasonally. To the extent possible, nature is diminished as a factor in production. Breeding, birthing, nurturing, fattening take place concurrently, year around, in environments designed for each, notwithstanding the seasons or other natural elements. Even in crop production, efforts must be made to minimize natural factors. Industrial agribusiness thrives where irrigation reduces vulnerability to drought.

Resource consumptive. In a fundamental sense, agriculture is a renewable system using biological processes without consuming natural resources in the production of food and fiber. But the industrialization of agriculture implies a different approach. In industrial agribusiness, resources are consumed in the process of converting them to finished products, by-products, and waste products. This is permissible because the industrial agribusiness lives for itself. It has no heirs. Its planning horizon is about as long as the depreciable life of its equipment. Conservation of resources occurs only if it can be justified as producing a favorable return on investment. Industrial agribusiness claims not to be unconcerned about conservation, but believes that the market place will determine the apropriate level of investment in conservation. Those farms that allow resource depletion to reduce their yields will be punished with failure.

Farmed as a business. Industrial agribusiness sees as its own values the economic virtues of efficiency, productivity, and competition. Sometimes, these values are expressed as social virtues as well: plenty, progress, and modernization are favorites. Generally industrial agribusiness is silent and occasionally disdainful toward community, neighborhood, and family. Frequently it is immodest in its claims of economic efficiency. Its favorite statistic is the number of people fed by the production from one farm, without so much as a nod to all those who supply the farm with its industrial inputs. When the industrial agribusiness becomes large enough to be socially conspicuous, it may develop a policy of community service for its public-relations value.

* * *

These two models, family farming and industrial agribusiness, are pure models representing the opposite ends of a continuum of farms in America. Neither system exists complete in the real world. Few farms typify either system. Many farmers, and probably most large commercial farmers, perceive themselves both as family farms and as industrial agribusinesses. Most feel the tension represented by two such contradictory sets of values. Most are pulled in both directions at once.

Generally, however, the weight of community sanction is with the family farms that most emulate the industrial agribusiness model. They have "progressive" images, considerable property (even if not paid for) that proves their worth, important friends, and most of all, political power. It is these farmers who get admiring stories written about them in the farm magazines, who win awards from small-town chambers of commerce (because they do a lot of business on main street), and who are considered top managers by agricultural experts. Their farms are on university tours and field days, seed companies want them to be their local dealers (for which they get their own seed much cheaper than the neighbors they sell to), and they are frequently elected to local school boards (where some may be less interested in education than they are in reducing property taxes). They are prominent.

The new industrial agribusiness is thus widely believed to be superior to the family farm. Its achievements are awesome. Its neighbors are humbled by its self-confidence. It knows more, does more, has more. Both its size and the process of getting big— growth—are not only legitimized, but admired. This star-struck fawning of the modern, progressive, industrial agribusiness is part of its mythos.

The center of gravity in American agriculture is thus moving along the continuum from family farming toward industrial agribusiness. This movement is pervasive and incremental, affecting nearly every farm in subtle and sometimes mysterious ways. Statistics on corporate farming, number and size of farms, or land tenure fail to convey the meaning of the change. Those data partially describe the effect but offer little insight into the dynamic of the change itself.

In the process, it is difficult to tell when a farm has stopped being a family farm and has become an industrial agribusiness. For example, one aggressive family farm in the plains grew rapidly by investing in irrigation in the 1960s and '70s. It grew so fast that it soon had over eight thousand irrigated acres, a cattle-feeding operation, and a farm-supply business. To acquire more working capital, the family farmer incorporated and merged his operation with an alfalfa processor whose stock was sold on one of the national stock exchanges. In a few years, the family farmer had lost so much money in cattle feeding and futures-market transactions that he had to accept a minority position in the company. Subsequently, the company was acquired by a conglomerate that held it a short time and then sold it to Texas oil interests. At the beginning of this high-speed transformation, no one would have quarreled with the claim that the farm was a family farm. At the conclusion, no one would have suggested it was anything but an industrial agribusiness. At many points along the path, however, you could have ignited a spirited debate by suggesting it was either.

As these changes unfold, the self-image of farming changes. Not long ago, most farmers in America clearly saw themselves and were seen by society as family farmers. The logic and values of industrial agribusiness frightened and disturbed them. But today, industrial agribusiness has gained a tight grip on the self-image of American agriculture. That grip is strengthened by one reality that industrial agribusiness now has to add to its mythos: the reality that it now dominates food production. Today, though most farms remain at least ambivalent about their identity, most food is produced on farms that have embraced industrial agribusiness. At what appears to be a rapid rate of transformation, it will be only a short while before even the cultural myth of the family farm is dead.

Consider, for example, the following statistics:

— Just under half the food in the United States is produced on the largest 4.1 percent of the farms and a third is produced on the superfarms that constitute the largest 1.2 percent (U.S. Department of Agriculture 1986). The first-ever survey of the biggest of the superfarms revealed that the four hundred largest produced one-sixth of the nation's food supply in 1986, more than all the farms in Iowa, Illinois, and Florida together (Smith 1987). By the year 2000, the Department of Agriculture projects that half the farm products will come from the top 1 percent (Lin, Coffman, and Penn 1980).

— The biggest farms rely increasingly on hired labor. Well over half the top 4.1 percent of the farms spend over $20,000 per year on hired labor, and half the superfarms spend over $50,000. (U.S. Bureau of the Census 1984).

— About 75 percent of the people who own farmland aren't farmers and they own about 43 percent of all farmland, according to a 1978 landownership survey conducted by the USDA. In the Corn Belt states comprising the heartland of American agriculture, less than half the farmland is owned by farmers. By contrast, in 1946, two-thirds of the farmland owners were farmers and they held 70 percent of the farmland (Daugherty and Otte 1983).

— Seventy percent of the cotton, 80 percent of the grains, 94 percent of the dairy products, and 98 percent of the poultry produced in the U.S. come from farms that receive most of their income from the sale of those products alone (U.S. Bureau of the Census 1984).

— In 1960, fewer than 5 percent shunned the open market for the certainty of contracts, and as late as 1974, only 9 percent marketed by contract. The USDA projects that by the year 2000, from one-quarter to one-third of all farms will market their products by contract rather than in open markets. Moreover, it is the larger farms that tend to prefer contracts (Linn, Coffman, and Penn 1980).

This gradual transformation from family farming to industrial agribusiness may not be best measured by such statistics, however. From within American agriculture, the change is seen in a thousand more subtle ways in the daily lives of people who farm or who live in rural communities.

As a result of the gravitation toward specialized grain farming in the Midwest, many farmers have had little more experience with livestock than the proverbial city slicker, and don't feel willing or able to handle animals. Some local 4-H groups have to go to non-farmers to teach farm kids how to work with animals.

Some farm families whose farms have become agribusiness-like won't let their children out to play in the farmyard when the hired help is driving heavy equipment. Their concern is not irrational. A recent university study indicates that the death rate from farm accidents has not declined in twenty-five years, that three-quarters of them are tractor accidents, and that many of the victims are children (Heinlein 1985).

The change is in the land, too. Once pristine regions of the country now experience environmental threats to safety and health from agriculture that are as serious as those urban areas suffer from heavy industry. Much of the damage is to the water that absorbs the chemicals used on farmland. According to the Nebraska Department of Health, eighty-one municipal wells in Nebraska—about one in five—are near or above tolerable levels of contamination from nitrate-nitrogen. The principal sources of nitrate pollution in groundwater in that state are agricultural chemicals and livestock wastes (Stansberry 1986). In Iowa, environmental officials reckon that up to half of that state's municipal water supplies are contaminated with pesticides or other synthetic organic chemicals (Bullard 1986). Perhaps most alarming, the heavy increase in the use of fertilizer and pesticides in the past thirty-five years has also been epidemiologically implicated in the high rate of certain cancers among farmers (Blair 1982).

It should not come as a surprise that the trend toward industrial agribusiness is accompanied by degradation of land and water resources. It is, after all, the stewardship of those natural resources that has made agriculture different from industrial businesses, and it is that difference that is eroding. If agriculture is to be made over in the image of industry, the way land and water are used will be changed. At the heart of the process of industrializing agriculture lie the changes in the relationship between people and land.

3.

Land, The Central Issue

Land, this nation's great natural endowment, has a special place in the American experience. Easy access to land, socially and economically, brought settlers to the New World, and the promise that those who worked the land might own it distinguished the New World from the Old.

Land itself had no intrinsic value, but offered instead a place on which to apply the one economic asset which nearly everyone had— the capacity to work. In the Old World, those without land had to sell their labor, and its fruits were subject to confiscation by the landlord. The term "farmer" derives from the French term "fermier," a progressive peasant who, toward the close of the feudalistic Middle Ages, was eager to produce for commercial markets. In order to farm at a commercial scale, however, the fermier had to rent land from a landlord. Significantly, a fermier was not a serf—he was not tied to the lord's estate—though his status was tenuous (Huggett 1975). His labor was his own, and if he could but get land, the entire product of his labor was his as well.

"Farmers" thus were landless people seeking an opportunity to own land, not for its own value, but for the value it imparted to their work. It was the equivalent of a job today.

This idea that people who worked the land could and should own it was thus rooted in the belief that economic opportunity should be widespread. It was a rejection of the feudal society in which rights for the many were few, while privileges for the few were many. Moreover, this new, popular right was made real in the

New World by the plain fact that there was a meaningful opportunity to gain access to and ownership of land.

The notion of individual ownership thus emerged as an alternative to the feudalistic seignorial system that lasted through the Middle Ages, and had residual effects well into the eighteenth century. Under this oppressive system, the masses of agricultual workers labored on small plots of land for their own use, paying a rent to the feudal lord of the manor. Besides their rent, they also worked about three days a week on the *demesne,* the block of land in the manor devoted exclusively to the support of the lord. The lord also monopolized essential services, such as ovens for baking bread, and mills for grinding flour, for the use of which the peasants paid. Though peasants had some personal rights, they did not have the right to leave the manor. They were their lord's labor force, without which his land was worthless (Painter 1951).

For the lord, of course, this was a pretty good deal. His manor was a fiefdom, a privilege to have and to hold, though not to "own." Instead, he was "possessor" of the land. No one considered feudal landownership as private property because the lord had no need to defend his privilege against the rights of others. Nor was feudal landownership thought of as public property, because the right to the product of the land was not owned by all. Feudalism simply meant that some had exclusive opportunities to exploit the efforts of others.

Private property, by contrast, was developed as a social right—the right of an individual to community protection from those who would vandalize or take land by force. It was instituted to ensure that the rights to property enjoyed by the masses would not be violated by those who chose not to recognize those rights. In a sense, government itself has evolved out of this need, at least in much of the Western world. John Locke argued that "the great and chief end of men uniting in commonwealths, and putting themselves under government, is the preservation of their property" (Locke 1821). Put simply, the concept of private property evolved as a community commitment to stop the meanest guy with the biggest stick from taking it all. Private property has no meaning outside the context of community, society, and government.

And it is a hollow right if few have a realistic hope of owning property. Realistic hope rested on the community's willingness to ensure that there was access to land for those willing to earn it. The New World, with its abundance of land, offered the new communities here the chance to make just such a commitment to its members.

It is not surprising then, that when the Puritans established the agrarian communities from which eventually emerged the family farming system, land was collectively held by the community. It was allocated to members on the basis of their contribution to the community and on their needs and ability to use the land. If you were worthy of membership in the community, you had a right to as much land as you needed and could use. You had a right to own that much, but not more than that much. If the community had authority over more land than was needed to support current members, the excess was to be held in common or reserved for future farmers. According to the covenant they established among themselves, those who were proprietors in the community—those entitled to a share in land—had both rights in the land and a responsibility to contribute to the common good by using it well (Bidwell and Falconer 1925; Lockeridge 1970; Cochrane 1979). Thus embodied in the birthright of the family farming system were both individual rights and community responsibilities for farmer-landowners.

During the colonial period, this covenantal relationship between land and people withered. The relationship became less communal and more individual. As the population grew and readily occupied land was taken, the original proprietors of communities gradually recognized that demand for land would bring a price. They grew reluctant to offer land to new settlers only on the basis of their worthiness to join the community. Soon, only those who could also pay could have some of the town's unappropriated land. Financial worth as well as social worthiness was necessary for anyone wanting land.

The growing population of new settlers and succeeding generations of colonists produced more pressure on the land. By the time of the Revolution, speculation in its value had become a business for those who had received grants from the Crown (Akagi 1963).

How to dispose of the nation's one valuable asset—land—thus became the central issue of the new republican government. Should it be offered free to those who would settle and improve it, or should it be sold to the highest bidder to help build the fragile nation's treasury and pay its debts? The debate raged for three-quarters of a century, and was never fully settled. Only when most of the best land had already been sold did Congress culminate the debate in the Homestead Act.

Over the period of this struggle, a social commitment to the owner-operated, working family farm evolved. But two developments tended to weaken this commitment. First, we ran out of good, easily accessible land. Second, new technology enabled one person to farm more land and to produce much more from each acre. Many of the new technologies not only made it possible to farm more land, but made it necessary to farm more land to pay for the technology—if only more land could be bought from others. The natural result was to increase competition for land. The great agricultural revolutions in machinery, genetics, and chemicals, each in its time, contributed to the transformation. Land changed from being a place to employ one's labor to a place to employ one's capital and technology. As agricultural productivity grew, so did the price of land.

In turn, as land increased in value, it provided the wherewithal to finance both new technology and acreage expansion. The ability to borrow against the value of land permitted the formation of farmer-owned credit associations that used the land as collateral for the issuance of bonds. The proceeds of the bonds were used to finance more machinery and more land.

Because land was the one input both limited in supply and essential to the use of these new technologies, it enjoyed first claim to the additional income which resulted from its use. Once the immediate farming and living expenses of the family were paid, all additional income from the increased production went to pay for land, either as ever higher mortgage payments or as higher rent to landlords.

Since nearly all the additional income from agricultural development was claimed by higher land prices and rents, most farmers benefited relatively little from this progress. They enjoyed relatively less improvement in their standard of living than did the rest of society, since most of their growing income went to pay for land—that is, for the right to farm. Of course, to the extent that those who survived this competition for land actually bought and paid for land that was rising in value, they accumulated wealth, but it was only "paper" wealth. It became a truism less humorous than ironic: Farmers live poor and die rich. The two groups benefiting most from these revolutions were consumers who received lower food prices resulting from expanded output, and landowners who received higher rents or higher market values for their land.

Naturally, those who had more capital to begin with could not only buy the new technologies but pay for the land with which to use it. Land prices thus constituted a claim on future incomes to be earned using the best technology, or put differently, a claim on someone else's future opportunity to farm. On the positive side of the ledger, this meant that land would serve increasingly effectively as a store of funds for retirement. To provide for their later years, parents rented or sold their land to their children (or others) who wanted to farm.

But on the negative side was the unavoidable fact that as land values rose, most people, including most people with the skills to farm, would be effectively denied the opportunity. They could neither inherit land nor make even the down payment on a suitable farm. This aspect of rising land prices as a manifestation of opportunity denied is the dark side of agricultural development. Land, in a word, came to be coveted.

Nothing about this process is mysterious. It merely reflects a market economy in which land is a limited commodity, a production input that must be paid for by those best positioned to use it profitably. In fact, reducing the number of people on the land is usually touted as a desirable goal of general economic development. This policy has certainly been viewed as progressive in North America. People unable to earn their living by farming were available to provide labor in the nation's burgeoning industrial plants. "Freeing" labor from the land to work in factories was supposed to make everyone better off by expanding the production of both food and other material goods. Jobs became for the masses what land had once been—a chance to earn a share of the growing prosperity.

But as industrial society has evolved, land has played an increasingly complex role in the economy. Its value is no longer tied only to its use as a food production input. Land now represents one of the few capital assets in our society that tends to appreciate in value. It appreciates because it is limited in supply, essential to food production, and subject to ever greater pressure from an increased population demanding more food. Land can't help it; it tends to increase in value because of developments in the rest of the economy. Such a striking fact implies that interest will grow in land as more than a farm production asset and retirement fund. It will become increasingly attractive as an investment for those who have no direct interest in food production at all, but who covet land for its value alone.

Indeed, land serves at least three functions which appeal to investors (Harrington et al. 1983):

— It is a *hedge against inflation* for those whose sole interest in it is to protect their money from the effects of general inflation.
— It is a *growth stock* whose current value reflects its potential to produce even greater income in the future than it does in the present. (Consequently, buyers must be willing and able to pay more for it than its current earnings justify in order to enjoy its future value.)
— It is a *tax shelter* for high-income persons because interest paid on land mortgages may be taken as a deduction and may more than offset the current taxable income received by the landlord from the land. The real increase in value of the land each year is not taxed until the land is sold, and until passage of the *1986 Tax Reform Act,* only a portion of the gain was considered to be taxable income.

These advantageous aspects of landownership, none related to the economics of food production, were the driving forces in the land market in the boom period of the 1970s. Their importance has since compounded. Far from being just a place of work or a place to employ new food-producing technologies, land has become a speculative investment commodity. It is like gold. As Richard Hofstadter (1955) observed even thirty years ago, American agriculture "loves not the land, but its value."

The obvious should be underscored here: Once land assumes these aspects, farmers—that is, those who produce income from farming—no longer hold any particular advantage in the land market. If land were only a production input and a retirement fund for farmers, they could pay for it by the income it produces, and no one else would have much interest in it. But when land serves as a hedge against inflation, a speculative investment, and a tax shelter, many will pay more for land than can be justified by the income it produces.

Of course, some farmers are in a position to gain from these aspects of landownership as well, not because they are farmers but because they are landowners. If they are able to borrow against their existing landholdings, or apply the income they receive from land already paid for to purchase additional land, they may become participants in the speculative land market. This behavior is not motivated by the enterprise of food production.

As land economics is separated from food-production economics, landownership gradually becomes separated from farm operation. This tension between use value and investment value of farmland forces a separation between ownership and operation in both crude and subtle ways. Most crudely, the separation is forced when outside investors outbid local farmers for available parcels of land. In the view of many family farm advocates, such absentee investors are almost proverbial villains.

But more subtly, and far more importantly, the forces separating ownership from operation of farms are as powerful *within* the institutional family farm as without.

As land grows in value, farmers want to hold on to it, even if they no longer farm it. They may reach retirement age, or they may not have enough land to produce an adequate income, or they may prefer other occupations. They, or even more likely their heirs, may be fed up with farming and eager to move to the city. But these farmers and their heirs want to keep the land as a good investment. Rather than sell it, they seek tenants to rent it. Even some retiring farmers with children who want to farm may resist selling such a valuable asset to the next generation.

Land-tenure patterns revealed in the data from the U.S. Census of Agriculture document this gradual separation of ownership from operation of farms. Over the past forty years there has been a steady growth in the portion of farms that are "part-owner" farms, meaning that the farmer owns some of the land in the farm and rents some. This is particularly evident among the medium and large-size farms whose expanding owners increasingly must rent land in order to farm more. The number of "tenant" farms (those owning none of the land they farm) has decreased, but almost all of the decrease has occurred on the small tenant farms, those too small to produce much of an income; larger tenant farms have remained a nearly constant portion of their size group. Meantime, "full-owner" farms (those owning all the land they farm) are increasing as a proportion of the smaller farms because at such a small size, only fully owned farms have much of a chance of surviving. Larger full-owner farms are declining as a proportion of all large farms because the farms that are expanding into the large-size category cannot do so by buying land—they must rent it. What were once full-owner, medium-sized farms are becoming part-owner, large-sized farms.

But these statistics alone cannot capture the significance of the trend toward separation of the land from the farmer. They do not reveal how it threatens to undermine the family farming system. *Within* the farm family itself, the allure of land as an investment produces changed values and behavior which inevitably alter the character of the family farm.

There was a time, not long ago, when the goals of most farm families could be summarized easily by order of priority:

— to pay for the farm, retiring all debt;
— to provide for the retirement needs of the parents;
— to establish at least one, perhaps more, children in farming, probably by selling the farm to them on favorable terms;
— to wean the other children, providing them a stake in life, probably by providing them an education.

To have lived such a life was full and rewarding. To have coaxed from the land such an abundance was a testament to the family farming system itself. More than a few accomplished all these goals.

But if land values are rising, these goals seem inadequate, particularly to those offspring who do not choose or are not chosen to stay on the farm. As the value of farmland rises, they may not find sufficient satisfaction in a mere start in life. They want their share of the farm's wealth. If a second child receives only a college education as inheritance from a fully-paid-for, 640-acre Iowa farm worth perhaps as much as $1 million, that child will probably feel effectively disinherited.

Yet for the parents and the offspring who wants to farm, there is a practical problem in redressing such a grievance. The farm is not big enough—it will not produce enough income—for all the children. Nor will it provide enough income for one to buy the others' heirship interest. To break the farm up into parcels for each to farm only ensures that none will survive. The key must be to keep the farm whole, as one farm unit, while dividing its value among the heirs. All manner of legal arrangements are sought to accomplish this challenge. Most popular is to incorporate the farm and to divide shares in stock among the family.

Equitable though this is, it opens a new set of problems. The off-farm shareholders have a different view of the farm from that of their sibling(s) who stay to farm. For them, the farm is an investment; they are tempted to think like landlords. They may very well be reluctant landlords at that, wishing their farm sibling could pay them off so they could take their inheritance and buy a home with it. They may even wish the farm sibling would give up the urge to farm so that the land might be sold and the inheritance realized for all. For the on-farm heir, the situation is no more pleasant. He or she is a tenant, renting land from this corporation in which he or she and others are stockholders. Each is tempted to farm the land for maximum current income.

The arrangement is particularly appealing to no one. None has much hope of owning the farm outright. None has much hope of realizing the cash value of their inheritance unless the farm is sold to someone with enough money to buy them all out of the farm.

Family tensions, as you might imagine, can become quite high in this setting. The nonfarm heirs don't understand farming, complains the farm heir frequently. The farm heir is unrealistic about staying on the farm, the others complain. The lawyers, accountants, and financial counselors they consult hear it all. The problem is compounded when people marry, have children, get divorces, go through life changes, encounter financial problems off the farm, or, more often, suffer losses on the farm. In a sense, the land becomes the enemy of either the farm or the family.

The consequences of this transition are many, but perhaps the most significant is that those who own land will become increasingly estranged from it or at best unfamiliar with it. I received a letter from a bookseller a few years ago that captures the poignancy of this process. He had recently acquired with his five brothers and sisters an ownership interest in a four-hundred-acre farm in Iowa. The farm had been in the family for three generations. Although his mother had been born on the farm, she had not lived there long and the letter writer himself had only a vague recollection of having seen it one time.

His reason for writing was simple: he wanted advice on his rights as an absentee landlord, a role with which he was unfamiliar and "not altogether comfortable." He did not "enjoy being so ignorant of the farm's condition and maintenance." It was his earnest desire to "exert influence for the good in my status." He was particularly worried because the nature of the trust instrument by which he acquired his partial interest was such that he could not sell it. "I am stuck with this for a long while," he wrote, "and would hope to make the best of the situation which, basically, seems unfair and unrealistic."

"What can one do who finds himself in this position and is truly concerned about the welfare of American farms?" he asked.

Clearly, it is difficult to characterize such an absentee owner as sinister or motivated by anything but goodwill. The forces dividing people from the land are potent, and they overpower the best of intentions. These forces are the undertow in the current which erodes the family farming system.

THE POLITICS OF INDUSTRIALIZING AGRICULTURE

A society giving up on its ideals invites political duplicity. Accordingly, the erosion of family farming from within means that it is always best to speak well of the family farm, even while fostering industrial agribusiness. The political sympathies of farmers themselves are torn between loyalty to family farming and the emerging dominance of industrial agribusiness. In this sense, family farming does not die in whole farm units, but a little bit at a time.

When, for example, broiler and egg production was moved from the farm to factories in the 1950s and '60s, the chicken was virtually eliminated from nearly every farm in America. Although it would have been difficult to blame the demise of a single farm on the loss of the chicken enterprise, many farms were changed. Without chickens to produce small amounts of cash for current expenses (chickens made "grocery money") and to provide a light-work enterprise for children, every family farm became less of a family farm and more of an industrial agribusiness. In such a process, the victims are hard to find, and the constituency for political resistance is invisible. On the other hand, the beneficiaries— consumers—are many, claim the industrial broiler and egg producers.

Many who profess to be a family farm in character are striving to become industrial agribusinesses. Some do so with glee, because they have made the transformation to that point of view; others reluctantly, because they must survive in a world increasingly oriented to industrial agribusiness. They have come to believe that what is bad for family farming as a system is nonetheless a necessity for their individual farm and, conversely, that some policies that sustain family farming may thwart their personal objectives. This tension between individual and social goals is inherent in any society. Ours takes the shape it does because our society is loath to impose limits on the behavior of individuals.

Not surprisingly, then, the changes taking place in agriculture are reflected in a changing politics. Family farming, which depends on dispersed economic power, open markets, and internal financing, requires public policies to police competition, prevent accumulations of wealth, and reduce barriers to entry for new farmers. These policies would attempt to preserve the system by keeping it open. Government would do for a family farming agriculture what the National Football League does for professional football—it regulates competition and balances the opportunities.

Industrial agriculture requires something different of government: that it minimize risk and secure markets in order to provide for the stable growth of industrial agribusinesses. Public policy frequently works to enhance exports and guarantee domestic markets, subsidize capital investments, and stabilize prices.

All of these policy tools are adaptable to either family farming or industrial agriculture, depending on how they are shaped and combined. Tax subsidies, generally designed to encourage the replacement of labor by technology for the benefit of industrial agribusiness can be used instead to reduce barriers to entry in a family farming system. Stabilized farm prices, now used merely to reduce price risk without disturbing the concentrated control over production by large industrial agribusinesses, could instead be used to maintain widespread ownership of farms. More on that in Chapter 9.

At the heart of the family farming versus industrial agriculture policy debate is the land issue. The land issue manifests itself politically in many ways.

In some ways, the interests of family farming and of industrial agribusiness separate easily. For example, one response to the concern over corporate farming has been a recent flurry of state legislation to prohibit corporations from owning agricultural land or engaging in farming. Now in nine states, these measures have attempted to exempt from the prohibition those "corporate" farms that are merely incorporated family farms. But where to draw the line? Legislatures (or the general public in the case of Nebraska where a constitutional amendment on this subject was adopted in an initiative-petition process) have had considerable difficulty deciding what is and is not a corporate farm or an incorporated family farm. But the criteria are fairly clear: Is controlling interest in the corporation held by members of a family or by unrelated persons; and even more crucial, do the shareholders who control the farm actually live and work on it?

Most of the states that restrict corporate farming have not faced up to these critical distinctions. They exempt corporations with a small number of shareholders, even if they are unrelated, and most do not require residency or direct involvement in the farm by shareholders. As a result, small groups of investors who may have no historic relationship with the land and no interest in establishing such a relationship are exempt from the corporate restrictions. They may be a small corporation, but they are hardly a family farm. These liberal exemptions may discourage corporate farming in a technical sense, but they do little to frustrate the development of industrial agribusiness.

But in other issues, the choices are more difficult. When do the vested interests of those who currently farm run against the public interest in preserving family farming? Nowhere, perhaps, is this dilemma more acute than in the area of estate and inheritance law.

Generally, the intent of estate and inheritance taxation is to force each generation to earn its own way by paying a substantial tax on inherited wealth. The tax is not confiscatory, though it may require the heirs to mortgage some or all of the estate in order to pay the tax. Then they, too, enjoy the privilege of paying off the mortgage, though it may not be as serious a challenge as the one their parents faced. They don't have to start from scratch, but the head start they get on the less fortunate among their generation is limited. Without such a handicap, those with inherited wealth would use their parent's estate as a financial base from which to acquire more, to the disadvantage of those who inherit little or nothing. With each new generation, the inherited advantage would grow. For farmers, the easier it is to inherit land, the more difficult it is to get it any other way. Thus, estate taxes are intended to avoid accumulation of wealth, if not prohibit it.

The logic of estate taxes is both direct and indirect. Directly, the tax forces heirs to buy back at least a portion of the inheritance, and retards their ability to compete for additional land. Indirectly, the fact that they are out of the market for additional land reduces pressure on land prices, making land more accessible to would-be farmers with none.

The estate tax thus cuts right to the heart of the origins of our national land policies, and the belief that if land is to remain available to those who will work for it, it cannot be allowed to accumulate in the hands of those who do not have to work for it.

Despite this logic, many family farm advocates support liberalizing the right to inherit. In America, it almost goes without saying that the right to property is an unlimited right, and that almost as sacred is the right to pass on to one's children that which one has acquired, without limit or interference. Generally, the rationale is also rooted in the economics of coveted land. It goes like this. If nonheirs cannot pay for land by farming it, how can heirs either? Thus, though some estate tax may be tolerable as a disincentive to accumulation of wealth, the tax must not be high enough to require the heirs to sell or mortgage a part of the estate in order to pay the tax. Otherwise, the tax would threaten the family farm. Among those who do not openly oppose the estate tax in principle, the issue boils down to a practical one: How much tax can the heirs afford to pay without losing the farm? For those who own farmland or will inherit it, the answer usually is: less than the current estate tax. What is good for the system of agriculture in which it is possible to pay for land by farming it, is bad for the vested interests of families who currently own farmland.

Thus, much of what is done in the name of family farming curiously works instead to preserve the vested interests of those family farmers striving to be industrial agribusinesses. Indeed, to save the family farm, a farmer will support policies and programs that contribute to the destruction of family farming.

Family farmers may know and agree on what is good for themselves as individuals, but they may separate politically over what they know and agree is good for family farming. Many have acquiesced to what seems the inevitability of industrial agribusiness and no longer support even the myth of family farming. For others, however, the conflict remains intense. For these, the choice seems to be to float with the current of self-interest or to swim against the tide for the principles they profess. It is an unhappy choice. It is the great dilemma of family farming.

4.

A Tale of Three Farms

Epochal changes in the economic organization of basic industries frequently go undebated until it is too late to alter their course. Sometimes they go unnoticed altogether until historians record them. Not so with the industrialization of American agriculture.

The tension between family farming and industrial agribusiness surfaced explicitly in the late 1970s. It was the immediate product of the 1977–79 farm protest which provided the political occasion to popularize an academic debate that had been going on for some time. What the protesters wanted was higher farm prices. What they got was easier (not cheaper) credit from federal agencies, something they were willing to accept, and a full-blown government study of the structure of American agriculture, something they might well have preferred to do without.

The term "structure" is academic shorthand. The structure of an industry includes everything that determines the relationships among the people who participate in it—the organization of productive resources, ownership patterns, and financial arrangements; the role of workers; the size and composition of the firms in the industry; competitive relationships among them; marketing methods; access to inputs; and all of the other factors that characterize decision-making relationships. *Structure* really refers to the parameters of economic power—who has it, how they use it, and how it affects the rest of us.

Economists have wrestled with the concept of structure for a long time. In a sense, the discipline of economics was born of the need to describe a pure structure—a market economy with pure competition as its controlling factor, one in which all parties are equal and power is absent. And it has evolved as a discipline which tries to understand and explain why it isn't that way at all. The very existence of a debate over the structure of agriculture reveals, however, that there *are* power relationships at work that frustrate the functioning of a theoretical free market. Among other things, economic power affects the distribution of income and wealth, distorts investment decisions, changes prices and employment patterns, and reduces efficiency.

Although the debate over the structure of agriculture ripened in the late 1970s, it by no means began then. Some of the nation's earliest political debates were over landownership, farm tenure, and the proper public-policy responses to the development of an imperfect market system. In a sense, North America has not enjoyed a "free market" since Queen Isabella subsidized Columbus.

Recent official concern over the structure of American agriculture dates to the 1930s, when economists and politicians became alarmed about growing tenancy, the erosion of economic opportunity, and the maldistribution of wealth in rural America. Out of a special committee on farm tenancy appointed by President Franklin Roosevelt emerged many of the New Deal programs to redistribute land and reinforce owner-operators. At the same time, studies of socio-economic problems in agriculture were freely sponsored by the Bureau of Agricultural Economics. One of the classic studies done under its auspices was Walter Goldschmidt's analysis of how land tenure and farm size affect the quality of community life in small towns (popularly known as the Arvin and Dinuba study). Since Goldschmidt's study drew negative conclusions about industrial agribusiness, it was controversial. It was politically suppressed, he was drummed out of the agency, and subsequently, the agency itself was dismantled (Goldschmidt 1978). The study of power is not appreciated by those who have it.

Since then, timidity has characterized much of the publicly sponsored research into economic structure. But in the late 1960s, such structural changes as the growth of corporate farming, the integration of the market for broilers and chickens, and the development of huge cattle feedlots prompted renewed interest among some economists in state agricultural colleges. A group of them established a committee to collaborate on a series of essays about the changing structure of agriculture. Quite correctly, they posed the question in simple, stark terms: Who will control U.S. agriculture? Included in the inaugural booklet published in 1972 were chapters on concentration versus dispersion, access to farmland, access to markets, and other subjects in political economics (Guither 1972). Subsequently, the same committee published a series of leaflets posing hypothetical outcomes to the question of who will control agriculture: a dispersed, open-market agriculture; a corporate agriculture; a cooperative agriculture; a collective-bargaining agriculture. To reassure that none of these pure models was likely to prevail, another option was also discussed: a mixture of all of them (Guither 1973).

Not surprisingly, this sparked little public response. Even the deluge of conferences, slide shows, and discussion groups sponsored by public extension funds failed to stimulate much debate about the structure of agriculture in the mid-1970s.

Such debate needed a political event to galvanize public interest. The farm strike of 1977–79 unintentionally provided it. Farmers protesting low commodity prices issued an ultimatum to Congress. If it failed to adopt legislation guaranteeing 100 percent of parity (a price for commodities that would represent the same purchasing power as those commodities had at a time when the farm economy was healthier) by December 14, 1977, the striking farmers would not plant their crop in 1978. They would "halt all Agricultural production and distribution immediately" and continue their strike until their demands were met. Striking farmers also threatened to cancel memberships in farm groups that refused to endorse the proposal (American Agriculture 1977). When the strike deadline passed, the demands were modified (the most significant modification was to drop the price demand to 90 percent of parity) and the threat to strike gave way to a more general protest, including an angry march on Washington, D.C., in February 1979.

The newly formed American Agriculture Movement (AAM) organized the protest, though it was best described as loosely organized. AAM spokespersons were plentiful, and they did not claim to represent the full spectrum of American agriculture. Instead, they claimed to represent the "real" family farmer, the fully commercial, well-capitalized farmer, one they might term "progressive." Big corporate farmers were not their constituency, nor were small farmers. One AAM spokesperson was widely quoted as saying that the movement did not need small farmers. All it needed was to organize the top family farmers who produced most of the food.

President Jimmy Carter's secretary of agriculture, Bob Bergland, got much of the brunt of AAM's anger. Bergland seemed to have too little sympathy for the AAM farmers, most of whom he probably included among the "high rollers"—a term he was fond of using. Moreover, he did not support parity. There were harsh words and confrontations between Bergland and the protesters. Some even called for Bergland's resignation.

Bergland was not about to resign and Jimmy Carter had no intention of firing him, but Bergland did have a problem. Any secretary of agriculture's main job is to woo the farm vote for the president. Convinced as he was that the AAM protesters did not represent the mainstream of American agriculture, but a group of heavily indebted farmers who had tried to borrow their way to riches in an inflationary economy, Bergland probably did not consider them to be a particularly heavy political burden. But in the minds of politicians, it is the public perception that matters: How to resist the AAM demands without appearing unsympathetic to family farmers?

That Bergland was defensive about the administration's family farm sympathies was evident in an interview with the *New Land Review*. At the peak of the AAM protest Bergland gave defensive answers to an interviewer's questions about the decline in family farming. He referred to "self-correcting mechanisms in the market place" that would prevent concentration of food production in a few hands. Tax laws were not a factor in consolidation of farms, he said. He saw no need for a government policy regarding the desirable number or size of farms. Inflationary land prices, the bane of family farming, would only be made worse by fulfilling the AAM demands for higher commodity prices, he argued. No, there was little or no need for policy change. Toward the end of the interview he summarized: "I don't see anything on the horizon that would clog up or destroy or in any way block the very strong system of family agriculture that we have in the U.S." (Center for Rural Affairs 1979).

But Bergland knew better. Two congressional agencies, the General Accounting Office and the Congressional Budget Office, had recently published reports on the subject, each questioning the role of government in determining the structure of agriculture (Schaefer 1978; Emerson 1978). This was to be Bob Bergland's legacy to agriculture: a clarion call for reform of agricultural policies that produce unintended consequences in the economic structure of agriculture. Besides, how better to diffuse the AAM protest than to challenge the forces behind the disintegration of family farming, some of which might be represented by AAM itself?

Less than three weeks later, an entirely different Bob Bergland appeared before the national convention of his old political allies, the National Farmers Union. He announced the undertaking of a major study of the structure of American agriculture. Such a study was needed because of an alarming concentration of agricultural production on a few farms, he said. Price- and income-support programs for farmers must be reevaluated to determine if they have worked to the "disadvantage of small and medium-sized farms." There was evidence, he said, that commodity programs, tax policy, and credit programs were responsible for the undesirable trend toward concentration, and he was concerned that many farm-program benefits contributed to higher land prices. "Surely," he concluded, "it is time to develop a national farm structures policy" (Center for Rural Affairs 1979).

Bergland acted quickly. He established a staff team and instructed it to conduct a series of hearings around the country to receive citizen testimony on the structure of agriculture. A hefty collection of background papers was prepared to encourage the dialogue (U.S. Department of Agriculture 1979b). Research papers, by experts within the Department and without, were commissioned. Other government agencies were encouraged to participate. The structure issue had found its moment in political time.

A TIME TO CHOOSE

When a term as academic as "structure" becomes central to a public-policy debate, it must be simplified for public consumption. The material gathered for the structure study was therefore both detailed and substantive, but the final report had to be direct, nontechnical, and readable. It was all three.

Published in the closing days of the Carter administration, *A Time to Choose* (U.S. Department of Agriculture 1981) might have seemed destined for oblivion as the babbling of a repudiated administration. The report had a role to play, however, for despite its origins as a lightning rod for political dissent, the study was serious and solidly analytical. Its theme was that critical changes were necessary to reflect new realities in agriculture. A time had come to choose between old and new policies.

Unfortunately, however, the report was written at a time when export demand was still strong, and *A Time to Choose* accepted as its premise the woebegone idea that the problem of surpluses had been solved. With strong demand in world markets and relatively high, if still too unstable, prices, agricultural income was no longer "pervasively or *chronically* depressed," the report reasoned. The disparity between incomes of farmers and those of nonfarmers had been narrowed by a combination of larger farms earning more, and smaller farms finding off-farm employment. With farm incomes stronger overall, the nation could now discuss the farm-structure problem in a rational way, without having to think first about food security or farm efficiency. We could now afford to have the kind of agriculture we wanted.

Free at last to say what might have been a heresy in the past, the USDA authors then revealed a number of important "informed judgments" they had reached:

— Tax policy is biased toward larger farms and wealthy investors.
— The marketing system is increasingly oriented to serve larger producers.
— Commodity price-support programs and credit services have been of more benefit to larger producers and landlords.
— There is little or no efficiency gain to be had from further expansion of large farms.

These general conclusions and others were based on an analysis of the size distribution of farms in the United States. Three categories of commercial farms with supposed common characteristics were identified (and a fourth category of rural farm residences was also noted). The categories were defined by the volume of farm products each sold, based on data from the U.S. Census of Agriculture.[1] The three categories described in *A Time to Choose* were therefore nothing more than a simple regrouping, or recombining of standard census classes.

1. This approach is convenient because the U.S. Department of Commerce uses sales-size intervals to classify data from its census of agriculture taken every five years. These data are widely used to measure economic conditions in agriculture. The census sales classes are tightly packed at the lower end of the spectrum—there are five classes of farms selling between $1,000 and $39,999 worth of products, but there are only two classes between that figure and $250,000

Nonetheless, the report's authors argued that these three kinds of farms—big, small, and medium—were important units of analysis for agriculture. What follows is a gross oversimplification of the farm-structure analysis that commonly develops from this approach, using more recent data than that presented in *A Time to Choose*. It is intended not to distort it, but to mimic the conventional wisdom assigned to it by so many others.

THREE FARMS

First, there are "small" farms. It has become common now to consider any farm that sells less than $40,000 in products a small farm. There are lots of these farms, but they don't produce much food. A whopping 72 percent of the 2,275,000 farms in 1985 were small farms by this definition, but they produce only 10.3 percent of the output of farm products (table 1). These farms seem to persist, and even seem to be growing in some parts of the country such as New England. They do so, reason the experts, because they really aren't farms at all; that is, the farm operators don't depend on farm income for their living. They are an odd collection of hobby farms, part-time farmers, back-to-the-land homesteaders, and oversized 4-H projects. This assessment rests on the evidence that, on average, these farms have sufficient nonfarm income, when coupled with their farm income, to raise total family income close to the national median. Some analysts pause briefly at this point to acknowledge that among this group are some who have little off-farm income, and who represent the remnant of farm poverty.

To its credit, *A Time to Choose* bothered to establish a distinction between "small farms" with sales between $5,000 and $40,000, and "rural residences" with sales below $5,000. This distinction spared the small farm from the harsh judgment that it was not really a farm at all, but it did not alter the conclusion that small farms don't depend on farming for most of the family's income. Most analysts have dropped the distinction and, with it, any consideration of the small farm as a part of American agriculture.

---

in sales, and only one class for farms with sales above that amount and below $500,000. All farms above $500,000 are lumped into one class. This particular classification scheme more or less is intended to parallel the distribution of farms, which is also skewed toward the lower end of the profile—there are more farms in each of the five sales size classes clustered between $1,000 and $40,000 in sales than there are farms in any of the sales classes above $100,000.

Table 1. Conventional View of the Structure of U.S. Agriculture

Farm Sales Size ($)	No. of Farms (1,000s)	% Farms	% Sales	Ave. Net Farm Income	Ave. Off-Farm Income ($)	Ave. Total Income
Small farms						
0–4,999	896	39.4	1.4	−4,188	22,644	18,456
5,000–9,999	268	11.8	1.5	−1,211	21,538	20,327
10,000-19,999	243	10.7	2.6	−1,978	18,916	16,938
20,000–39,999	230	10.1	4.9	−48	14,333	14,285
Total	1,638	72.0	10.4	−2,789	20,729	17,940
Medium farms						
40,000–99,999	323	14.2	15.7	6,566	10,347	16,913
100,000–249,999	221	9.7	25.2	36,660	10,551	47,211
Total	544	23.9	40.9	18,792	10,430	29,222
Large farms						
250,000–499,999	66	2.9	16.6	99,661	11,447	111,108
500,000 or more	27	1.2	32.2	640,010	15,448	655,458
Total	93	4.1	48.8	256,537	12,609	269,146

Source: U.S. Department of Agriculture. 1987

At the other end of the spectrum are large farms, those with sales of over $250,000. These are fully capitalized, modern farm operations, frequently referred to respectfully as "efficient" or "progressive." They represent the full flowering of the forces reshaping American agriculture. These are the farms that followed the advice to "get big or get out." Although a small portion of the farm population, only 4.1 percent of the farms in 1985, they produce the lion's share of the farm products—48.8 percent. And they seem to be quite healthy for it. They garnered over three-fourths of the net farm income that year, and their income from farming alone is high enough to place them among the high-income brackets in the nation. Many have nonfarm income alone that places them near the median! Indeed, these are farmers who have made their way to the promised land.

Finally, there are those "in-between" farms. Some call them "medium," others "moderate," or "family" farms. They are neither too small to write off as a nonfarm, nor big enough to be among the chosen. With sales between $40,000 and $250,000, these farms constitute 23.9 percent of the farms, and produce 40.9 percent of the sales.

For many, these "in-between" farms are a real dilemma. Many of them are certainly big enough to require most of the farm family's labor and management resources, allowing little time to earn off-farm income. But many of them are too small to produce an adequate family income from the farm alone. Others may have a spouse who works away from the farm earning more than the farm. Certainly, these farm families *think* they are farmers. They pour most of their energy into farming, but many get most of their livelihood elsewhere. Many simply don't get a lot of income from either source. Their average total family income may be less than that of many small farms not so dependent on farm income. According to the new conventional wisdom, they have only two choices: scale down the farming operation in order to expand off-farm income opportunities, or expand the farm to become more "efficient." They are economically ambivalent.

They may also be an endangered species. As medium farms choose between bigger farming and nonfarming, the number of large and small farms increase while the number of medium-sized farms declines. This cleavage of agriculture into large and small farms with the middle withering away is a phenomenon frequently dubbed by the experts as the "disappearing middle," and the result, a "dual agriculture."

Significantly, however, to many proponents of this point of view, this merely suggests that farm policy has done what it was supposed to do. Some have gotten bigger and are better off for it. About half the food is now produced on fewer than 5 percent of the farms that together earn nearly three-fourths of the net farm income. They really don't have the same economic problems as smaller farms. They represent the emerging industrial agribusiness.

By contrast, most of the operations still counted in the census of agriculture are too small to be taken seriously as farms. If they have economic problems, they are not *farm* problems, and the evidence is that because of substantial off-farm income, their problems are minimal anyway.

Thus, the only farms that really are farms and really do have income problems are the in-between farms. But unlike just a generation ago, these struggling middle-sized farms are no longer a majority of the farms or the source of most food. We may have legitimate concerns about them as victims of progress, as the remnant of traditional family farming, but the "good news" is that agriculture has matured to the point that these farms can be treated as an economic-welfare problem, not a food-production problem.

This partitioning of American agriculture into three distinct kinds of farms based on sales has come to characterize much of the public discussion of farm policy. Precisely which classes of farms are categorized as small, medium, and large varies somewhat according to the whim of the analyst and the purpose of the analysis. But the small-medium-large trinity that was persuasively presented in *A Time to Choose* has now become the usual way of looking at agriculture.

The policy debates that flow from this analysis are fairly easy to anticipate. Since these three kinds of farms are fundamentally different, they have different policy needs. While some consensus exists over the policy needs of big and small farms, it fades over what to do with the middle.

Large farms, the reasoning flows, have captured all the economies of size available in agriculture. They make use of the best technologies, they manage money well, they adopt new ideas quickly. They need little public support since they operate as "efficiently" as current technology permits. Certainly the public has nothing to gain by encouraging them to expand further, since they are already big enough to operate efficiently, and they hardly need income support to provide a decent standard of living.

But because these farms are capital-intensive and rely heavily on borrowed funds to make large investments, they do require a steady cash flow to meet current expenses. They are very sensitive to fluctuations in market prices and to sluggish demand for the commodities they produce. They therefore need government policies both to expand demand (such as aggressive export policies) and to minimize price variations.

Moreover, because these are really agribusinesses, they are more influenced by general economic conditions than are traditional family farms. Interest rates affect them significantly, as do inflation, tax policy, and the value of the dollar, which helps determine the relative price of U.S. farm products in foreign markets. For industrial agribusinesses, macro-economic policy is probably more important than farm policy.

Small farms, by contrast, don't have farm policy needs, since they really are not farms at all. Increasing farm prices, for example, would do little to help them, because they produce too little to benefit much from higher prices. Their needs are more social than economic, according to this analysis, and social needs are best handled by social, not economic, legislation. Farm policy, of course, is economic legislation.

Medium farms present the real policy challenge. To some, if

progress is permitted to continue, these farms will be forced to either expand or scale back into the part-time category. This change is fundamental to a progressive, rational economic system, and ought not to be resisted by public policy. If necessary, these farms should be eased out of agriculture gracefully by programs that soften the human suffering associated with the transition. Modest income supplements might be provided, but nothing that would interfere with the competitive nature of the system that must eventually work against them. This view is most widely held by classically trained economists, many practical politicians more worried about budget deficits and the consumer price index than farm policy, and quite a few well-established farmers and their organizations.

To others, the disappearing middle is a tragedy that signals the end of the family farm. As farms get bigger, it becomes increasingly difficult for the medium-sized farms to compete, and even harder for beginning farmers to start at a competitive size. Some, unwilling to give up on the family farm, argue that while income supplements are a form of welfare that is inappropriate for farming, price supports at levels guaranteeing that these farms can make a decent income are needed to "save the family farm". In this tradition are some of the more populist farm organizations, especially many of the newer grassroots protest groups that emerged in the Midwest during the crisis of the 1980s.

Yet others contend that the protection of medium farms is necessary, but they stress that this is impossible to accomplish if price levels for commodities are raised for every producer regardless of size or need. Medium farms should be protected therefore with income supplements paid directly from the U.S. Treasury and carefully targeted to those farms with income needs. Among those with this view are many liberal economists, some farm-state politicians, some church and rural advocacy groups. My own organization, the Center for Rural Affairs, when trapped in this debate, seeks refuge in this corner.

The point is that there are all kinds of ways suggested for dealing with the dilemma of the disappearing middle. Clearly, some view the disappearance with more alarm than others, but most recognize that something must be done. In fact, since it is the disappearing middle that carries the family farm mantle of virtue, nearly every farm program proposal is described by its proponents as one that will help save the medium-sized family farm. In fact, one proposal actively considered by members of the U.S. House of Representatives Agriculture Committee in deliberations over the 1985 farm bill was to provide most benefits to medium-sized farms, cutting back benefits to both large and small farmers. In the jargon of farm politics, both "big" and "small" have lost their virtue. "Medium" is in as the center of sympathy. In a nutshell, that is the political legacy of the debate Bob Bergland launched over the structure of American agriculture.

THE NEW CONVENTIONAL WISDOM

In politics, truly new ideas rarely enjoy the public confidence necessary to become public policy. Instead, when there is a need for significant policy change, leaders search for notions that have gained sufficient currency to become the basis for new policies and programs. A new conventional wisdom, untarnished by association with failed policy, not new ideas, is what the successful politicians search for in troubled times.

The "three farms" approach filled that bill. With it, *A Time to Choose* was not offering a radical new analysis of contemporary agriculture, but a crystallization in popular terms of an emerging consensus among experts about the changes taking place in agriculture. Even if the authors' recommendations about policy changes were not widely accepted, the report presented a simple framework for evaluating farm structure that was.

Government economists, university researchers, farm organizations, and newspaper editors have all crafted their arguments on the theory that American agriculture has been partitioned into "three farms." Understanding this uniform framework that now dominates analysis of farm problems is important because it shapes and limits the political debate upon which policy choices are made. The analysis is so widely accepted that it must be invoked to defend whatever position one chooses to argue. Once the pattern of analysis becomes standard, necessary assumptions are made without challenge, and they become less well understood with time and usage. Raw data from which reasonable people might build many conflicting conclusions tend to be homogenized and reported in standard formats which fit the prevailing way of looking at things. We tend to see what we expect to see. Other possibilities are obscured.

Most important is the conclusion implicit in the new conventional wisdom, one that is attractive in its simplicity: *Agricultural policy has worked.* The problem was too many people dividing up the pie; the solution was to make half of them bigger farmers and half of them nonfarmers. That has been accomplished. All that remains is to clear up a few residual problems. If some of the remaining farmers would only learn that they could earn more income outside agriculture, they would leave the farm, turning their land resources over to those who would then be able to expand, make better use of new technologies, and enjoy a decent income. How to make that happen is where the new conventional wisdom admits to no conclusion.

In sum, the new conventional wisdom now sets the parameters of the farm-policy debate. It contains these widely accepted notions:

— American agriculture has matured. It is now structurally differentiated into three clearly separable groups (big farms, small farms, and medium farms), and each group has its own, different needs.
— Larger farms produce most of the food and are most efficient. They do not need or deserve direct public support; they need price stability, export programs, and a general economic climate of growth.
— Smaller farms aren't really farms at all, don't really have income problems, and can't be helped by farm programs anyway. They should not be considered in farm-policy discussions.
— Medium-sized farms are under the most pressure as they struggle to produce an adequate farm income from an inadequate farm. Most of the people who farm them would be better off farming either bigger or smaller. What to do with them is the big policy issue.

BEYOND THE NEW CONVENTIONAL WISDOM

As far as it goes, the new conventional wisdom has merit. Its most important contribution is that it has legitimized the question, Who benefits from farm programs? That question has been underemphasized for far too long.

But there are more than a few problems with the simplistic nature of this notion that the world of American agriculture now consists of three neatly defined kinds of farms. By focusing attention on the size distribution of farms only, more important changes taking place in American agriculture are obscured. By focusing on the "problem" of medium-sized farms, we miss the problems of industrialization. Some faults in the "three farms" approach are merely measurement and accounting problems.

First, using the volume of sales as a measure of farm size has some limitations. Since the sales-size intervals are based on gross income from the sale of farm products, they can be easily distorted by changes in commodity prices. A farm producing 2,000 market hogs for sale in a year when the average hog sells for $110 grosses $220,000 a year and is considered a medium-sized farm. A year later when the average hog sells for $130, the same farm, with no change in output, grosses $260,000 and is considered a large farm. Is this farm, which experienced an 18 percent increase in gross income a different farm? Can conclusions about the success or failure of policies designed to help medium-sized farms be drawn from this change? Are there fewer medium farms and more large farms as a result of this change? The answer to all these questions is no.

This phenomenon of "floating intervals" does offer some additional insight into the industrialization of agriculture. In industrial economics, sales volume is a reasonably valuable tool for measuring the size of a firm because the prices of industrial products fluctuate little. But farm commodity prices commonly fluctuate by 15 to 20 percent in a year, so for a given farm, a sales-size category is not very reliable over time. As differences in the size of farms become more extreme, the sales-size criteria becomes a more effective tool for measuring the growing differences. This explains much of its popularity despite its limitations.

Second, the classification obscures major differences between farms with similar volumes of sales but different mixes of crops. A commercial cattle feedlot is in the business of buying cattle that already weigh 600 to 800 pounds and feeding them rich diets of expensive feed grains which the feedlot also must purchase. If it markets about 500 head of cattle per year, it would gross about $250,000 in sales and would therefore be in the sales-size class generally considered to be large farms. But since it buys both the feeder cattle it feeds and the grain with which to feed them, the value it adds to the economy is only the difference between these purchased inputs and the value of the fattened cattle it sells. Its net income is very low.

On the other hand, a farm-feedlot that raises both the cattle and the feed grains, then feeds the grain to the cattle, may also sell 500 head and gross $250,000, but it has produced considerably more economic activity and would ordinarily receive considerably more net income. While the $250,000 commercial feedlot is small for such operations, the farm-feedlot is not. But the sales-volume classification system masks the difference. The dollar value of the products sold from the farm does not necessarily measure the contribution it makes to the nation's economy.

The sales-size approach produces a third measurement problem. Average income figures reported for farms of various sales-size categories obscure important income variations *within* the classes. Off-farm income is particularly subject to variability, especially at the lower end of the scale where it most affects judgments about the economic condition of the farm operator. Lumped together in some of those smaller sales-size classes are part-time hobby farmers with off-farm professional incomes, semi-retired farmers living on social security, and some beginning farmers who farm limited acreage and try to make ends meet with a part-time job. The average off-farm income of farms with sales between $10,000 and $19,999 may be about $19,000, as table 1 indicates, but the average may describe the actual circumstance of none of them. Do most of the 247,000 farms with sales between $20,000 and $40,000 have off-farm incomes sufficient to reach the conclusion that they are really too small and too well off to be considered farms with income problems?

Very little is known about the distribution of off-farm income among farmers, but a USDA survey in 1979 indicated that over two-thirds of the farms in each of the sales categories under $40,000 earned less than the average shown in table 1 (U.S. Bureau of the Census 1982). A similar survey in 1984 produced similar results (Ahearn 1986).

But there are more than mere measurement problems with the "three farms" approach. There are also conceptual and analytical problems.

The actual distribution of farms is continuous, of course. Each farm has a specific volume of sales, and that is its sales size. But for analytical purposes, it is necessary and convenient to group them. The selection of certain sales-size intervals to define "large," "medium," and "small" is entirely arbitrary, and the upper and lower sales-size figures that define each interval are arbitrary as well. The larger the groupings and the fewer of them there are, the less similar the farms within a given class must actually be.

70

With the nine census classes consolidated into three farm sizes, the lines of demarcation between them must be harsh. The relationships between small and medium and between medium and large become distorted. Farms that are really quite similar are made to look different by the classification alone. A farm with $45,000 in sales is more like one with $35,000 in sales than it is like one with $245,000 in sales, yet the arbitrary classification of farms into three groups leaves it analytically lumped with the larger farm, not the smaller one.

This problem is compounded by the fact that farms are not evenly distributed within the sales-size classes. They tend to congregate toward the lower end of each class. There are therefore far more medium-sized farms with about $45,000 in sales than there are medium-sized farms with $245,000 in sales. *Most medium farms are more like small farms than they are like large farms.*

In other words, the "pie" that constitutes American agriculture can be cut up to support nearly any conclusion one wants to draw about small, medium, and large farms.

For example, when the USDA published an analysis of the farm-credit crisis in 1985, it broke faith with the standard classification scheme (Harrington and Stam 1985). Instead of categorizing farms with sales between $250,000 and $500,000 as large farms, it grouped them with a medium-size class which it called commercial family farms. That was an important adjustment, since farms in this class had the worst debt-to-asset ratio. Lumping those farms with medium-sized farms allowed a single, simple conclusion to be drawn from the study—one that was widely reported by the news media: Medium-sized family farms are the ones most in trouble.

A reasonable person could have easily looked at the same USDA data and reached a much different conclusion: The larger the farm, the more likely it is to be heavily indebted. But such a conclusion would not fit the new conventional wisdom's widely held belief that large farms are efficient and healthy, and that medium farms are destined to disappear because they are inefficient. Perhaps the USDA economists saw what they wanted to see, then fit the data to their conclusion. Better to change definitions of "medium" and "large" than to allow the facts to challenge conviction.

Another conceptual problem with the "three farms" approach is that it leaves the unmistakable impression that the structure of agriculture is one-dimensional, and that the distribution of farms measured by the value of their output is the only structural characteristic that matters. Although the volume of sales is critical in the power relationships among farms, the ownership and management structure, the land base, the tenure of the operator, the financial structure, and the diversity of crops (or the lack thereof) are just as important. There are many "structures" of agriculture, and they must be viewed simultaneously. The more included, the richer the analysis. Looking at only one dimension of the structure of agriculture is like buying a house on the basis of a newspaper photograph.

It only takes a little more information about these other structures of agriculture to change one's perspective. In reviewing the status of the family farm in Nebraska, agricultural economist Bruce B. Johnson included labor in his analysis (Johnson 1983). He assumed that a family farm must be one which sold over $20,000 in farm products, controlled management decisions within the family, *and* received the lion's share of its labor requirements from the family. If a farm hired more than 150 worker-days of outside labor, it would not qualify as a family farm.

The validity of that assumption aside, its inclusion as a variable and its impact on Johnson's conclusions were significant. Over 10 percent of all farms in Nebraska would have otherwise qualified as family farms in this analysis, but for the fact that they hired too much labor. Not surprisingly, these were larger-than-average farms, producing nearly 37 percent of the state's farm output. Had Johnson not included the labor dimension in his analysis, he would have concluded that three-fifths of the farms in Nebraska are family farms and that they produce 84 percent of the state's farm products. With the labor variable included, Johnson found that *less* than half the farms in Nebraska are family farms and they produce less than half the farm products.

These are more than academic matters. It matters whether you assume that average income for a sales class of farms is typical; it makes a difference which sales groups you combine for small, medium, and large farms, and it surely alters the picture to consider the importance of other factors as well as volume of sales in defining those terms. In fact, using the same database from the census of agriculture and USDA surveys, it is possible to arrive at a significantly different view of the structure of American agriculture. To do so, however, we must give up some of the comfortable assumptions of the new conventional wisdom.

First, rather than use averages as the measure of any variable, we choose instead to chart variables on a graph showing how they

Figure 1. Characteristics of Farm Operations by Size

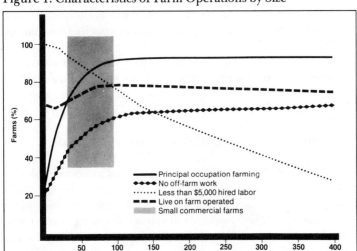

change over various farm sizes measured by sales. We still must use average values for each variable, but instead of assuming that the average typifies the entire class, we can now show how that variable changes, approximately, over the full range of the class. Doing so does not correct the problem of skewed distribution within the class, but we have escaped much of the distortion of averages.

Second, we abandon any predetermination of what a small, medium, or large farm is, and any commitment to define those terms as mere combinations of census sales classes.

Third, we include some information beyond farm and off-farm income. We consider the principal occupation of the farm operator, the number of days worked off the farm, the amount of money spent to hire others to work on the farm, and whether the farm operator lives on the farm he or she operates. The 1982 census of agriculture reports all of these data by sales-size class. They are charted in figure 1.

This organization of data reveals a striking cluster of farms somewhere within the range of $20,000 and $100,000 in sales (the shaded area in figure 1). These farms include the larger of those farms usually considered small and the smaller of the farms usually considered medium sized. We might call this group "small commercial farms." They exhibit the following characteristics:

— Their total family income averages below or very near the national median income, in the $15,000 to $25,000 range.
— From 60 to 90 percent report that their principal occupation is farming.
— From 40 to 60 percent report no days worked off the farm (and from half to three-quarters work less than half-time off the farm).
— From 75 to 95 percent spend less than $5,000 on hired farm labor.
— From 70 to 75 percent live on the farm they operate.

The figure also reveals that within these approximate sales-size ranges, the overall reliance on farm income and other characteristics of commercial farming grow with increase in sales volume. Time spent in employment off the farm is declining, while money spent on hired labor is increasing. Those who are farming are more apt to consider themselves farmers. Significantly, above $100,000 in sales, the rate of change in most of these variables is considerably slowed. This suggests that those above $100,000 in sales represent a more homogeneous group, while those below a more diverse group. It seems to offer little support for the conventional practice of grouping those in the sales class below $100,000 with those in the class above.

These small commercial farms may be small compared to the larger farms that produce most of the food, but they are clearly serious, commercial ventures. For the most part, these farmers spend most of their time farming, they think of themselves as farmers, they live where they farm, and they don't hire anyone else to farm for them.

Most of these farms may be too small to earn an adequate income in the economic environment within which they farm, but if they moonlight to supplement their farm income, it is probably out of necessity, not by preference.

Nor are these farms an insignificant part of the farm economy. In 1982, they had stewardship of about 315 million acres of farmland (about 32 percent of all land in farms), and of about 160 million acres of cropland (about 36 percent). They produce about 27 percent of the total output, and they constitute 28 percent of all farms. Significantly, 38 percent of all people in the United States who consider their principal occupation to be farming are within this group. And 63 percent of the people who consider themselves farmers *and* sell over $20,000 worth of farm products are part of this small commercial farm group.

Among these small commercial farmers are many families who live in the irony of poverty amid substantial resources. The average value of all physical assets (excluding the home) on farms with gross sales between $20,000 and $100,000 in 1982 was over $511,000, about three-fourths of which was in the form of real estate—primarily farmland. Moreover, about 83 percent of that asset base was in the form of equity. These farms owe relatively little. In fact, according to a USDA survey taken during the farm credit crisis of 1984, such farms as a group have proportionally the lowest debt-to-asset ratio among farms in America (Harrington and Stam 1985).

In short, these small commercial farms are a major source of financial resiliency, if not prosperity, in American agriculture. They are not the agriculturally insignificant residual of progress that orthodox analysis makes them out to be.

Splitting the small and medium-sized farms at $40,000 in sales, as most analysts do, divides in half this group of small commercial farms and thus obscures an important perspective on the structure of agriculture. This group is not comprised of farms too small to be considered real farms, nor does it represent a minority of the farm population. It is, in fact, *the largest group of commercial farms in the nation.* Moreover, this group is not free of income problems. Most small commercial farms receive well below the national median income.

But the point here is not to substitute one pie-cutting scheme for another. There is no "right" way to look at the structure of American agriculture using sales-size criteria alone. Each of us will tend to see what we want to see. Like the Rorschach test used to assess personality by analyzing responses to ink-blot designs, what we see from sales-size data may say more about us as analysts than it does about American agriculture.

More important, this kind of analysis rests too heavily on a series of data that represents a slice in time. No matter which dimensions are included, they must be measured "standing still" on the day the survey is taken. But things are changing rapidly in American agriculture. And they are changing across all dimensions at once. Farms are growing, and they are not just growing bigger. They are growing more specialized, more industrial, more powerful, more complex. The shape of the lines in figure 1 says more about the dynamics of change in American agriculture than do the numbers in table 1, but neither reveals the nature of the competitive relationships among classes of farms, or their policy needs.

It is here that the new conventional wisdom misleads most seriously. Its most serious flaw is in the giant leap it takes from separating farms by sales size to assuming that the needs of each of the "three farms" in the model can be independently met by a dispassionate Congress. This all-things-to-all-people approach is politically appealing, but entirely impractical in any other respect.

Though there may be parts to the whole of agriculture, it is nonetheless a unified whole, and the parts interact dynamically. The unifying fact is that farming operations that make up the whole compete for limited land and for limited markets for farm products—for limited opportunities to farm. No policy that benefits one part can therefore be expected to be neutral with respect to the other parts. Policies that encourage expansion or reduce risk on large, highly leveraged farms cannot be without consequence for smaller farms, especially for beginning farmers entering the land market for the first time. Likewise, policies that protect the incomes of smaller farms must frustrate the expansion plans of other farms. The needs of these groups may be separable, but the means of meeting those needs are not necessarily compatible.

When farms were more or less alike, or at least seemed that way, it was easy to talk in simple terms of what was good for agriculture. Efficiency, rationality, productivity, and income were the issues. One policy for all of agriculture was reasonable. But with the growing recognition that farms are not the same, comes growing awareness that all do not benefit in equal measure from the same public policies. *A Time to Choose* made the point. Not many others have since. The structure issue means that fairness must be considered in farm policy today.

Any policy for agriculture must recognize the differences among farms, regulate the competitive environment, address the distribution of income and resources, and redress the inequities among farmers. That challenges the comfortable neatness of the new conventional wisdom, which speaks simply of three sizes of farms, the needs of each, and the harmonious programs that can give something to each. Bob Bergland was right: We need a national farm structure policy.

This policy should recognize that the size distribution of farms is but one aspect of the structure of American agriculture. The static issue of counting farms or measuring their sales is far less important than the dynamic one of fair competition, economic opportunity, growth and expansion, and the exercise of economic power. These are public policy issues. Who farms, under what conditions, and for what rewards are at stake, and these are determined as much by the fickle laws of the state as by the immutable laws of economics.

To be fair, the debate Bob Bergland and the American Agriculture Movement sparked over the structure of American agriculture did address such issues, but incompletely. To the dismay of many who care about them, it turned them into a series of clichés about "three farms." The term "structure" has gone from being academically esoteric in 1977 to fashionable in 1980 to trite today. But the issues it embraces persist. Indeed, as the farm crisis swells, questions multiply. Whom to help with financial aid, and why? And as American agriculture continues its structural transformation toward industrialization, the course becomes more irreversible and the consequences greater.

Perhaps we are blind to these dynamic relationships and their policy implications because we have simply accepted the view that bigger is better. For those who have, the questions this chapter raises about farm structure may seem irrelevant. Industrial agribusiness is not a soothing concept, but after all, isn't efficiency in food production our top priority, and aren't these big, on-the-way-to-becoming-industrial farms more efficient? Isn't that why they expand and gain more control of agriculture? Isn't bigger better, after all?

The answer is: not necessarily.

5.

The Myth That Bigger Is Better

The emergence of industrial agribusiness is a product of the tireless quest for efficiency in agriculture. In America we believe that bigness delivers efficiency.

Efficiency is always measured in the cost of inputs *per unit of output*. The fewer inputs used to produce a bushel of corn or a hundredweight of pork or a bale of cotton, the more efficient the farm. Since most experts believe that as the size of a farm increases, it can use its resources more efficiently to produce at a lower cost, "bigger is better" becomes axiomatic.

Of course, there is also a theoretical peak efficiency. Take the challenge of finding the most efficient way to rid a field of weeds. In most cases, controlling the weeds using a chemical herbicide will cost less—including the cost of the machine used to spray it—than it would cost to control the same weeds by hand labor. But, that would be true only if the farmer has enough acres to justify investing in the sprayer. With very few acres, the farmer could not pay for the sprayer from the additional income received as a result of the increase in yield attributable to the weed control. That farmer would be better off weeding by hand. However, that farmer might not be better off than the farmer who acquired more land, bought the sprayer, and paid for it from the additional yield per acre from many more acres.

Efficiency, therefore, involves optimizing available resources in two ways. First, more productive resources (i.e., those that accomplish the same result at a lower cost per unit of production) must be substituted for less productive ones. And second, more productive resources must be used at a scale that keeps them fully employed—that maximizes their income-earning potential. Thus, there are two great sins in managing for economic efficiency. One is to use the wrong resources; the other is to use the right resources, but below their potential. Weeding by hand is one sin; not farming enough land to pay for the sprayer is another.

As technology changes, the size of an optimally efficient farm changes, too. As new technologies are developed, the number of acres and volume of production one farmer can manage tend to expand, too. The relationships between size and efficiency are expressed as *economies of size*.

It should be emphasized that a farm can be inefficiently operated at any size if it combines resources in impractical ways. A farm that produces fewer bushels of corn per dollar expended because it uses too much land and not enough fertilizer might be just as inefficient as one that uses too much labor and too little machinery, regardless of the number of bushels each actually produces. But there is a theoretically optimum combination of inputs producing an optimum volume of output. That is the solution to the efficiency puzzle.

What happens beyond that point of peak efficiency if the farm continues to grow? Once the lowest cost per unit of production is achieved, further expansion may result in higher costs per unit. Farms can get less efficient as they grow. This is called diseconomy of size, the downside of efficiency. Diseconomy may occur primarily because of the human factor in production. As farms become larger, making use of more land and machinery, it becomes necessary to add hired labor. Even under optimal conditions of goodwill between management and labor, the fact is that there is a cost involved in communicating instructions between those who make decisions and those who must implement them. That cost is worth paying only when the farmer hasn't enough time to do the work, such as when extra labor is needed to harvest perishable crops at the right time. Ask any farm manager: the farm operated by the one who makes the decisions has an advantage over the one in which management must direct labor.

Moreover, quality of the management itself may not be able to keep pace with the quantity of land and other resources being managed. Technology may permit things to be done bigger, but it does not necessarily assure that they will be done well. Management quality is the critical, and most nearly immeasurable ingredient in size efficiency.

The perfect farm is one in which all resources are fully used in just the right combination to produce a bushel of corn (or pound of cotton, or hundredweight of milk) as cheaply as possible. Economists search for such a farm by measuring how the cost of producing a single unit of production varies with the size of the farm. The one with the lowest cost of production is the winner. If that does not sound like the perfect farm to you, step aside. In the economic theory of agriculture, the quest for perfection is the quest for efficiency. Some people might bridle at the notion, but economics loves dispassion.

CONSENSUS ABOUT ECONOMIES OF SIZE

The study of economies of size is important because it provides a measure for how close to theoretical efficiency farms are actually operating, and whether the cost of producing food on these farms is reasonable. If resources are not being used efficiently, public policy ought to encourage adjustment, or at least not discourage it.

Studies in this field are voluminous and there is a familiar pattern to the findings. The consensus emerging from these studies was best summarized by J. Patrick Madden in 1967 and has been scarcely modified since. Figure 2 shows a standard cost curve reflecting this consensus. There is some disagreement among economists over the location of the curve (i.e., how high or low actual costs are on farms of a particular size), especially with respect to some crops (Hall and LeVeen 1978). But the *shape* of the curve and the interpretation of it (i.e., the relationship between size and efficiency) are generally agreed upon by economists. The consensus is summarized in six points:

— Very small farms operate inefficiently (have high costs) because they are guilty of excess capacity—too much idle equipment, underutilized labor, and other resource-squandering practices (point A, figure 2). They produce too little for the resources they consume.

— As farms become moderately large, however, they rapidly gain in efficiency, making better use of all those inputs. In fact, most of the economies of size are achieved at relatively small volumes

80

Figure 2. Standard View of Economies-of-Size

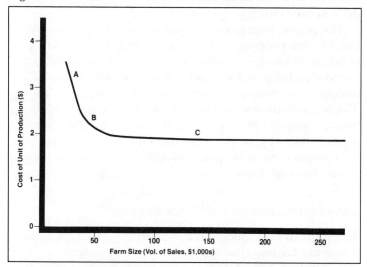

of output. Under current circumstances, farms producing as little as $45,000 worth of output (at point B, figure 2) have captured most of the economies of size, i.e., they produce at costs within 10 percent of the most efficient operators. Beyond that size, not much more efficiency can be gained by getting larger (U.S. Department of Agriculture 1981).

— Peak efficiency (lowest cost of production per unit) is gained on most types of farms when one or two people are kept fully employed using the best technology. Though the figures vary greatly depending on the crop, on average, the volume of sales necessary to accomplish this level of efficiency today is about $133,000 (point C, figure 2). By most standards, that is considered a mid-sized farm today.

— Beyond peak efficiency the cost of production does not change much. Most economists believe it remains about the same or even increases very slightly because of diseconomies of size due to management inefficiency. This is especially the case for farms operated over large areas where weather and other natural factors are more difficult to monitor, or for farms requiring highly skilled labor and close supervision. Where labor can be routinized, simplified, and easily supervised, as in large feedlots, for example, and where more of the natural risks can be controlled by management, as in animal factories, management diseconomies may be minimal.

— Even though costs per unit of production may increase slightly as farms expand beyond the point of peak efficiency, many continue to expand anyway. They do not gain in efficiency, but they do gain in total net profit. This is possible because even if costs do increase slightly and thus the profit margin on each unit of production decreases slightly, there are more total units of production to sell, and thus more total profit. If the costs increase too much, of course, they may exceed the price the farmer can get for each unit of production. At that point, expanding not only reduces efficiency, but profits as well. But most economists doubt that this ever occurs in agriculture.

— Some large farms enjoy certain market economies, also known as pecuniary economies. These are cost savings in the form of special discounts on the inputs they purchase and special price premiums on the commodities they sell. These discounts and premiums have the effect of substantially increasing the profitability of the larger farms. One study concluded that large wheat farms may receive as much as $.10 per bushel more and spend as much as $1.84 per acre less on inputs as a result of these market economies (Krenz, Heid, and Sitler 1974). But these cost savings are a result of the market power of these farms and of the economic advantages their bigness offers the companies who do business with them, not their own internal efficiency. Dealers and processors simply want their large volume of business enough to pay more for it in discounts and premiums.

This assessment has become almost standard. A number of implications flow from it. If most efficiency is gained at about $45,000 in sales, and nothing can be gained in efficiency after about $133,000 in sales, then most food in America is produced on farms operating very near or above peak efficiency levels. About seven-eighths of the food is produced on farms which market over $40,000 in sales. Moreover, since nearly half of the food is produced on farms marketing over $250,000, it is safe to say that half the food comes from farms that are *larger than they need to be* to be fully efficient.

From the point of view of the public, then, American agriculture must be considered big enough. There is really little public purpose in encouraging further farm-size expansion. That is precisely the conclusion reached by the USDA in *A Time to Choose.*

But from a private point of view, no farm is ever big enough as long as diseconomies of size do not threaten the prospect of further profit from further expansion. If costs increase due to diseconomies, they may exceed the selling price of the commodity being produced. Then the farm will have expanded too much, will be operating inefficiently, and will lose money. But since the consensus is that little or no diseconomy of size exists, that won't happen. More expansion means more profit. Why not expand?

At the other end of the spectrum, the small farms are an enigma. Operating as inefficiently as they supposedly do, they must lose money on everything they produce. Why do they persist? And why are there so many of them? Economists have anguished over them.

Some explanation must be found that is consistent with the theory of economies of size. Many have been brought forward. One is that these small farmers really can't do anything else, or at least don't think they can, so they don't move out of agriculture even though they should, rationally. Another is that the money they have invested in buildings, equipment, and machinery cannot be salvaged for use elsewhere because they can't be used in any other business and there isn't much of a market for used farm goods. So these farmers hang on because they can't get their money out of the farm.

Lately, it has become fashionable to theorize that off-farm income makes it possible for many of these inefficient operators to subsidize their farm. They farm because they want to, not because they have to, should, or are good at it. And they are willing to pay a price in reduced standard of living in order to do so. They "exploit" their own family labor, accepting less for their work than they could make elsewhere, some because they can afford to, some despite the fact they really cannot. To each his own, but they are no credit to efficiency, so the argument goes.

Some experts have been known to get downright hostile about small farms. They berate them for being irrational, inefficient, a burden to society, selfish hoarders of land and other resources that bigger farmers could use better. They harangue, discredit, blame. This pejorative view of small farms is a form of scapegoating that is especially handy in explaining why large farms get into financial trouble from time to time.

Scapegoating the small farm has become more popular lately as the public has begun to question giving federal farm-program benefits to large farms. In a widely read 1983 article in *Science* magazine, for example, the prominent agricultural economist Luther Tweeten wrote about the economics of small farms. Tweeten's purpose was to debunk eight "more or less conventional assertions concerning small farms"—that they provide a higher quality of life, use energy more efficiently, take better care of their soil, and have been disadvantaged by federal farm programs, for example. His dispassionate conclusion that "the evidence provides no basis to accept any of the eight small farm hypotheses" was richly spiced with a few passionate assertions along the way, including his description of small farming as a condition of "poverty, discrimination, underemployment, and squalor" (Tweeten 1983).

Less than a month earlier, Tweeten had revealed that his real concern was not the plight of small farms, but the political threat they pose to larger farms. In an interview for *Farm Futures* magazine, one of a growing number of trade publications catering to large farms, the author of the article attributed to Tweeten a concern that "a movement of small farmers could create powerful political pressure to redirect government funds to try to save small-scale agriculture." Tweeten believes, the article continued, that "commercial farmers have a stake in offsetting the 'mythology that is so rampant' concerning 'alleged advantages of small farms'" (Skolda 1983). These comments place the *Science* article in perspective as an attempt to scapegoat small farms so as to keep the benefits of farm programs going to larger farms.

Could it be that what gets under some people's skin is not only that small farms persist, but that their persistence challenges the notion that bigger is better, as well as the political privileges for some that rest on that notion?

Let's look again at this notion that bigger is better.

LOOKING AGAIN AT ECONOMIES OF SIZE

Evaluating economies of size requires that a number of assumptions and judgments be made about what to include in the analysis as legitimate costs of production and how to measure those costs. Further decisions have to be made about how to measure the size of the farm. Throughout the analysis, choices are made that reflect the values of the analyst. The results, of course, appear as mere numbers, as sterile and objective as can be. Looking only at the numbers is therefore not enough. It is necessary to understand the assumptions that underlie them. Usually, though not always, the assumptions underlying formal studies are stated, even if only in appendices, footnotes, and obscure portions of the text.

But the general public, predisposed to believe that bigger is better, does not (and sometimes cannot) evaluate the underlying assumptions of economies-of-size studies. We only hear the general conclusion that bigger is better, and our biases are reaffirmed. Time and again, journalists, politicians, and other opinion shapers simply regurgitate the phrase "bigger and more efficient farm" as if the public only had to be reminded that, of course, one characteristic implies the other. But these studies are the intellectual foundation that supports our collective bias, and they provide the political rationale for national policies that encourage farm expansion. It is worth our time to examine their underlying assumptions.

When we do, it isn't difficult to detect a pattern. Assumptions are consistently biased in favor of larger farms and against smaller farms. The bias is not necessarily born out of prejudice. Most economists really try to be objective. Few are smitten with the need to scapegoat small farms. But since most seem to begin with a belief that bigger is better, they design studies that confirm their belief. Four systematic biases frequently lurk within efficiency studies. They are briefly outlined below.

Social and Environmental Costs Ignored

Most efficiency studies ignore social and environmental costs because these costs are external to the farm. The study of economics is the study of selfishness and therefore economists tend to ignore costs that the farm can force others to pay. Economists are particularly inclined to discount the value of the future, and therefore to ignore any costs that must be absorbed by the next generation of farmers and consumers. The record of U.S. agriculture with respect to these costs is largely unknown, though they are suspected to be quite high. What, for example, is the cost of a ton of topsoil washed away by careless farming practices? Since as much as one-half of the topsoil in major portions of our most productive areas of the Midwest has been washed or blown away, it is a serious question. Equally serious questions surround the cost of groundwater depletion, pesticide contamination, and the displacement of farmers.

Our concern for the moment though, is whether these costs are higher on larger farms, and whether the results of efficiency studies would be altered if these costs were included in the analysis. The plain answer is that we do not know. However, some studies suggest that the separation of ownership from operation of farmland—characteristic of large-scale, industrial agribusiness—does adversely affect soil conservation. Ervin (1982) found that erosion rates for cropland and pasture were 40 percent higher on rented land than on owned land, despite the fact that the rented land was less erosion prone. The reason was simple: conservation practices were more common on owner-operated land. Another study confirmed that full owner-operators are more likely to invest in conservation than were nonoperator landlords (Baron 1981).

Social costs of farm consolidation are also rarely considered in economies-of-size studies. Yet they have been widely documented. The classic study in this field was the controversial Goldschmidt study done in California in the 1940s (Goldschmidt 1978) mentioned earlier. Comparing two nearby communities of similar size and physical endowments, one with a modest-scale, owner-operated farming environment and the other with a large-scale, absentee-owned farm system, Goldschmidt found startling differences in the character of the two communities:

— The small-farm community supported nearly twice as many business establishments as the industrial-farm community and two-thirds more retail trade.
— Expenditures for household supplies and building equipment were three times greater in the small-farm community.
— There were 20 percent more people per dollar of agricultural crop sales in the small-farm community, where half the breadwinners were self-employed. Two-thirds of the people in the industrial-farm community were agricultural wage laborers, with fewer than one-fifth of paid workers self-employed.
— The small-farm community had four elementary schools and a high school while the industrial-farm community had but a single elementary school.
— The small-farm community had three parks and two newspapers compared with one corporate-owned playground and one

newspaper in the industrial-farm community; the small farm community had twice the number of civic organizations, churches, and church-goers.

Are these conditions typical only of California? Not at all. A 1986 study done at the University of California–Davis for the Congressional Office of Technology Assessment (U.S. Congress 1986b) reviewed the relationship between poverty and agricultural development in two hundred of the richest agricultural counties in the nation. The study found that as farm size increases, so does poverty, and that the faster farm size increases, the faster poverty increases. Midwestern studies have found similar patterns between farm size and social relations. One study of the long term development of rural Nebraska concludes that the overall rural population, the number of retail stores and service establishments, the size of the civilian work force, and school enrollment are all a function of the *number* (and therefore the size) of farms in a local area and not the *volume* of farm goods produced in that area (Swanson 1980).

A summary judgment is in order. It comes from University of California–Davis sociologist Dean MacCannell who has studied the relationship between agricultural structure and social conditions in California as closely as anyone and has lead an effort to update the Goldschmidt findings in a series of contemporary studies. In reviewing the results of his own work as well as that of others in the Midwest and South, he concludes: "Everyone who has done careful research on farm size, residency of agricultural landowners and social conditions in the rural community finds the same relationship: as farm size and absentee ownership increase, social conditions in the local community deteriorate" (MacCannell n.d.).

What is the cost to society of dislocating, relocating, and retraining farm families pushed off the land by expanding farms, and dismantling or restructuring the rural communities that are supported by those farm families? No one really knows. A branch of economics known as welfare economics devotes itself to questions of how to evaluate the net cost and benefits of economic change. But welfare economists so far have not taught production economists how to include these costs in the efficiency formula. So, in the dispassionate language of economics, they remain "externalities."

But the fact that quantifying social and environmental costs is difficult does not alter the fact that they are real. Surely if they were not real, they would not have their own name—externalities. If they were not largely ignored in economies-of-size studies, the size of an optimally efficient farm would be deemed smaller than it now is by economists, and diseconomies of size would be more widely acknowledged.

Imputed Costs Inflated for Small Farms

A more tangible problem with economies-of-size studies is how to deal with costs that are not paid out in cash by the farmer, but are absorbed internally in the farm. The best examples are labor, management, overhead, and a return on the farmer's investment in land, machinery, and buildings. These are real and unavoidable costs, but no survey of farmers can provide a realistic estimate of these costs. Farmers tend to overlook many of them, and like economists, farmers aren't really sure what some of these costs are. So these are costs that economists impute according to their wits, not according to farm records.

Most economies-of-size studies rely heavily on such imputed costs, which are estimated for hypothetical farms of various sizes. In the jargon of economists, these are "synthetic" farms, and studies using this approach are appropriately referred to as engineered.

But are these imputed costs the same for all farms of all sizes, and if not, how do they vary by farm size? Is an hour of labor worth the same on big farms as on small? Are the management costs the same on large and small farms? Should they receive the same rate of return on investment?

Many economists say yes to all these questions. When imputing management costs, for example, they assume that there are *no diseconomies of size in management,* and that the cost per bushel of managing a farm that employs five people and two million dollars in assets is the same as the management cost per bushel of a weekend farm with fifty thousand dollars in assets. Commonly, the imputed management cost is a flat percent of gross sales—usually about 5 percent (for an exception, see Moore 1965).

That these costs are not the same is apparent to most farmers. Farmers will think hard, for example, before expanding the farm by adding on a parcel of rental land far removed from the home place. They know that the additional problems of scheduling machinery use, breakdown and repair time, and timeliness of planting and harvest—all diseconomies of size—are heightened on such checkerboard farms. Sometimes, economists see this, too (Johnston 1972), but not often.

The potential for management inefficiency is heightened where the number of factors that are beyond the control of managment increases. The unpredictability of weather, the difficulty of monitoring actual field conditions over large expanses of territory, and the complexity of managing simultaneously for many different crops at once have frustrated big farms.

Where industrial agriculture claims its advantage is in being able to reduce the number of factors beyond the control of management by specializing in single crops and replacing the uncertainty of nature with the certainty of technology. Large hog factories are good examples of this claim and of its limitations. If animals can be kept in closed quarters, their environment controlled and their feed delivered automatically according to their computer-determined needs, management can be efficiently provided to large numbers of animals. But, if disease problems can't be controlled in such buildings, the management problems proliferate. If the quality of the management is insufficient to prevent the death of many pigs, the management cost per pig actually sent to market can get very high.

Labor costs, like management costs, are similarly imputed in most economies-of-size studies. In the most imprecise studies, the farmer is assumed to require a fixed labor income from the farm—say $12,000 per year—regardless of how much time is actually spent farming. On part-time farms, charging this full wage to the farm's small output makes it appear very inefficient. And since most economies-of-size studies only consider synthetic farms that produce one or two crops, the problem is compounded. Smaller, more diversified farmers spend less than full time at each of many enterprises, but an efficiency study that imputes a full-time labor charge to each enterprise implies that the small farmer has nothing else to do with his or her time. This analytical abuse is so discredited that it has been largely discontinued.

Now, for the most part, a farmer's labor is assumed to be worth the same as hired labor, and the cost of providing the labor is charged to the farm at that rate on the basis of the number of hours worked by the farmer. That seems proper. But is it?

A better way to put a price on a farmer's labor is to ask first what the farmer would be doing if not working on the farm. For a big farmer, time is probably better spent in the farm office, managing the operation, than out working on the tractor. This is especially true if the farm is so large and technically and financially complicated as to suffer potential diseconomies of size in management. If the farmer isn't minding the store, things might go wrong in a big way. For the big farmer, managing mainly means controlling money and technology. The cost of ignoring this chore can be quite high, and every hour a bigger farmer spends in manual labor is time lost to management. The imputed cost of labor on a big farm should reflect that.

On a small farm, where land and labor are likely to be more important than technology and money, management chores are different. The most important decisions the smaller farmer has to make involves how to use his or her own labor. Closeness to the land may be necessary to squeeze every bit of value from the time spent working it. The tractor seat might well be the best place to think, because what's seen from it affects the farmer's decisions. This kind of symbiotic relationship between labor and management means that management time is not compromised by time spent in the fields on a small farm. The cost of working isn't measured by any loss of management attention, as is more likely on the larger farm. And what are small farmers to do with their time if it's not spent in the fields? Rent out the farm and stand in an unemployment line? Given the alternatives, the time a smaller farmer spends at work doesn't cost much at all.

Put simply, the small farmer is both manager and worker, and the distinction between the two roles is both less noticeable and less important than on larger farms. The big farmer is an investor in a big business, and ought to (and usually does) worry more about managing a return on investment than working up a sweat on the tractor.

The cost of capital investments on different-sized farms is also difficult to measure. The temptation is to say that all farms must eventually reinvest in buildings and equipment that wear out over time. Each crop therefore should be charged with the cost of setting aside funds to replace such items. The easiest way to do this is to calculate the depreciation of the item—its cost divided by its useful life.

But what does the economist do with pesky, resourceful small farmers who don't spend much money on such items, preferring to salvage used equipment, remodel old barns, and generally to use labor, which they have, versus capital, which they don't have? These farmers simply won't have much depreciation. They maintain old buildings and equipment and use them much longer than is commonly believed to be their useful life.

To make life easier, if not more realistic, the economist is inclined to ignore these habits of small farmers and to assign enough cost to *every* farm to replace worn-out capital goods with new ones. Obviously, the cost of the smaller operation is seriously overstated while the cost of the more capital-intensive one is more accurately reflected.

By imputing costs these ways, the economist separates the farm into its component parts—labor, management, and capital—and requires that each be costed separately. While this format may fit the world of the industrial agribusiness, it grossly distorts the world of the working family farmer. The working farmer enjoys an efficiency based on harmony among these parts. Such efficiency doesn't reveal itself in the engineered world of the economist, but it does in the persistence of small farms in the real world.

Small Farms as Miniature Big Farms

This tendency to inflate imputed costs of small farms extends into a related bias—that small farms are only miniature big farms, different only in scale, not in character. For example, in constructing budgets for machinery, crop rotations, and other characteristics of the farm, economists simplify things by assuming that farms of all sizes produce the same crops using the same technology and the same mix of inputs.

The problem is that farm inputs can't be mixed like cake batter. You can't add just a tablespoon of tractor power or a dash of prime farmland. Farm inputs are not perfectly divisible. You buy another whole tractor and another 40 acres, or you don't. This "lumpiness" of inputs can cause inefficiency anytime an input is bought that can't be fully used because the farm lacks the other resources necessary to make full use of it. The cost of this underused input must then be charged to fewer units of production than it is capable of contributing to (or than it would contribute to if used on a farm that made more complete use of it).

Engineered economies-of-size studies have tended to assume that smaller farms operating with the same mix of inputs and producing the same mix of crops, must have excess investments in machinery, buildings, and other lumpy inputs. Again, they ignore small farmers' tendency to buy used machinery or remodel old buildings, or the possibility that many small farmers pay to have certain machinery work done for them by other farmers (who themselves have excess machinery capacity looking for a place to be used). They just assume that every small farmer goes running down to the implement dealer to overinvest in machinery.

This problem of lumpy inputs is worsened when economists assume that farms of all sizes use the same technology. Take hog production technology. Surely a farmer who builds a hog farrowing barn capable of farrowing hogs year round but produces only two litters of pigs per year will be less efficient than a farmer who uses the same building to its full capacity by farrowing more often.

But the small farmers might well choose a different system altogether (i.e., a different technology) for producing their smaller number of pigs. Because the technology for producing hogs has changed so fast in recent years, many alternative methods are actually operating in the real world today. Research at the University of Tennessee (Johnston 1984) reveals just how important it is to evaluate each of these systems on its own terms. Three types of hog operations were evaluated: a small system using low-investment facilities and farrowing an average of 29.4 sows twice a year; a moderate-sized system using remodeled buildings and farrowing an average of 63.6 sows; and a large, high-investment, total-confinement system farrowing 106.5 sows. The small system competed quite well with the large system, but the mid-sized system was far and away the most efficient. This analysis, moreover, gave the large system the benefit of the doubt in one crucial assumption: interest rates (a much larger factor in the capital-intensive large system) were figured into the cost of the systems at 8 percent. We haven't seen 8 percent interest on farm loans in a good many years!

In their tendency to make small farms in the image of large farms, economists almost always ignore the advantages small farmers gain from diversification. They tend to consider diversification of crops only when it improves the cost effectiveness of capital-intensive equipment, usually where the same large machinery can be used over two crops in a rotation. Where the crop combination may improve the efficiency of labor but compromise the efficiency of large-scale equipment, it is ignored. There are studies on the efficiency of farms growing corn and soybeans, but not of those growing corn, soybeans, oats, hay, hogs, and cattle.

Diversification is an efficiency strategy because it allows the more complete use of some inputs, such as general-purpose tractors and buildings, over several crops grown in different seasons. It also allows farmers to use their time better. For generations, for example, farmers have farrowed pigs in the barn in the spring and fall, before and after planting and harvesting corn. Keeping yourself and your buildings and equipment busy is one of the many small economies that make a difference in farming. It is too small an economy to be noticed in most economies-of-size studies. Reducing all farms to specialized farms simplifies the economist's analytical problems, but it prejudices the outcome against the versatility of small farms.

Interestingly, students of *industrial* economics have recently rediscovered the value of diversification as part of the explanation for mergers among major corporations. The advantages of diversification include using the same facilities to produce more than one product, use of one product to aid in the production of another, and sharing certain intangible assets, such as research and planning (Bailey and Friedlaender 1982). The efficiency of doing several things together seems to exceed the efficiency of doing each of them separately. This discovery has led to the coinage of a new phrase to describe the efficiency of diversification. They call it economies of scope (Panzar and Willig 1975, 1981). Welcome to barnyard economics.

In agricultural economics, a bias against diversification persists, reflecting the conviction that doing one thing well on a large scale is more important than doing many things well on a small scale. It is a function of our fixation with maximums, and of our indifference to optimums. Economics tells us a great deal about the peak efficiency of growing corn in Iowa, but not much about how to make a living farming there. Studying economies of size in this way is like evaluating a group of basketball players only on their ability to "slam dunk" the ball. The biggest guy will do it best. But can he also play defense?

Output, Not Input, the Measure of a Farm

Perhaps the subtlest, most common, and cruelest bias against smaller farms in efficiency studies lies in the choice of how to measure farm size. This problem is present not only in the engineered studies, but in many studies using data from actual farms as well. In both cases, gross volume of sales or some other physical quantity of output is routinely used as the measure of a farm. The efficiency question then becomes: How much output is necessary for a farm to be most efficient?

This nearly automatic equation of volume with efficiency squares with a general attitude that more of anything good must be better. Absorbed with production, we lose sight of the fact that our purpose is not to measure how much is being produced, but how much it costs to produce it. And in doing so, we forget that *output* is only one of the two variables that determine efficiency. The other is *input*.

It is the ratio of the two—the number of units of inputs required to produce a unit of output—that we are trying to determine. Plainly, it is possible to measure the size of a farm by either variable. Why should farm size be measured exclusively by the volume it produces and never by the inputs it consumes? Isn't the size of a farm best described by the resources it has at its command and the inputs it consumes? Aren't these the appropriate efficiency questions: How well do farms use their resources (the inputs at their disposal) to produce food? At what level of resource use is food most efficiently produced?[1]

In a way, many seem to have twisted economics around. Instead of asking how farms of various sizes can use their resources as efficiently as possible, they want to know how big a farm should be to achieve efficiency. Instead of looking at what farmers do to achieve as much efficiency as they can with what they have to work with, most analysts prefer to describe what farmers could do if they only had more to work with.

The difference is significant, because as long as volume of output is the economist's measure of farm size, smallness will be viewed as a reflection of management inefficiency. Consider two farms consuming an equal amount of resources—the same land, equipment, seed, fertilizer, labor, and other inputs. One is better managed and produces more than typical farms using the same volume of resources. This farm has a relatively low cost of production. The other farm is poorly managed and produces less than typical farms using the same resources. It has a relatively high cost of production. But despite the fact that these farms consume equal levels of economic resources, they are usually not considered to be of the same size precisely because they produce different volumes of output. The "smaller" of the two farms will always be implicitly less

1. This approach has also been suggested by David Holland.

94

Figure 3. Efficiency of Farm Size Measured by Sales Volume

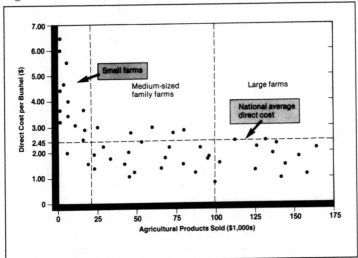

Source: Miller 1979.
Note: Each point represents one wheat farm, 1978.

efficient than the "larger" of the two farms as a matter of definition, though when measured by the inputs they consume, the two
farms are identical in size.

Sharp differences in cost of production among farms with the
same volume of output confirm my point. Figure 3 (Miller 1979)
shows this variability. The fact that the variability is greater among
small farms supports the argument that the practice of measuring
farm size by sales is biased against small farms. The worst managers with cost of production above four dollars are all in the small
farm category, quite naturally, partly because if you squander resources so badly that your average cost of production is that high,
you obviously aren't going to produce much. But some of the best-
managed farms with costs of production below national averages
are also in the small farm group, proving that small resources can
be managed efficiently. The average cost of production for all farms
with low volume of sales, however, masks this significant difference. When the orthodox economies-of-size line is drawn to reflect average costs as in figure 2, this vast difference between poorly managed large farms and well managed small farms is lost. They
all become just poorly managed small farms.

By the same token, the average efficiency of each larger farm

The Myth That Bigger Is Better 95

category is overstated by the inclusion of smaller, efficient farms in the category. At the end of the spectrum are "large" farms almost all of which are below national average costs. There are no inefficiently operated "large" farms with above average costs in figure 3 partly because such farms would tend to have relatively lower sales volume, pushing them back toward the medium size category.

Using sales as the measure of size thus forces each progressively smaller farm-size category to carry the burden of the inefficiently operated larger farms, while each progressively larger farm size category benefits from the relative efficiency of well-managed smaller farms. This means that in most efficiency studies, many "small" farms are really just poorly managed larger farms, and many "large" farms are really well-managed smaller farms.

This bias is systematic and mathematical. In every instance where two farms consuming equal inputs have different levels of output, the less efficient will be considered the smaller of the two and its higher costs will be included in the cost figures for smaller farms. The more efficient will be considered the larger and its lower costs added to the figures for larger farms. It is as if the economist were an unwitting traffic cop, ordering inefficient farms to the left, efficient farms to the right in figure 1. No matter where on the scale this discrimination occurs, the result is the same: on average, every farm is made to appear less efficient than the ones in the next larger group.

In essence, the economist has proven by this analytical approach that inefficiency produces smallness, but what the economists, the general public, and policy makers have concluded is that smallness causes inefficiency.

To illustrate this point more graphically, in figure 4 I've rearranged the data from figure 3 so that the horizontal axis is not "value of products sold," but "value of direct resources consumed." To make this conversion, I had to assume a price of wheat ($3.75 per bushel) and estimate the numerical value of the points in figure 3.

Figure 4 is different from figure 3 in several important ways. First, a greater percentage of the "smaller" farms have costs of production below the national average (five of sixteen small farms instead of two of fifteen). This shows that it is possible to farm efficiently on a small scale. By contrast, a significant number of the largest farms now have costs above the national average. Half operate at no better than average efficiency. That is important be-

Figure 4. Efficiency of Farm Size Measured by Resources
Consumed

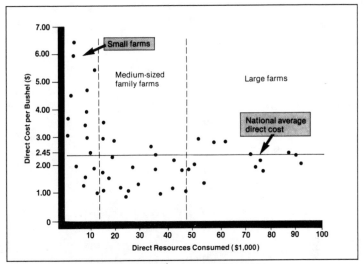

Source: Based on data used in figure 4, from Miller 1979.
Note: Each point represents one wheat farm, 1978.

cause it implies that diseconomies of size have begun to appear. The
lowest cost of production appears among the small- to medium-
sized farms. In fact, few of the medium-sized farms have costs above
the national average. Over three-fifths of the medium farms have
costs under $2.00 per bushel, while fewer than one-third of the
large farms can make this claim. And nearly as high a percentage
of the small farms do that well.

This suggests that small farms can be very competitive in the use
of resources, that peak efficiency is gained at much lower levels than
is conventionally assumed, and that beyond these levels, real inefficiencies begin to appear.[2]

Actual records of farmers in Iowa cooperating with the Iowa
Farm Business Association's record-keeping program support this
assessment. Instead of comparing the performance of farms
grouped according to their volume of sales, the program groups

2. Assuming a different wheat price does not alter the analysis. It shifts the dots
horizontally by a proportional amount, elongating or compressing figure 4, but
does not alter the relationship between them.

Table 2. Farm Size and Efficiency, Iowa, 1976–83

	Acres Farmed				
	100–179	180–259	260–359	360–499	500 or more
Year	Gross Product per $100 Invested ($)				
1976	18	17	17	18	16
1977	18	18	17	16	15
1978	23	22	21	20	20
1979	19	16	17	18	18
1980	20	19	18	18	17
1981	16	15	14	14	14
1982	19	17	16	16	14
1983	15	16	17	16	15
Average	18.5	17.5	17.1	17	16.1
	Gross Product per $100 Expense ($)				
1976	140	147	156	148	153
1977	142	154	160	155	150
1978	185	191	195	188	185
1979	152	137	162	166	168
1980	160	158	172	168	162
1981	125	123	120	127	125
1982	134	129	128	134	128
1983	105	126	135	135	131
Average	143	146	154	153	150

Source: *Iowa Farm Costs and Returns,* Cooperative Extension Service, annual reports, 1976–83. Iowa State University, Ames.

them by the number of acres in the farm. Since land is the largest single input, and since variation in land quality within Iowa is much less than it is in many other states, this is a reasonable way to compare Iowa farms. Moreover, the records indicate that the total value of investment in the farm and the total expenses consumed by the farm vary directly with the number of acres farmed.

The results for the years 1976–83 are presented in table 2. Small farms, when categorized as such on the basis of the resources at their disposal, get *more* output per dollar invested than do the large farms in Iowa. In fact, the larger the farm, the lower the output per dollar invested. Small farms don't do as well on the basis of output per dollar of direct cash expense, but it is still medium-sized, not large farms that operate at peak efficiency. And though not the

Table 3. Farm Size and Efficiency, U.S. Crop Farms

Size	Ave. Harvest (acres)	Ave. Per Farm Gross Sales ($1,000s)	Ave. Per Farm Net ($1,000s)	Ave. Per Farm Assets ($1,000s)	Efficiency Ratios Net as % of Gross Sales	Efficiency Ratios Net as % of Assets
Small	142	70	13.9	389	19.9	3.6
Medium	312	98	16.5	677	16.8	2.4
Large	578	154	25.3	1,088	16.4	2.3
Very large	919	233	37.9	1,581	16.3	2.4
Largest	1,790	454	95.2	2,861	21.0	3.3

Source: Congressional Budget Office 1985.

best, small farms receive only 7 percent less than the best output per dollar of cash expenditure. This suggests that the cost of production difference between large and small farms is not all that great, and that inefficiencies do begin to creep into the larger farms.

The same point is confirmed by data not usually available from the census of agriculture but specially requested for a study of commercial crop farms by the Congressional Budget Office (CBO) in 1985. Studying only farms with over twenty thousand dollars in sales that produce the major field crops involved in farm programs, and measuring farm size by acres, not sales, the CBO found that small crop farms tended to be more diversified and to have rates of return similar to *or better than* larger farms (table 3). The small farms were most efficient at squeezing net income out of their farm assets. They were second only to the largest farms in the proportion of their crop sales they were able to keep as net income. Noting that federal farm programs provide larger benefits to larger farms and that this policy is sometimes defended as encouraging efficiency, the CBO concluded that "there is no persuasive efficiency argument for preferentially supporting the incomes of large farms."

Our habit of measuring farm size by volume of output is largely analytical convenience. It is easier to measure output because it is physical—bushels, gallons, pounds. Moreover, output measures can be standardized across farms that produce different kinds of crops simply by measuring the value of farm sales. By contrast, measuring input is very complicated because there are so many intangibles like the management factor, and because many inputs are capital items whose costs are difficult to evaluate for a single crop.

Convenience is compelling in agricultural economics because data are so difficult to find and farms are so diverse and variable.

But making things simpler for the economist is no justification for faulty conclusions. In an age when careful use of scarce and fragile natural resources is far more important than flooding the market with food surpluses, resource consumption, not output, should be the measure of a farm. More conservation, not more production, is needed.

* * *

I know a farm couple named John and Theresa Fleming whose life embodies this view well. They started farming in the 1940s on 240 acres, a moderate to large farm at the time. Sobered by the experience of so many others in the Great Depression, John and Theresa farmed very conservatively. They rotated crops, growing corn, oats, hay, and later, soybeans. Every acre was farmed according to strict rules of conservation so as to preserve every drop of scarce water that fell on their dryland farm in northeastern Nebraska. They contoured, terraced, and strip-cropped; if a drop of water left the place as runoff, they were chagrined. John once told me proudly that you couldn't "find a straight line" on the place where water would run off, carrying precious topsoil with it. He used fertilizer sparingly, and pesticides almost never. He bragged that the yield on the hilltops (where many farmers get lower yield due to erosion) didn't vary from the yield on the bottoms, and that even in the drought years, his conservative methods paid off with yields good enough to meet expenses. He never got top yield, but he always got enough to stay in business. He always got what he knew he could afford to try for.

And, of course, the Flemings raised hogs as well, carefully judging whether the trade-off between corn and hog prices dictated raising more hogs or selling more corn. Sometimes, it didn't make much difference, because there wasn't any profit in either.

But they stayed in business, partly because they kept their costs low. John and Theresa farmed this way through the 1950s when farmers were advised to get big or get out, through the 1960s when they were supposed to adapt or die, and through the boom 1970s when good managers were supposed to borrow and expand. They continued to farm with modest equipment—a two-bottom plow, a two-row planter, and a one-row corn picker. In 1982, they were still farming that 240 acres with the tractor they had bought in 1952.

100

There wasn't any secret to it. Their strategy can be summarized as management for survival. But others weren't much interested in their old-fashioned ways, John will admit. For years he served on the local soil conservation district board urging greater care, cautioning against irrigation investments. His views were considered eccentric.

Did the Flemings suffer for it? Maybe, in the view of some, but not in theirs. They have raised thirteen children on that farm (*good* children, they'll insist I add), sent several of them to college, and lived comfortably themselves. I don't know of a more spacious, warm farmhouse, a better-kept barn, or a neater front yard.

In 1983, as the farm crisis deepened, John went to his local implement dealer and bought the couple's first tractor since 1952, one of the few tractors the dealer sold in 1983. I asked John if he didn't know there was a crisis, and that farmers didn't have any money. He looked at me as if I were out of my mind.

There must be something to the way John and Theresa farm. It isn't very progressive, farm-management advisers will say, and it isn't the most efficient, economists will conclude. But you'll not convince them of it.

The twin effects of the four analytical biases described above is to overstate the cost of production of small commercial farms like the Flemings' and to understate the costs of larger farms. The shape of the efficiency curve in figure 2 should probably be more accurately drawn as in figure 5.

The implication of figure 5 is that small farms can be managed very efficiently, the inefficiency of some small farms notwithstanding, and that diseconomies of size begin at very moderate levels and rises more rapidly than most experts acknowledge. The actual performance of small farms shames the assumptions underlying most economies-of-size studies. In the real world, small farms compete well, and big farms evidence creeping inefficiency.

There is an even larger implication. The conventional view has been that the way to improve efficiency in agriculture is to employ more technologies that increase inputs while expanding output. Figure 5 suggests that resource-conserving technologies have more to offer many farms in America than output-enhancing technologies do. I'll discuss this in Chapter 9.

But a major obstacle in appreciating the efficiency of farms like the Flemings' is that political antagonists confuse the economic and political power of large farms for technical efficiency. Their ar-

Figure 5. Revisionist View of Economies of Size

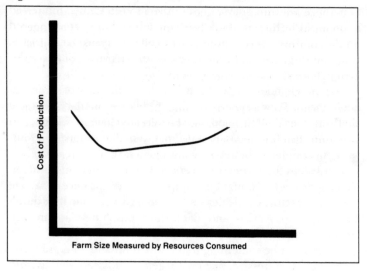

gument is: large farms exist and are gaining ground, therefore they must be more efficient. This inductive reasoning seems compelling. But it fails to recognize that factors other than efficiency are determining success. Tax policies have favored large farms and federal farm programs provide advantages to them. These and other examples of public policy biases in favor of larger farms will be detailed in Chapter 7. These are privileges parading as efficiency.

Significantly, one agricultural economist (Plaxico 1984) has noted that large farms seem to dominate production only of certain specialty crops, such as fruits and vegetables, and of crops that depend on the purchase of livestock or grain from smaller farms. In many instances, the domination may result as much from economic and political power as from efficiency. With respect to fruits and vegetables, the presence of government marketing orders is a major factor. For fat cattle, tax policy has been a major factor leading to large feedlots. There are several implications. One is that very large farms depend on smaller farms for cheap inputs, and some of their perceived efficiency is but a reflection of the efficiency of the smaller farms that supply them with those inputs. Another is that if all farms produced only the commodities grown on the largest farms, we might be comfortable with our myth of efficiency, but we'd get awful tired of grapes and watermelon.

The purpose of this critique of economies of size is not to deny that there are some economies of size in farming, or to discredit economists' efforts to describe them, but rather to challenge the smug, comfortable conclusion that small farms must be inefficient and that there are no losses of efficiency as farms continue to expand. There is less to economies of size than meets the eye.

But if bigger isn't necessarily better, is it possible that in some ways it's not even as good? It's one thing to argue that small isn't bad and that small farms should be tolerated in the national farm economy. But it is quite another to suggest that our growing reliance on big farms for our food supply may be a risky and expensive proposition. A further look at the big farm economy is appropriate.

6.

Chasing the Myth: Big-Farm Blues

The farm crisis that began in the early 1980s has two faces. Its human face is that of thousands of farmers going broke, most of them the typical mid-sized farmers that most of us think of as family farmers. The other face is financial. It is less visible and less emotional. It is also more concentrated on a small number of larger farms.

The crisis is widespread. Many farms of all sizes and types are in trouble. Few farmers are making much money. But it is apparent that not all farms are equally likely to be in extreme financial trouble. Generally, the larger the farm, the more likely it is to be having financial problems, and the more serious its problems are likely to be.

A paradox follows. Since there are many more mid-sized farms than large farms, most of the *farmers* in trouble are mid-sized farmers, despite the fact that, as a group, they are less likely to be troubled than their larger neighbors. But though the larger troubled farms are fewer in number, they have the lion's share of the *debt* that is not likely to be repaid. They are the ones who borrowed to expand rapidly.

But there is a further paradox: among the biggest farms that are not in trouble are those that are wealthy enough to prey on their financially weaker neighbors of all sizes.

As the farm crisis deepened in 1984, the USDA released a report (Harrington and Stam, 1985) describing farms at various stages of

Table 4. Financially Stressed Farms, by Size of Farm

Sales ($1,000s)	Stressed Farms as		Debt on Stressed Farms as	
	% of Class	% of All Farms	% of All Debt	% of Troubled Debt
$500 plus	15.3	.2	4.9	20.7
250–499	12.6	.5	4.2	17.7
100–249	9.2	1.2	5.9	24.9
50–99	8.7	1.2	3.9	16.5
Under 50	5.0	3.4	4.8	20.3
All farms	6.6	6.6	23.7	100

Source: Harrington et al. 1985.
Note: Calculations are for farms with debt/asset ratio greater than .7 as of Jan. 1984.

financial difficulty. The authors assumed farms with debts in excess of 70 percent of the value of their assets to be under extreme financial stress. The report revealed that 6.6 percent of the farms in the nation holding 23.7 percent of all farm debts were in extreme financial stress (table 4). It also showed that as farm size increased, the likelihood of being stressed did, too. The biggest farms were almost twice as likely to be in extreme stress as small commercial farms with sales under $100,000. And although financially troubled farms with sales over $250,000 constituted only .7 percent of the farms in the country, they held 38.4 percent of the debt most likely not to be repaid—the debt on extremely stressed farms.

But notice in table 4 that small and medium-sized farms in trouble far outnumber the larger farms in trouble. Of the 6.6 percent of the nation's farms in extreme stress, 5.8 percent have sales below $250,000. Most of the troubled debt is held by big farms, and big farms are more likely to be in trouble, but most of the troubled farms are not big farms.

And notice, too, that the farms in trouble within all farm sizes have more than their proportional share of the debt. Only 3.4 percent of the farms in the nation are small farms that are in trouble, but they have 4.8 percent of all debt and 20.3 percent of the troubled debt.

Finally, notice that almost 85 percent of the largest farms were *not* in extreme trouble in January 1984. Those financially strong big farms stood ready to acquire the farms of the failing of all sizes. A few sick barracudas don't stop the healthy ones from feeding on the tuna.

As the crisis deepened, more farms in every category fell into extreme hardship. Whereas the value of both assets and commodities fell, the debt load and the interest rate did not. It became harder for all farms to make ends meet or to convince their creditors that their collateral was worth enough to cover debt. Still, the basic pattern to this crisis remains the same: the crisis is widespread in human terms, but concentrated in financial terms on a few farms, especially the largest farms.

Why is it that so much trouble can be lodged among such a small group of farms that are disproportionately large farms—the very farms so many believe to be most efficient? These are farms that should have the lowest costs of production, if as we have been taught, they suffer no diseconomies of size. If bigger is better, why is it that a greater proportion of the largest farms are in financial trouble than any other size group, and that the proportion of farms in that condition drops with each declining sales-size category?

THE LEVERAGE TRAP

Part of the reason is that being *big* is not the same as being *wealthy.* Nor is *being* big the same as *becoming* big. In both cases, debt makes the difference. It is the process of trying to become bigger that has put many farms of all sizes on the brink of insolvency.

Many of the big farms that dominate food production in America aren't southern plantations or rich estates or "new" farms created out of whole cloth by rich investors and corporations, though some of them are. Most of them are expanding family farmers who use debt to finance their expansion, chasing the myth that bigger is better. Between 1945 and 1978, the proportion of farm real-estate transfers financed by debt doubled from 44 percent to 89 percent, and the portion of the purchase price that was financed increased from 57 percent to 76 percent (Lins and Barry 1980).

Since most of the purchases were made by expanding farms, it is not surprising to find that, on average today, the bigger the farm, the heavier its debt load. The most common measure of this is the ratio mentioned above—the ratio of debt outstanding on a farm to the market value of its assets. Debt as a percentage of assets for farms of various sales-size categories in 1984 are presented below.

Farm sales size	Debt as % of Assets
Under $5,000	11.0%
$5,000–$10,000	12.6
$10,000–$20,000	14.9
$20,000–$40,000	16.7
$40,000–$100,000	21.0
$100,000–$250,000	23.3
$250,000–$500,000	26.7
$500,000 plus	38.1

Source: USDA 1987.

The ratio of debts to assets is particularly helpful in describing financial vulnerability because the higher the debt load, the less tolerance the farm has for economic disruptions. In fact, as debt grows on a farm, risk of trouble grows even faster. Since most farm expansion was debt financed in the 1970s, this fact has particular meaning for our understanding of the crisis of the '80s. The principle of increasing risk by debt-financed expansion is demonstrated in table 5 (adapted from a similar table in Nelson and Murray 1967).

Consider four hypothetical farmers with the same amount of owned capital (equity). They operate four different-sized farms with various levels of borrowed capital, as indicated in the first block of numbers in table 5. Farmer A borrows none and operates a small farm. Farmers B, C, and D each borrow progressively larger amounts to farm larger. By borrowing, they hope to get more or better equipment, or to farm more land in order to make fuller use of the equipment they already have. They either believe they can farm more efficiently at larger levels, or at least no less efficiently. They are sure that higher levels of output will earn them more profit. The additional income they earn by farming larger on borrowed capital will more than pay for the cost of borrowing it, they hope. This is the principle of leverage.

The second block of numbers in table 5 shows what seems to be the happy results of farmers B, C, and D's strategy. Each successively larger farm earns a higher net income paying interest (charitably assumed to be 5 percent), and therefore earns a higher return on the owner's own capital invested in the farm. The more borrowed, the higher the return. This is good money manage-

Table 5. Why Debt-Financed Expansion is Risky

	Farm A	Farm B	Farm C	Farm D
Owner's capital	$100,000	$100,000	$100,000	$100,000
Borrowed capital	0	35,000	100,000	200,000
Total capital	100,000	135,000	200,000	300,000
If return on capital is 8%, then:				
Gross return to capital	8,000	10,800	16,000	24,000
Less interest on borrowed capital (5%)	0	1,750	5,000	10,000
Net return to owned capital	8,000	9,050	11,000	14,000
Rate of return on owned capital	8%	9.1%	11%	14%
If return on capital is –8%, then:				
Gross loss on capital	–8,000	–10,800	–16,000	–24,000
Less interest on borrowed capital (5%)	0	1,750	5,000	10,000
Net loss on owned capital	–8,000	–12,550	–21,000	–34,000
Rate of loss on owned capital	–8%	–12.6%	–21%	–34%

ment as well as good farming. These are the good times. Farmer D is praised as progressive, farmer A is denounced as laggard. Farmers B and C are urged to follow the lead of farmer D. The government is told to keep its nose out of agriculture. An 8 percent gross return on capital makes geniuses and brave talk abound.

But come the bad times—and they always do, sooner or later—and the formula for success is turned on its head. Farming aggressively, debt-expanded farmers boost production, so farm prices fall precipitously. Gross return on capital used in the farm falls from + 8 percent to – 8 percent. The same farmers now fare far differently, as the third block of numbers illustrates. Each farm's rate of loss on capital is the same, but the farms that have borrowed lose not only on their own capital but on the capital they borrowed as well. The losses must come out of the farmer's pocket, not the lender's. That is what risk is all about. Moreover, the lender must still be paid interest (still charitably assumed to be 5 percent), and the larger the amount borrowed, the greater the interest payment.

Thus, the larger the debt-expanded farm, the larger the loss.

Even worse, once leveraged, *the rate of loss on owned capital grows much faster in bad times than the rate of profit during good times*. In good times, farmer D earns 14 percent compared with only 8 percent for farmer A. But in bad times, farmer D loses at a rate of 34 percent—over a third of the farm's $100,000 equity in one year—compared with only 8 percent for farmer A.

The rate of loss, the magnitude of the debt, and the ratio of the debt to the equity all affect the ability of these four farms to weather the hard times. Obviously, a farm that loses a third of its equity in one year cannot withstand too many such years! Many farms will try to reduce family living expenses during hard times and cut back on some operating expenses, but belt tightening may make little dent in such large losses. Moreover, as the ratio of debt to equity grows, the lender will get very nervous, especially if the borrower's only hope of survival is to roll over the debt, adding the losses on to the amount owed. This increases interest payments and threatens to add to the repayment difficulties of the borrower.

By contrast, the farm with little or nothing borrowed still has options. Belt tightening can still make a difference, and the lenders are not so reluctant to lend the funds necessary to survive, both because the amount required is small and because the borrower has plenty of owned capital to secure the small debt.

This simple example only considers one misfortune—a fall in farm prices. There are many other risks for the leveraged farm. If interest rates increase, its costs are increased in proportion to its debt; if drought reduces yields, its losses are multiplied in the same manner as a fall in crop prices. The point is, when things go wrong, they go wrong in a big way on debt-financed farms. The loudly proclaimed advantages of leverage are real, but the disadvantages are real, too. In the good years, the advantages are magnified as the debt increases; in the bad years, the disadvantages veritably explode as the debt grows. The old saying that a financial genius is anyone with a short memory in good times bears repeating.

This leverage trap goes far toward explaining the woes of so many farms in the 1980s. Among farms in trouble during the early stages of the crisis, the most common characteristic was that they had borrowed heavily either to expand, to start farming, or to buy their first piece of land. Later, as expansionist behavior forced farm prices down, others had to borrow heavily, too, to cover operating expenses for the next year's crop. Not all—probably not most—were chasing the myth that bigger is better, but the ones who borrowed most cavalierly boosted land prices and expanded output, setting the terms others had to meet. Those trying hardest to get into the superfarm category simply took on debt with little restraint. But like the neighborhood bully, their size proved to be more flab than muscle. Swelling debt made these big farms look "bigger and more efficient" than their capacity to cope with difficulty justified.[1]

The extremely stressed farms in table 4 are more highly leveraged than the hypothetical farmer D in table 5. Moreover, according to the USDA report on which table 4 is based (Harrington and Stam 1985), the average annual cash deficit of the largest farms (those with over $500,000 in sales) under extreme stress in 1984 was over $35,500 (even after adding off-farm income averaging over $28,600) while that of the small commercial farms in trouble was only $688 (despite a more meager off-farm income averaging only about $11,250). It will be difficult for the large farms to cover over $35,000 in annual losses for long. But for the smaller farms, a combination of belt tightening and lender patience is a possible solution to their problems, particularly if they can increase their off-farm income even a little.

The leverage trap also sheds new light on the efficiency issue. The fact that farmers expand seems to prove that bigger is more efficient. But this ignores the reality that some farm inputs, especially land, "cost" more to some than to others. For the well-established farmer with no debt on land, taking on some debt to buy more land is merely a way of leveraging the wealth he or she already has tied up in land. But for the beginning farmer, or for the farmer trying to expand rapidly on a narrow equity base, land cost is a much bigger factor. The annual mortgage payment with interest can be crippling in hard times. Both the established and the highly leveraged farmer might manage the land efficiently and consume identical volumes of other inputs, but due to debt have sharply different cash expenses.

Although in the abstract world land costs society nothing, farm-

---

1. Significantly, the textbook by Nelson and Murray from which table 5 was adapted is an older one, already in its fifth edition by 1967. More recent textbooks on farm finance also have sections on leverage, but none of the ones I reviewed included an analysis of the consequences of leverage during periods of losses. Farmers might note that the welfare of textbook writers does not vary with rates of return on leveraged capital.

ers live in a real world where they bid against each other for the right to farm. In that real world, financial prowess plays a greater role in determining who can get land than does efficiency in farming it, especially in boom-bust times. If you have land, it is easier to get more, not because you are more efficient, but because you can afford to play the leverage game in boom times, and because you can weather the fall that follows.

OPERATING AT FULL THROTTLE

Besides tending toward debt obesity, large farms also have substantially less flexibility than smaller farms. They tend to have more long-term investments in land, buildings, and equipment. These investments are considered fixed costs because they must be paid for each year—whether they are actually used or not. Big farms are able to enjoy whatever theoretical advantages there are in economies of size precisely because they make aggressive use of such capital investments. The downside, however, is that these farms have fewer options about how to operate, how much to produce, and how to reduce costs. Their production pattern is rigid.

The reason for this is that capturing peak efficiency requires investment in enough equipment, machinery, and land to achieve the minimum cost per unit produced. As we have seen, however, the farm must continue to use those inputs to produce precisely that much output—and no less—to remain efficient. Once a big new hog building is constructed, it must be fully used to be used efficiently. Since the mortgage on the building must be paid whether it is fully used or not, the cost of having it is fixed in annual payments for many years to come. If the number of animals produced in the building is reduced, the building cost *per animal* is effectively increased.

For example, a 1982 survey of hog producers in seven prime pork-producing Iowa counties showed that the one-third with the lowest profitability had almost twice as much fixed cost per farrowing crate as the one-third with the highest profitability. In addition to these higher fixed investments, the low-profit group used their facilities less thoroughly, weaning an average six fewer pigs per crate per year than the high-profit group. As a result, their fixed cost per pig actually produced was higher than that for the high-profit group by an even wider margin than their fixed cost per crate. These high-investment farmers had $12.33 more fixed costs for each pig they produced than did their more efficient counter-parts. Overall, the survey showed that farmers with the highest investment in facilities would have to wean *five times* as many pigs per crate each year to cover their fixed costs as would farmers with minimum investment. Obviously, given their profit performance, not many were able to do so (Mobley 1984).

Large farms also have less flexibility in the use of variable costs, costs that can be shaved simply by reducing production. Some examples are fuel, fertilizer, seed, interest on short-term debts, animal feed, and hired labor. Once the hog building is built and the farmer is committed to keeping it in use, the cost of heating it and of keeping it in good repair, of feed for the animals in it, and of borrowing money to meet all these expenses become more or less fixed as well. In the case of the larger animal factories, one of the most expensive of these costs is that of keeping a good manager hired to run it. Large farms have a way of converting variable costs into fixed costs.

This inability to cut back means that larger farms have fewer management options. They manage sophisticated technologies by formula, and because the formulas themselves are sometimes complex, the management function appears complex, too. Management is held in very high esteem in the world of industrial agribusiness. But the fundamental management decisions about what and how much to produce are obviated by the decision to invest in high fixed-cost capital items. That decision must be lived out in full production for many years—until these investments have produced the income to pay for themselves, or until the operation is broke.

In other words, farms that operate at a scale large enough to reach theoretical peak efficiency are able to operate efficiently only at *that* volume of production. They can produce efficiently at only one speed—full throttle. Any less vigorous pace reduces efficiency, increases costs, and reduces profits, or worse, increases losses.

But what happens when the cost of inputs necessary to their operation increases? Their vulnerability is painfully apparent, as the early 1980s have shown. It is precisely the input that large-scale farms depend on most—borrowed money—that has spiraled in cost so sharply in recent years. They are stuck.

Farms with fewer long-term investments, fewer annual fixed costs, and more flexibility in reducing their variable costs by cutting back on production may operate at less than full efficiency.

But they may operate close enough to full efficiency to be competitive, and they may weather economic storms better and compete longer.

ALL THEIR EGGS IN ONE BASKET

Another form of production rigidity that reduces the ability of big farms to withstand hard times is specialization. Big farms tend to use single-purpose equipment, buildings, and machinery, and they tend to invest in land at prices that obligate them to produce a high-value cash crop.

Continuing the example of hog production, the "best" technology available for producing hogs is a system of very specialized buildings and equipment that, when fully used, produces hogs in conveyor-belt fashion. But the buildings are designed to do just that and only that. If hog prices were sharply reduced and the hog farmers who own these facilities tried to produce other crops for awhile, they would find themselves with an expensive, empty building. The building won't do for cattle, sheep, or chickens without substantial remodeling. In fact, the buildings are so specialized that one designed to fatten adult hogs isn't suitable to nurse young pigs, and still another can be used effectively only to handle pregnant sows.

Farms that use technology designed to produce one product tend to forsake alternatives. The investments they make in specialized equipment, machinery, and buildings and the management skills these specialized facilities require are so great that those who commit to them can't afford to give much money or attention to more than one enterprise. They might produce one or two closely related crops, but they think of themselves as corn growers, or hog producers, or dairymen, first, and as farmers only second. Wedded as they are to a single crop, they are vulnerable to even slight changes in the price that crop brings or in the cost of inputs required to produce it. All their eggs are in one basket.

Because these specialized farmers produce only one crop, they must purchase more inputs, including some inputs that more diversified farmers could produce for themselves. The cattle-feed-lot operator, for example, must buy corn, and is vulnerable to any increase in its price. Similarly, specialized corn growers lose the advantages of soil fertility and weed and insect control they could have from rotating several crops.

Table 6. Production Expenses as a Percent of Gross Sales

Year	All Farms	Farms with Sales over $100,000	Farms with Sales under $100,000
1960	71	88	68
1965	74	89	70
1970	76	87	70
1975	78	85	72
1978	79	85	71

Source: Lins and Barry 1980.

Having to purchase more inputs is a characteristic of industrial agribusiness that shows up clearly in historical data. At no time since at least 1960 have production expenses as a percent of gross sales on larger farms been less than 85 percent (table 6). Among smaller farms during the same period, production expenses have never been more than 72 percent of gross sales.

Farms with high production expenses will be hardest hit by a slump in commodity prices. Consider the effect of a 10 percent fall in commodity prices. A farm with $70,000 in sales and $56,000 in expenses (an 80 percent ratio of expenses to sales) would fall to $63,000 in sales and still have half its profit left. But a farm that grosses $300,000 in sales and has production expenses of $270,000 (a 90 percent ratio) will lose all its profit if commodity prices fall 10 percent.

The expanded, more specialized farm has less slack, and its margin of error is smaller. Locked into one or two crops, heavily invested in high-cost equipment, and dependent on a specified range of purchased inputs, these farms are economically brittle. When things go wrong, they go wrong in a big way. The old virtue of resiliency that characterized the family farm in America is being traded for the sake of the self-proclaimed efficiency of the industrial agribusiness.

SHIFTING RISK

Farming has always been risky, made so by weather and unstable markets. But in the past, the risk has been largely controllable by the cautious management practices of the farmer. In a business environment loaded with uncertainty, the business that survives is the business that is prepared for anything. A farm that cannot tighten its belt when times are hard, or can't shift production from one crop to another, or relies too much on a crop whose price varies too much, or depends too much on particular inputs whose availability and prices are unreliable, is a farm that can't weather storms. For generations, farmers have learned to be cautious, to be frugal, to borrow little, and to produce several crops to protect against both natural and economic disasters that might ruin one or the other of them. Think for a moment about the everyday maxims for a cautious life that originate from the farm: Don't count your chickens 'til they're hatched. Don't put all your eggs in one basket. It's too late to shut the barn door after the horse is gone. Don't cry over spilled milk. Make hay while the sun shines.

The fact is that many of us don't have the foggiest idea what some of these sayings mean literally on the farm. But we understand them figuratively as everyday rules for survival—don't count on outcomes you can't control, avoid putting all your resources where a single catastrophe might cost you everything, take preventive measures so you won't have to take corrective measures, plan for the future rather than moan over the past, and take advantage of opportunity before it is too late. These are lessons for life that American agriculture has offered to our society. And it has been the internal capacity of farmers to withstand ill fortune by following such rules that has given American agriculture its reputation for toughness and practicality. If family farming is known for anything, it is its resiliency in the face of difficulty.

It is precisely this feature of American farming that is most painfully lacking in the emerging industrial agribusiness. Stretched to the limit using specialized equipment to produce single crops for special markets; heavily indebted; dependent on a narrow range of particular inputs, especially energy and money; and deeply invested in sophisticated technology geared to do only one thing, produce more of the same, industrial agribusiness is becoming what farming has taught society not to be. It has all its eggs in one basket, counts on a full hatching of all its chicks (to pay for that expensive basket, of course), is too busy buying more horses to keep the barn door closed, and has too many hay fields to cover before it rains. Every once in a while, things are bound to go wrong, and when they do, they can go wrong in a big way for a big farm.

The risk these big farms suffer has a real cost. We all recognize the cost of risk in our own lives when we buy car insurance. And we also recognize that not all drivers have the same risk or pay the same cost. Younger drivers, men, those who get speeding tickets or who have had accidents in the past, and people who don't have dependents are riskier than others. For those with more risk, the cost is higher. Acutuarial science promulgates the statistics and assigns different insurance premiums to various drivers based on the cost of the risk they represent to the insurance company.

One of the simplest ways of measuring risk in agriculture is to evaluate the variability of farm income experienced by farms of various sizes and types. In *A Time to Choose,* USDA economists did just that. They generated a statistic known as the coefficient of variation to describe how much net farm income varied by size of farm during selected time periods since 1960. The larger the coefficient of variation, the wider the fluctuation. They found that farms with sales over $100,000 had 50 percent greater variability in income during the period 1960–72 than any group of smaller farms, and twice as much variability in the period 1973–78. The authors concluded that overall instability in farm income was increasing in American agriculture, and that the problem was particularly acute for larger farms because of their greater reliance on purchased inputs and and high fixed costs. It was one of the less heralded findings of *A Time to Choose* (U.S. Department of Agriculture 1981).

The cost of risk is rarely included as a cost of production in efficiency studies. There are, of course, all kinds of good reasons why. The cost is difficult to measure and the proper accounting period for it is not a single crop season. Risk is incurred over time, especially on farms that make heavy long-term investments in the "best" technology when the economic conditions for such investments are ripe. If the cost of risk were evaluated as part of the cost of production for each crop, the vaunted efficiency of bigger farms would moderate considerably. We might well discover that over time, the risk-reducing management strategies of smaller farms would be vindicated by economists. John and Theresa Fleming might someday come to be seen as the real progressive farmers.

But in the meantime, the public will increasingly be expected to share in the cost of this financial risk. Implicitly, that is what happened in 1983 when the federal government engineered a payment-in-kind program to give surplus commodities back to the people who had produced them in return for agreeing to cut back on production. It was no accident that the $50,000 limitation ordinarily placed on payments to individual farms was waived to assure that the biggest farms got the full benefit of this classic bailout scheme. It was they who needed it most. Some farms got over $1 million worth of commodities. One corporate irrigator in Nebraska got over $3.2 million. Overall, "risk" cost the U.S. taxpayer about $9.8 billion that year.

We can expect similar episodes in the future. As food production concentrates, it will become imperative to save the big farm when it gets in trouble, not because it is more efficient, but despite the fact that it isn't. There will be periodic crises and ever more demand for expensive bailouts to save the "most efficient" farms from the reality that bigger isn't better.

BRITTLE FARMING IN NEBRASKA

The kind of vulnerability to which the big farms that increasingly dominate American agriculture are subject is evident in the case of irrigated corn farming in Nebraska.

In the 1950s, Nebraska pioneered in the development of the now widely used center-pivot irrigation system. A big overhead-sprinkler system anchored in the middle of a field, this engineering marvel rotates in a circle, like the hands of a clock. Because it can roam up and down low hills as it travels around its circle, and because it can travel at variable speeds, sprinkling water at just the right rate for varying crop and soil conditions, this oversized lawn sprinkler made irrigation possible on land too hilly and soils too sandy for conventional irrigation methods. By the 1960s, the center pivot was "proven" technology and it became widely popular in the boom of the '70s. With it, much of the semi-arid plains of states like Nebraska were transformed from cattle grazing to crop production.

The center pivot can be used to irrigate nearly any crop, and some farmers use it to boost hay or wheat yields. A few even use it on soybeans. But mostly, in Nebraska, it is used on corn, still the champion cash crop here. Mainly because of the center-pivot system, Nebraska increased its corn acreage by 35 percent and its corn production by 44 percent from 1972 to 1982. In some counties where corn had been little grown before, the transformation was startling. In Rock County, for example, corn acreage more than tripled from 10,300 to 37,700, and production zoomed from a little over 1.1 million to nearly 4.1 million bushels (Nebraska Department of Agriculture 1972–82).

With the center pivot, an acre of range country capable of producing the equivalent of a few dollars per year in beef cattle can generate $400 worth of corn. Of course, you *have to* generate a lot of money to pay for the system. One center-pivot system (capable of irrigating 132 acres, or the circle within a 160-acre quarter section) plus the well and related equipment typically cost about $50,000 through most of the boom 1970s. That's more than some of the land itself was worth. With such a high fixed cost, which with interest could run over $8,000 in annual payments, the machine had to be kept busy producing a high value cash crop—corn.

While these machines were installed by family farmers of nearly every description, they had a particular appeal to expansion-minded farmers, nonfarm investors, and corporations. Research in the middle of the boom years revealed that one-third of the land irrigated by center pivots in seven counties in Nebraska was owned by nonfamily farm corporations, partnerships, or investors. The corporate operations averaged about twelve times as large as family farm irrigators in the counties studied (Center for Rural Affairs 1976). In fact, it was largely the controversy over such corporate irrigation development that sparked passage of a state constitutional amendment in 1982 banning corporate farming in Nebraska.

The overall commitment that Nebraska made to this kind of irrigation during the boom 1970s is stunning. In 1972 there were 2,733 pivots in Nebraska. In 1984, there were 25,216. Nebraska farmers and other investors have embedded well over $1 billion in the equipment alone (Sheffield 1984). Having made these expensive investments in irrigation on land with extremely limited alternative uses, the Nebraska irrigator (and other irrigation investors) has little choice but to produce one huge corn crop after another.

And to whom is this huge crop of corn to be sold? In the 1960s, corn had been in chronic surplus, but the '70s export boom promised big new markets, especially for Nebraska. Nebraska's special advantage was its location on the western edge of the American corn belt. In the past, this location had been a disadvantage to Nebraska because it made it the furthest state from the Gulf Port export facilities. But with the advent of the unit train, composed exclusively of big grain cars that could be shipped almost nonstop from Nebraska to export ports on the Pacific Coast, Nebraska had an alternative route to the surging Japanese corn market. During the export boom, with shipping facilities at the Mississippi Gulf Port full to overflowing with business, the unit train to the Pacific Coast was a particularly attractive alternative to the traditional river barge to the gulf as a method of moving grain to Asia. It made Nebraska the closest (in time and money) major corn-producing state to the growing Japanese market. In 1976, the Pacific Coast export facilities handled about 1 percent of the U.S. corn exports, but by 1982, thanks primarily to the Japanese grain binge and the unit train, they shipped 13 percent. About three-quarters of that 13 percent came from Nebraska (Strange 1983.)

Nebraska's farm economy has changed markedly as a result of its increasing commitment to capital-intensive irrigation. Once, the health of Nebraska's farm economy hinged on the disposable income of middle-class America—the principal variable in consumption of red meat, which had long been the main money earner on the state's diversified crop and livestock farms. Unemployment in major industrial cities was bad for Nebraska farmers, and still is. But increasingly, the economic indicator of importance in Nebraska is the value of the Japanese yen relative to the U.S. dollar, the principal determinant of where Japan goes shopping for corn. Unemployed auto workers in Detroit may not eat much meat, but they are not as important as good trade relations with Japan to some Nebraska farmers who have wedded themselves to the corn export market. Bring us Toyotas, Nissans, and Hondas, and we will sell you corn.

When the sorry 1980s arrived, the inflexibility of these irrigated farms and their vulnerability became obvious to all but their most zealous defenders. The costs soared for fuel, fertilizer, and money (interest rates)—three of the things center-pivot irrigated farms needed most. Cash operating expenses for an acre of pivot-irrigated land in north-central Nebraska jumped from an estimated $178.10 (of which $7.67 went for interest on operating loans) in 1977 to $190.82 per acre by 1983. Short-term interest rates jumped from 9 percent in 1977 to 14 percent in 1983, and since these higher rates had to be paid on the larger loans needed to meet the other rising costs, the interest expense on operating loans jumped 63 percent to $12.48 per acre (Bitney et al. 1977; Jose et al. 1983).

But most irrigators had little choice but to continue to pay these operating expenses. The fixed cost of their investment—the irrigation equipment and other machinery, real estate taxes, and interest on land— was estimated at $129.88 per acre in 1983. That cost had to be paid whether the land was farmed or not.

That $129.88 estimate must seem extremely conservative to some bitter investors in irrigation. It is based on an assumed long-term land mortgage interest rate of 6 percent on land valued at $350.00 per acre. Many boom-era irrigators bought land in north-central Nebraska for as much as $1,000 per acre, borrowed up to 85–90 percent of the purchase price, and paid interest rates as high as 14 percent. Their fixed costs would have been closer to $230.00 per acre.

Some irrigators did farm in areas with enough rainfall that they could choose to leave the center-pivot system idle and still farm. If the drop in yield that would result reduced total income less than the additional cost to run the system, it was wise to shut down the pivot. But most had no such choice; once the investment was made, the system had to be used to help pay its own way. That was especially the case for those who had chosen to develop range land in the semi-arid Nebraska plains known as the Sandhills. The land they had developed wouldn't produce a corn crop without irrigation, and other crops wouldn't meet the costs of operating the pivot. So, as long as the corn crop paid for the cash expenses and covered at least some of the fixed costs, they irrigated.

But soon, the sagging export market lightened demand on the Gulf Port facilities, forcing down their fees for moving grain by barge. States better situated than Nebraska to use Mississippi barge services once again had an advantage over Nebraska in getting corn to Japan. By 1983, Nebraska was swimming in a sea of corn it couldn't sell.

For many Nebraska irrigators, the agony was over by 1985. Interest had eaten them up and corn prices persisted too low. Land values had fallen so much that their bankers were unwilling to renew their operating loans. Many could no longer afford to operate the pivots. A telling statistic sums up their fate. Only about 5 percent of the land in Nebraska is irrigated by center-pivot systems, but more than a third of the land taken over by lenders to satisfy uncollectable debts is irrigated by the rotary systems (Baker et al. 1986). An ill wind had snapped these brittle farms.

By 1985, in Rock County, about 10 percent of the center pivots installed in the boom years lay idle or had been removed altogether (Looker 1985). A local conservation agency was deluged with requests to help pay for sowing land back to range grass at a cost of about $70 per acre. In 1986, when the federal government offered landowners a chance to place their land in a conservation reserve for ten years in return for annual rental payments, Rock County irrigators rushed to sign up. About 10 percent of the cropland in the county was enrolled in the first year of the program, the government paying as much as $52 per acre per year for land that had fallen in value to as little as $30 per acre (Dorr 1986). Two Production Credit Associations serving the area failed as numerous irrigators defaulted on large irrigation loans. One of the most aggressive irrigation developers alone defaulted on over $8 million in loans (Dorr and Flanery 1985).

This story can be retold about pork producers who invested too heavily in big, new buildings ("pork palaces"), or about Iowa corn farmers who paid as much as $3,500 per acre for land, or about dairy farmers who upgraded and expanded their dairy barns. Cummulatively, this grief extended into the entire farm sector. By the middle of the decade, the entire Farm Credit System, a farmer-owned cooperative lender that collectively represents one of the nation's largest financial institutions, was on the verge of failure.

Technically, big farms capitalized for full production of specialized crops for specialized markets might be efficient, but only in the narrow, short-run sense in which armchair economists measure efficiency. Like a high-speed race car, industrial agribusiness is capable of tremendous bursts of output, and we mistake output for performance. Now we are discovering about these kinds of farms what many teenagers and their sorry parents have discovered about fast cars. They're hard on the pocketbook, and they're not safe.

THE CRISIS IN PERSPECTIVE

It would be wrong to leave the impression that the crisis in agriculture in the mid-1980s is nothing more than the product of imprudent borrowing by incautious farmers. Most who borrowed did so with care, many with little choice if they wanted to farm at all. Rising interest rates, falling inflation, sagging exports—all caught them off guard. Given the general economic conditions of the 1980s, agriculture would have been in trouble, though far less trouble, even had expansionism not been so prevalent among farmers in the 1970s.

But the behavior of those who aggressively chased the myth of industrial agribusiness contributed significantly to the malaise of the entire farming sector. Absentee investors and nonfarm corporations found land an appealing, inflation-proof investment and were willing to pay more than could possibly be justified by farm income alone. "Young tigers" among farmers, schooled in the blessings of leverage, borrowed heavily to buy the best, the latest, and the highest-priced of everything from machinery to land, and ran the risk of losing everything. Some well-established farmers saw an opportunity to make money not by farming, but by buying land and watching it appreciate. These gamblers, whether individually culpable or not, set the pace that others who had to compete with them for land and markets had to match. The expanded, debt-bloated farm soaked up available land, credit, and markets—out-bidding, overproducing, and eventually, undoing its neighbors and itself. As costs rose and prices fell, the crisis matured, turning its wrath from the plungers who were guilty of expanding too much too rapidly to those who were merely swamped in their wake. The crisis of the mid-1980s reveals that where competition for productive assets is based only on ability to pay, those who believe that bigger is better victimize many who actually are better.

Who wins, then? The winners include those who sell out when land is priced high, of course. For the most part, these are retiring farmers. But it also includes those who are poised to buy land at bargain basement prices from those who are losing it. Included in this group are those who did not expand in the 1970s when land was overpriced, or those who expanded early in the boom, when land prices were lower, borrowed at modest interest rates, and stopped expanding well before the economic fortunes shifted in the 1980s. There are also wealthy investors waiting in the wings of every crisis for land prices to bottom out before they invest. Others, such as corporate farms, are financed by nearly inexhaustible sources of shareholder equity capital rather than debt, and can buy land at will in a weakened land market.

These winners are in a position to profit from the financial difficulties of others, not because they are more efficient at food production, but because they have money. There is, nonetheless, a temptation to mistake their financial strength for economic efficiency. After all, our system praises the latter but rewards the former. Doing so lets us reconcile the success of a few with the failure of many. Some of those who defend cannibalism within the farm economy as "progressive" would even insist that the right to fail is the most cherished right of a free economy.

For the rest of us, the question is whether we want a food system premised on might rather than performance. With such a system, most must eventually fail, and the rate of failure will be heaviest among those who accept the premise and try hardest to make the myth that bigger is better work for them. That is the lesson of the financially troubled big farms and their financially strong colleagues.

The smaller farms in trouble are a more complex group. Some are in trouble because they, too, are chasing the myth that bigger is better, struggling to be part of the big-farm world. They borrow against meager assets, expanding in proportion to their capacity to borrow. Still small, or maybe now big enough to be considered medium, but heavily in debt, they are in the leverage trap as well. Others are beginning farmers, or farmers who bought land from their retiring parents, or otherwise found themselves choosing between buying or renting land at inflated prices and not farming at all. They had to borrow at inflated interest rates and sell their crops in depressed markets. They were the victims of the aggressive behavior of the few who set the pace, an economic system that works like a treadmill, and public policy that makes a virtue of greed.

In defense of all farmers who now know they borrowed too much, no matter the reason, it should be said that there has been plenty of encouragement for this kind of farming over the years. Many lenders encouraged borrowing in the 1970s. Imagine the spectacle of several hundred farmers assembled at an annual meeting of the Farm Credit Banks in Minneapolis at about the peak of the boom belting out "Go, Go, Grow!" to the tune of "Three Blind Mice" (Dorr and Flanery 1985).

The drum beat has also been offered by officialdom. Secretaries of agriculture have applauded "progressive" farmers, and chided the "inefficient." County extension agents, 4-H clubs, Future Farmers of America, state departments of agriculture, and farm organizations have too often chanted the rhyme of expansion, growth, and efficiency. With the enthusiasm of a carnival huckster, the University of Nebraska has peddled the benefits of irrigation without cautioning about the risks. A Nebraska farmer needed a strong will to stay out of the irrigation carnival tent in the 1970s. Industrial agribusiness has too many promoters and apologists.

Now, of course, many of these promoters are rushing to rewrite history. Ignoring their own culpability, they wave an admonishing finger at farmers. A 1986 USDA report urged farmers to "reconsider the advantages of diversification," arguing that specialized agriculture and economic uncertainties don't mix. It counseled farmers to diversify by producing several commodities whose prices vary along complementary patterns, so all are not likely to be low at the same time. And it suggested farmers produce several crops that make use of the same machinery, if possible (Associated Press 1986b). Oh well, hindsight is better than no vision at all. But you can't help but wish there were a USDA apology for all the bad advice of the 1970s to go along with this new advice.

You might also wish that the federal government would acknowledge its own role in the making of this farm crisis. Instead, it only denies it. Former Office of Management and Budget director David Stockman offered nothing more than recrimination when he argued before the U.S. Senate that farmers don't deserve federal crisis assistance because they borrowed as "consenting adults." His choice of that phrase was curious. "Consenting adults" is a phrase usually used to describe people engaged in vices that damage only themselves. Usually, when such activities are organized on a large scale, however, they become crimes and matters for public concern. The public intervenes, not to punish the consenting victims so much as the organizers. Sex among unmarried people is one thing; organized prostitution requires a pimp. It's the pimp society tries to stop.

You might say that in this agricultural crime of vice, the pimp as much as any other was the federal government. It was the government that abandoned acreage reduction farm programs in the 1970s, promoted exports, permitted inflation, encouraged tax-motivated investments, and then, in a reversal, throttled inflation, and drove up interest rates. Each of these acts encouraged the predatory behavior among farmers that contributed to the crisis. The public surely has some responsibility.

The proper questions are: What responsibility? To whom and toward what? Should loans of heavily indebted farmers be guaranteed? Should interest rates be subsidized? Should lenders be required to write down the amounts owed, or be bribed to do so? Should the few most in trouble be relieved despite the fact that doing so will require commitment of scarce resources that could be used to assist many more farmers whose needs are so much more modest? Ultimately, all these questions reduce to a single one: How should the losses be shared among farmers, lenders, investors, and the public?

124

In resolving that issue politically, the most important principle to keep in mind is that while the economic system rewards ventures with success and punishes them with failure, the political system has the capacity for greater restraint. Politically, it is possible to save farmers who are in trouble, without rewarding the behavior that got them in trouble. In the case of many, this will require a scaling down of farm size, and perhaps of ambition. In the case of many more, this will require policies to help them save enough to start over. Most of all, it will require giving up the notion that everything everyone acquired with leverage must be saved for them. It is crucial to assure that expansionist behavior is not validated by policies that rescue it from its consequences.

It is not necessary, however, to determine whether a fallen farmer is in trouble because of greed, stupidity, or the betrayal of government. Only a vindictive spirit is preoccupied with those differences. It is only necessary to assure that the leverage trap into which so many fell is left tripped and unbaited.

TOO MUCH CAPITAL, NOT TOO MUCH LABOR

Public intervention in this crisis is complicated by its very nature. The conventional wisdom has always been that farm crises are evidence of too many people trying to make a living farming. But this crisis is clearly one of overinvestment, overexpansion, overcommitment, and overindebtedness. So much money has been invested in land, machinery, equipment, and buildings, that people are going broke trying to pay for these investments. This is a crisis of capital. The excess resource that must be removed from farming in America is capital, not labor.

Whose capital, then, will be squeezed out of agriculture during the current shake-out? Will it be farmers' capital, bankers' capital, or investors' capital? If farmers lose their capital, of course, they lose their farm. But more so than in any previous crisis in agriculture, the chances of broke farmers being offered a chance to farm for hire on someone else's land—perhaps the land they once owned—are good.

What does this tell us? It tells us that the labor and management skills of many of the people who are losing their farms are still needed in American agriculture. The president of the nation's largest professional farm-management company reported in 1987 that two-thirds of the farms his company manages for lenders who have taken them over to satisfy debts are actually farmed by tenants who formerly owned them (Fruhling 1987).

In effect, the shake-out is not so much a shake-out of farmers who farm as it is of farmers who own. Consider these facts: Between 1982 and 1986, the total number of people working on farms in 14 farm-belt states declined by 13 percent. But the number of people working on farms they own fell by 16 percent, while the number of hired workers fell only 6 percent. Moreover, the number of steady hired workers (those who work a minimum of 150 days per year) actually increased. In those four years, the proportion of workers on midwestern farms who had no ownership interest in the land they worked increased by 9 percent (U.S. Department of Agriculture 1986).

This is truly a financial crisis, not an economic one. The productivity of agriculture is not primarily at issue. The ownership of farms is. The issue before the nation is not how many farmers we should have, but whether farmers should own the land they farm.

"It's the wave of the future," said an Iowa real-estate broker lining up investors to buy farmland. "The family farm as we know it is not going to exist to a great degree. The land will be owned by people who hire someone who owns the equipment and will do the farming" (Anthan and Hyde 1985).

If the industrialization of agriculture proceeds, this issue will become moot. Gradually, the notion that people who farm should own the farm will become as antiquated as the notion that people who build cars should own car companies. Those with financial might will have prevailed, and agriculture will have made the transition from family farming to industrial agribusiness.

7.

Living the Myth

The myth that bigger is better might be a harmless curiosity if it were only an academic prejudice or an article of faith among some farmers. But it is so widely accepted that it penetrates both public policy and individual behavior. Public policies are shaped that encourage farmers to chase the myth by enlarging their own farms. Some resist, but to the extent they do they are considered quaint, laggard, or unprogressive. American society and American agriculture live the myth that bigger farms are better farms.

Usually, the bigger-is-better influence in public policy is subtle. Explicit favoritism toward industrial agribusiness is rare. Instead, farm programs, tax rules, credit services, and other instruments of public policy are weighted to seduce individual farmers to expand. Such policies are consistently designed to nourish the ambitions of the growth-minded farmer, to chide the reluctant, and to disdain those who are satisfied with enough. All farmers, no matter the current size of their farm, are encouraged to expand, to become "more efficient" for their own good as well as that of the public. And the policies offer no limits on how much expansion is good. There are no policies of restraint. No farm is big enough; every farm is too small. Growth, not simply bigness per se, is the policy objective of American agriculture.

Most farm policy is loudly proclaimed to benefit the small family farm. Nearly all farm legislation is said to address that purpose. Candidates for office never leave accolades for the family farm out of their repertoire. If praise constituted policy, the modest family farm would be entrenched in America. But the words of praise and promise for the family farm have been substitutes for effective policies to enhance it.

EMPTY VICTORIES

The most naked case of public hypocrisy is the sorry history of the Reclamation Act of 1902. It was the intent of Congress to populate arid regions of the West by providing enough water to irrigate only 160 acres for "actual bona fide resident[s]" on the land. Instead, in most of the big reclamation projects, absentee land speculators, corporate farms, and other unintended beneficiaries established their interests early and enjoyed a long period of lax enforcement of the acreage and residency limitations in the law. In the 1970s, when the issue was forced into court by small-farm advocates, these intruders on the dole were able to persuade Congress to gut the law in their favor. Having finally been exposed in open violation of the rules, they simply used their political muscle to get the rules changed. The result is that none of the high public purposes for which the law was enacted (and public funds spent) were ever fulfilled. Privilege simply overturned principle.

An equally empty victory for the family farm was the payment limitation law first passed in 1970. Ostensibly, it restricted the amount that any recipient could be paid under federal commodity programs. It was passed because corporations, foreign investors, and even state governments were being paid by the government to cut back on food production just when public attention was being focused on the problem of hunger in America. Some of the biggest payments were being made in the very counties where federal aid for hunger relief was most needed and most meager (Strange 1982). Overall, the top 20 percent of the farms were getting over half the benefits of most commodity programs in the 1960s, while the smallest 40 percent of the farms were getting less than 10 percent (Bonnen 1968).

The reason for the concentration of payments is plain. The payments are based on the farm's production output—the larger the farm's output, the larger the payment. The income needs of the farmer are not considered. Rather than change the basis for the payments, however, Congress simply capped them to avoid the continuing embarrassment of making huge government checks out to wealthy people and institutions.

Initially, the limitation was set at $50,000 for each of several eligible crops a producer might grow, a level so high as to offend (i.e., to affect) scarcely anyone. Later, when it became evident that the biggest farms were circumventing the limitation by artificially splitting their farms so as to be eligible for more than one payment of up to $50,000, the limit was lowered to $20,000 and applied to all crops in combination. This did not really frustrate the farm-splitting tactic. It just increased the number of splits required to accomplish the same purpose. This harassment might have had some effect, but the fact is that the $20,000 limit remained in effect only during the boom period of the mid-1970s, when commodity prices were so high that no payments were made anyway. When prices fell and the austere payment limitation actually threatened to target public payments only to small and modest-sized farms, the limitation was raised again to $50,000.

Even that generous liberalization was not enough, however, to accommodate the avalanche of federal payments for which some big farms were eligible in 1983. That year, the government paid farmers not only in cash, but in surplus commodities as well, and the Reagan administration arbitrarily suspended the payment limitation on crops paid in kind. Once again, hardly anyone suffered under the ostensible limitation. Later, the General Accounting Office (GAO) of the Congress opined that this decision was illegal, but no one in the Congress or the judicial system did anything about it.

In 1986, with crop prices falling and farm-program payments rising, efforts to avoid the limitation by farm splitting became more common than ever. Moreover, Congress exempted significant portions of the payments from the limitation altogether, rendering it nearly impotent.

Thus, despite the payment limitation, the biggest farms still get most of the payments the government makes directly to farmers. The largest 10 percent of the wheat farms got about 43 percent of the government payments in 1982, for example, while the smallest 10 percent got but 1.4 percent. The top 10 percent of the cotton farms the same year got about 40 percent of the payments, the bottom 10 percent, 1.2 percent. For corn, the largest 10 percent got over a third of the payments, while the smallest 10 percent got only 1.2 percent (U.S. Senate 1984).

The situation was no better in 1986, especially in the programs for commodities grown by the largest farms—cotton and rice. A General Accounting Office report predicted early in 1986 that 40 percent of the payments to be made that year would be exempt from the limitations (Knight-Ridder 1986). At the same time, the GAO predicted that the top 12 percent of the cotton growers would each receive over $50,000 in payments because of exemptions, and that together, they would garner a plump 55 percent of all cotton payments. The king of the big payments was reported to be agribusiness giant J. G. Boswell Co. of California, which could count on ringing up over $10 million in federal farm-program payments, primarily for cotton (Associated Press 1986a).

Payment limitation or not, the benefits of these programs are simply proportional to farm output—the bigger the output, the larger the benefits. The more you expand, the more you get, whether you need the money or not.

This regressive nature of farm-program payments is frequently defended on the grounds that farm programs are economic programs designed to adjust production goals, not social programs intended to redistribute income. Many of the payments are made only if farmers agree to take some of their land out of production in order to reduce surpluses and stabilize farm prices. If the payments are based on the income needs of the farmers rather than these production-adjustment objectives, big farms won't cooperate, and their refusal to take land out of production will result in even greater surpluses, lower prices, and more farm trouble. To prevent this, Congress allowed those affected by the limitation to reduce their land retirement proportionally, again thwarting the social purpose of the limitation.

But the fact is that payments have almost always been higher than would be necessary to bribe farmers to take land out of production. As early as 1972, economists at USDA estimated that 46 percent of the payments made to farmers were in excess of the income they would have received from actually farming the land they had removed from production. That 46 percent constitutes an income supplement, not a payment-for-production adjustment (Miller 1974). The portion of the payments that has supplemented rather than just replaced lost income in recent years is probably much higher. Whether Congress likes it or not, farm-program payments are a form of income maintenance, not merely production adjustments. But they do not redistribute income from the rich to the poor. The rich get richer.

The history of the payment limitation can thus be succinctly stated: The limitation is usually set so high that it affects almost no one, and if it threatens to discourage participation in acreage-reduction programs by driving larger farms out of the programs, it is raised or suspended. In short, Congress doesn't really mean to target the benefits of commodity programs to family-sized farms. It only wants to leave the impression that it does. Payment limitations are now a political ritual in every farm bill—obligatory and meaningless. Living the myth that bigger is better sometimes requires living a lie.

COMMODITY PROGRAMS ENCOURAGE EXPANSION, SPECIALIZATION

The distribution of direct payments under the commodity programs is easy to analyze, but the programs reinforce the growth bias in more subtle and powerful ways as well.

Since the programs only support prices for a limited range of field crops, especially corn (and other grains used in animal feed), wheat, rice, and cotton, they encourage production of these crops. Assured of a certain price for the crops covered by the program, farmers are inclined to limit their risk by producing only those crops. Farmers are understandably less inclined to diversify into other crops or livestock. A bird in the hand is worth two in the bush.

Specialization means more dependence on large-scale, expensive, specialized equipment. That, in turn, requires more production (and more land) to generate the income to pay for the equipment. In the meantime, other commodities are not supported and get less attention from farmers. For the expansion-minded farmer, the commodity programs are therefore an inducement to specialize while expanding.

The Congressional Budget Office reached just that conclusion in a special report on how diversity in crop farming affects farm-program goals. Researchers found that as farm size increased, the farm's dependence on its principal crop substantially increased as well (table 7). They concluded that "to the extent that public policies have reduced risk and uncertainty, it is very likely they have encouraged specialization and growth in farm size" (Congressional Budget Office 1985).

The result is a steady erosion of diversified crop and livestock farming and a growth of large-scale, specialized grain farming. This is especially true in states like Iowa where land and climate are especially amenable to grain farming. Between 1969 and 1982, the

Table 7. Specialization by Farm Size

	Percent of Harvested Acreage Devoted to Principal Crop					
Farm Size	Corn	Wheat	Soybeans	Cotton	Rice	Sorghum
Small	34	26	45	44	61	34
Medium	51	46	54	58	67	49
Large	58	59	60	66	69	57
Very large	62	65	65	69	61	63
Largest	67	73	73	67	67	72

Source: Congressional Budget Office 1985.
Note: A farm is a "corn" farm if it harvested only corn or planted more acres to corn than to any other crop. Farm size is based on amount of land devoted to the principal crop.

land harvested for crops in Iowa increased by 25 percent from 19.3 to 24.1 million acres, while cropland used for livestock pasture fell by 38 percent from 4 to 2.5 million acres. In four short years from 1978 to 1982, during which farm programs steadily supported commodity prices, the number of farms specializing in grain production in Iowa increased 7.3 percent, whereas the number of livestock farms (most of which in Iowa also produce grain for their animals) fell 16.7 percent. During the same period, the number of Iowa farms with over 500 acres of harvested cropland increased by 29 percent, while the number of smaller farms fell by 10 percent (U.S. Bureau of the Census 1984). Obviously, this trend toward specialization cannot be blamed on commodity programs alone, but by selectively supporting only major field crops, they have tended to accelerate, not retard, the trend.

Commodity programs have also influenced the competition among farmers for land. This is probably the most mysterious aspect of farm programs to many people, and the most beguiling of their inequitable effects.

Because these commodity programs reduce the risk of price declines and lure farmers into putting all their eggs in one basket, they also lead to expansion. Farmers (and others) who might otherwise balk at the prospect of having to buy or rent more land are given confidence by the commodity programs that farm prices will remain relatively stable. It is the stability in prices, as well as the absolute level of the price support, that diminishes risk. A farmer or investor will not only make investments that might not otherwise be made, but will pay more for land than could be justified in a less stable economy.

Of course, what such expansion-minded farmers and investors are doing is trading price risk for political risk. The expansion strategy is based on the premise that the government will make good on its promise to support prices at anticipated levels, not just in the year the land is purchased, but for as long as the buyer must meet mortgage payments on the land. Generally, that has been a relatively safe bet, though many caught in the 1980s farm crisis would disagree.

For the most part, expansion plans bolstered by farm programs tend to be self-rewarding. Because expanding farmers or investors bid more for land than they might if there were no commodity price supports, the price of land tends to increase more than it otherwise would. As a result, all land inflates in value, and the farmer who has expanded enjoys not only the risk-reducing and income-enhancing benefits of the price supports, but the increase in the value of land as well.

That increased land value is only "paper" value, of course. You can't eat land values. But increased land value means more wealth to be enjoyed when the land is eventually sold, and more borrowing power in the meantime. The borrowing power alone may be of greatest immediate importance to the expansion-minded farmer, for he or she can use that borrowing power to finance the purchase of more land. You don't have to eat land values if you have lots of land and the value is going up.

In fact, as long as the process continues, such a farmer is inclined to spend as much of the additional income from price supports as he or she can afford on yet more land from which to earn yet more return. It's a vicious cycle that rewards only those who can afford to play the game in the first place. Others are disadvantaged in the competition for land. Latecomers must buy land at inflated values, making entry into farming difficult. Those who rent land must pay inflated rents, and those whose farms are small frequently must use the additional income from farm programs to pay for farm operations or to meet their family living expenses. Everyone experiences higher land costs one way or another, raising costs of production and leaving less net income per acre. For the larger well-established farmer, that's good news because higher land prices mean more collateral to borrow against. For the struggling farmer, higher land costs result in an even lower standard of living. Eventually, it means failure for many, and riches for a few. In essence, the rich use the additional income from the commodity programs to prey on the poor, outbidding them for land and, eventually, for the right to farm.

Bidding commodity-program benefits into higher land prices is referred to as capitalizing benefits. In 1970, one of the few research efforts to estimate this phenomenon concluded that the capitalized value of farm-program benefits was $16.5 billion, about 8 percent of the total value of farmland at that time (Reinsel and Krenz 1972).

Farm programs do not have to work this way. It is possible to tie the benefits to people, rather than to land. This can be done if the payments are limited in amount and available only on limited quantities of production, and if eligibility is limited to farmers who actually work the land and have inadequate incomes. It is also possible if production cutbacks, when required, are *mandatory,* and the right to produce is allocated on the basis of the farmer's income needs rather than on the basis of how much production capacity he or she already has.

But as long as the object of programs is to protect the price of commodities and the benefits are distributed in proportion to the number of acres farmed, most of the benefits will end up in the pockets of the biggest farmers and landowners. We'll get back to the important relationship between commodity prices, land prices, and farm programs later.

USING PUBLIC CREDIT TO FINANCE FARM EXPANSION

Almost from their inception in the 1930s, commodity programs have tended to fuel farm expansion by providing regressive benefits and reducing the risk of expansion.[1] By contrast, government farm-credit programs began with a clear intent to encourage widespread ownership of land, but they too have gradually given way to the growth bias. As these programs have been liberalized to serve ever larger, more aggressive farmers, including many who can't hide behind even the loosest use of the term "family farm," their original purpose has been forgotton or forsaken. Instead of

1. Much of the research credit for this section goes to my colleagues at the Center for Rural Affairs, especially Gene Severens, Jerry Hansen, Nancy Thompson, and Annette Higby.

steering a steady course in the service of family farming, they have drifted into the mainstream of farm credit, financing expanding industrial agribusinesses.

The federal government's role in the financing of farming operations has grown and changed. From the Ordinance of 1787 through the Homestead Act of 1863 and culminating in the Reclamation Act of 1902, the principal federal role was to make land easily accessible to would-be farmers. Throughout this period, the policy of the nation was more or less well-understood: disperse publicly owned lands to small and modest-sized landowners who would operate the nation's farms as yeomen farmers—owner-operators. This family-farm policy was frequently frustrated by speculators' schemes to monopolize land on the frontier, and prior to the Civil War, by compromises with the southern states' demands to extend plantation agriculture to the Southwest. But the Jeffersonian dream of settling the nation's hinterland with working farmers who owned the land they farmed nonetheless captured the heart, if not the soul, of American farm policy in the nineteenth century.

Later, when the nation ran out of land to give away or sell cheap, the government's role in financing agriculture shifted to the provision of credit. High interest rates made it difficult for new farmers to carry loans for increasingly expensive land in the early 1900s. The federal response in 1916 was to adopt a successful European model for providing long-term land mortgage credit. Twelve land banks were established with capital provided by Congress and given authority to sell bonds to investors, using the proceeds to make loans to farmers. Borrowers had to buy the equivalent of 5 percent of the loan in land-bank stock, and in this way, the original capital was repaid to the U.S. Treasury.

The loans were long-term and, more important, were to be amortized—payments were to be made in equal installments that combined both interest and principal, allowing the borrower to build equity slowly, at a pace that was manageable. This innovative, long-term land mortgage system was attractive to farmers for whom high interest rates on short-term land loans had become ruinous. In the first fifteen years of operation, two-thirds of the land banks' loans were for conversion of existing mortgages. During the Great Depression, it was to the land banks that the federal government turned to administer the early debtor-relief programs.

The land banks also served as the model for another federal

response to the changing credit needs of farmers during the depression. The collapse of many rural banks left farmers without short-term operating funds just when those who survived the initial collapse in land prices needed them most. At the same time, farmers' needs were growing for intermediate-length credit to finance new machinery, such as tractors, that could not be paid for from the earnings of a single year. In 1933, Congress established twelve Federal Intermediate Credit Banks (FICBs) to meet these needs in the same manner that the land banks financed land purchases.

The function of both the land banks and the FICBs was to free the farm economy of its dependence on internal financing through the income that could be earned on the farms themselves, and to introduce debt-financing based on prospective future income. Looked at another way, these credit institutions were designed to finance the competition for land and new technology.

There were bound to be those who were victimized, and the depression economy produced many. John Steinbeck immortalized them in his graphic description of displaced farmers who had been "tractored out"—forced to leave the land by expanding farmers who had the money or the borrowing power to purchase the latest equipment. Throughout the 1920s and '30s, there was an alarming increase in tenancy as established farmers lost their equity in land and young farmers were unable to buy land on terms they could afford. Many were on relief.

There was a government response to this, too. First, under strictly executive authority, the Roosevelt administration established the Rural Resettlement Administration (RRA) to provide opportunities to those for whom agriculture was the occupation of last resort (or the work they knew best) by providing acreages to farm, frequently in cooperatives composed entirely of the dispossessed. Later, the RRA was renamed the Farm Security Administration (FSA). The FSA offered rehabilitation loans for up to five years to tenants for operating capital to strengthen their bargaining position with landlords otherwise inclined to push them off the land in favor of bigger, more established operators.

These programs were reinforced by the findings of the Presidential Commission on Farm Tenancy, which advocated further measures to help tenants become owners. The Commission's report led to the landmark Bankhead–Jones Farm Tenant Act of 1937, which provided forty-year loans for tenants, farm laborers, and sharecroppers to buy land. The act also solidified into law the rehabilitation loans and provided that annual payments would be varied according to the borrower's ability to pay, as farm income fluctuated. Loans were limited in amount to twelve thousand dollars in order to ensure that the funds would be widely spread among eligible borrowers. Loans were also made to break up large plantations into smaller farms (10 percent of the real-estate loans made under the act between 1939 and 1948 were for this purpose) and to finance group purchases of equipment that was too expensive for an individual small farmer (Schickele 1954).

These provisions were passed in recognition of the fact that the playing field had to be leveled if those with an uphill climb were to participate in the rebuilding of a depressed agricultural economy. The government was intervening, not on behalf of all farmers, but on behalf of the disadvantaged; not only to help them, but to foster a more widely owned farming system. The purpose of these programs was to increase farming opportunities in the face of economic inequality.

But by the early 1940s, with farm prices rising, the zest for agricultural reform had given way to milder ambitions. The goal gradually became helping small farms grow large enough to make their own way in an increasingly profitable agriculture. In 1942, the first FSA loans were made to enlarge and develop existing farms by clearing land and other means. In 1946, these purposes were officially written into law with another provision that the loan-size limitation be made flexible to reflect local conditions. That permitted larger loans to be made to expanding farmers. The same act laid to rest the FSA and established in its place the Farmers Home Administration (FMHA). Two years later, a provision allowing the agency to guarantee private loans to farmers as well as make them directly from the U.S. Treasury effectively doubled the size of FMHA almost overnight (Schickele 1954). In some respects, the erosion of the original federal farm-credit purpose of equalizing farming opportunities had already begun.

Still, the federal government had been established as the so-called lender of last resort to give people a hand up in farming. Several themes characterized this role. First, loans could be made only to family-sized farms that could not get credit elsewhere and loans were to be limited to amounts that such farms could reasonably use. Second, loan terms were generous. Interest rates were to be below prevailing rates, even below the interest rates paid by the federal government in the bond market. Loan payments were allowed to vary depending on farm income, and could even be deferred during difficult times. Third, FMHA borrowers were to get management assistance as well as credit. And fourth, borrowers were expected to shift over to conventional, commercial credit sources as soon as they were able.

Thus, FMHA's mission was clear. It was to provide *interest-subsidized loans in limited amount to family-sized farmers who could not get credit elsewhere but who, with management assistance, could be expected to graduate to commercial credit.* The federal role was carefully targeted to serve farmers whose opportunity to farm was constrained by their inability to command commercial credit.

But during the same period, the seeds of a very different form of government farm credit were also sown. In 1936, Congress established the Disaster Loan Program—later known as Emergency Disaster (EM) loans—to help farm families deal with the immediate economic devastation from natural disasters. Later, from 1953 to 1961, Congress authorized FMHA to make loans up to $2,500 to protect farmers from *economic* disasters, such as low commodity prices, and in 1974, it was permitted to guarantee private loans of up to $350,000 to livestock producers stressed by low prices.

The EM loans became particularly popular in the 1970s because, unlike other FMHA loans, they had no loan size limit and looser eligibility criteria. Moreover, the interest rate was favorable—3 percent. Big, rapidly expanding farms found the FMHA door open, or at least unlocked.

But emergency loans to remedy only natural disasters were not sufficient to satisfy the appetites of many expanding borrowers. What about man-made disasters, like low prices, high costs, and other misfortunes of risk-taking farmers? When the American Agriculture Movement threatened a farm strike in 1977, it was precisely because of these grievances, and it was clear that the traditional FMHA loans could not serve many of these protesters. Many were either too big to be eligible for FMHA services, or they could get commercial credit, or they needed larger loans than FMHA was authorized to make. Nevertheless, they expected federal help in their time of need.

That help could only be justified under the rubric of emergency loans. Since these big farms were surely among the most "efficient" in America, they must be in trouble through no fault of their own. Instead, their current misfortune had to be the product of malicious government behavior— deregulated energy prices, trade embargoes, the abandonment of farm programs during the boom years. If government was to blame, surely government could help during the economic emergency it had helped create.

Pressure mounted and in 1978 Congress passed an Economic Emergency (EE) loan program to be administered by FMHA. In startling contrast to the agency's traditional purposes, loans were no longer limited to family-sized farms. To qualify, borrowers did not even have to rely on farm income for their livelihood. Loans were still limited in amount, but not nearly so limited. Under the EE program, borrowers could get up to $400,000, twice the amount available for the agency's regular real-estate loans, and four times its regular operating loans.

At the same time Congress eliminated the interest subsidy on most of FMHA's regular (as opposed to emergency) loans for family-sized farms. Then, as if to make amends for doing so, Congress also created a limited-resource loan program. It would offer interest-subsidized loans to family-sized farmers who could not afford the new, nonsubsidized interest rate. At least 25 percent of FMHA's regular loans were to be made to this loosely defined category of limited-resource borrowers, but effectively, that minimum percentage soon became a maximum. The agency's traditional clientele, farmers who could not afford commercial credit, had simply been given a new name—limited-resource farmers— and a much smaller share of the agency's credit services. All the fanfare about the limited-resource loan program could not hide the fact that it was nothing more than a paltry residue of the FMHA's original purpose.

In short order, Congress had effectively increased interest rates on loans to most of the family-sized farmers borrowing under FMHA's regular programs, while opening up the agency's services to much larger farms.

The effect was quickly evident. Within a year, the agency's loan portfolio began to reflect a sharply different clientele as shown in a chart published by the Center for Rural Affairs, reprinted here as figure 6. EE loans were made in larger amounts to older, better-established farmers with higher net worths and more farm assets, and they went to fewer minorities than the agency's regular loans. Nearly three-fourths of FMHA's regular operating-loan funds went to borrowers with income below $12,000 and a net worth of under $120,000. The agency's traditional real-estate loans also went to

Figure 6. Comparison of FmHA's OL and EE Programs, 1979

In a nutshell:		Operating Loans (OL)	Economic Emergency (EE)
The regular OL and the EE programs both provide short term operating credit to farmers, but for different purposes...	1. Purpose	The OL program is part of FmHA's basic permanent loan program begun in the 1940s to promote opportunities for small low-income farmers.	The EE program was created in 1978 as a temporary program to meet credit shortages and unfavorable relationship between production costs and product prices; scheduled to automatically expire in September 1981.
in different amounts...	2. Limit	$100,000/loan	$400,000/loan
at different funding levels...	3. Total $ obligated	1979 $894.8 million 1980 $874.8 million 1981 $875.0 million (estimated) 1982 $1.325 billion (Reagan budget)	1979 $3.089 billion 1980 $2.185 billion 1981 $2.850 billion (estimated) 1982 Program to expire
at different interest rates...	4. Interest rate	Regular OL program: Cost of the money to the government. Currently 14%. However, 25% of the loans must go to "limited resource" or low income farmers at reduced interest rates.	EE program: Cost of the money to the government. Currently 14%.
and to different farmers.	5. Need	OL borrowers must need to rely on farm income. Nonfarm income is permissible only if it will be phased out after 3 years.	EE borrowers need *not* rely on farm income. They need such credit to maintain viable farms. May have on-going nonfarm income up to 50%.

Commentary	Item	Not larger than family farm.	EE borrower can operate larger than family farm. "Preference" for family farm but no enforcement mechanism.
As a result, FmHA now serves a much different clientele:	**6. Farm size**		
Proportionately fewer young farmers...	**7. Farmers' ages**	Under 30 — 48.8% 30–49 — 37.1 50 and over — 14.1	Under 30 — 25.9% 30–49 — 57.2 50 and over — 16.9
fewer minorities...	**8. Farmers' races**	White — 89.3% Black — 8.3 American Indian — 1.2 Hispanic — .9	White — 96.9% Black — 1.9 American Indian — .5 Hispanic — .9
The loans to these new clients are much larger...	**9. Farmers' loan sizes (avg.)**	1980 — $27,160 1981 — 30,420 (estimated)	1980 — $48,688 1981 — 54,540 (estimated)

10. Net worth

	Not larger than family farm.			EE borrower		
	Below $50,000	$50,000–200,000	$200,000+	Below $50,000	$50,000–200,000	$200,000+
Nation	78.4% (74.1)*	19.4% (22.7)	2.1% (3.2)	40.3% (26.5)	43.9% (41.0)	15.8% (32.5)
Cornbelt	76.0% (73.7)	21.3% (22.4)	2.6% (4.0)	37.8% (23.6)	43.8% (40.9)	18.4% (35.6)
Southeast	80.7% (76.5)	17.6% (20.9)	1.5% (2.7)	56.0% (16.1)	43.1% (34.8)	9.9% (22.4)
Pacific	54.8% (51.1)	37.2% (39.3)	8.0% (9.6)	20.5% (16.1)	49.1% (39.7)	30.4% (44.4)

and go to borrowers who have higher net worths... (note that one-third of the EE funds go to farmers with net worths above $200,000)

11. Assets

	Not larger than family farm.			EE borrower		
	Below $100,000	$100,000–200,000	$300,000+	Below $100,000	$100,000–200,000	$300,000+
Nation	74.8% (67.7)	20.3% (24.8)	4.8% (7.5)	24.9% (12.0)	43.1% (31.7)	31.9% (56.2)
Cornbelt	68.5% (64.4)	24.5% (26.0)	7.1% (9.5)	21.5% (9.5)	42.0% (30.2)	36.1% (60.3)
Southeast	78.2% (68.6)	17.8% (24.4)	3.9% (6.9)	36.0% (19.0)	40.2% (36.5)	23.8% (44.4)
Pacific	55.8% (57.4)	30.6% (27.7)	13.6% (14.9)	10.9% (5.6)	37.1% (23.0)	52.0% (71.5)

and who command more assets. (note that over half the EE funds go to farmers with assets over $300,000)

Source: Center for Rural Affairs, *Small Farm Advocate*, 1981, 2(4): 7.

*Percentage figures are the proportion of total borrowers who fall within a particular group. Figures in parentheses are the share of total loan funds received by each particular group of farmers.

Chart prepared by Center for Rural Affairs based on information provided by USDA.

predominantly low-income, low-net-worth farmers. By contrast, over 70 percent of the EE loan funds went to borrowers who either had incomes above $12,000 or were worth over $120,000. Over a quarter of it went to farmers who had both higher net income *and* higher net worth (Hughes et al. 1981).

Together, the two emergency loan programs (EE and EM) had not only opened the FMHA door to a very different class of borrower, but they had opened it wide. By 1979, the EE program constituted 40 percent of the agency's outstanding farm loans, while the EM program consumed another 37 percent.

In contrast to this exuberant growth in the big-farm emergency programs, the new limited-resource loan program languished under administrative neglect. FMHA officials themselves were clearly confused about who was eligible for the program's subsidized interest rate. In the early 1980s, the congressional mandate requiring that at least 25 percent of the traditional loans go to limited-resource borrowers was lowered to 20 percent. Even that diminished mandate was studiously ignored by the Reagan administration, which only spent half the limited-resource funds available, and officially opposed congressional reauthorization of the program.

As the farm crisis deepened in 1985 and its political consequences became more ominous, the administration started making limited-resource loans with abandon, easily reaching the 20 percent quota. The loans appeared to be made almost indiscriminately, since by then, the main eligibility criteria—that the borrower be unable to pay the regular interest rate—could arguably apply to nearly all farmers. The administration cynically continued to support elimination of the limited-resource loans.

The administration also supported elimination of the EE program, and Congress agreed in 1984, but not before removing one of the most vital distinctions between it and the regular loan programs. Congress raised the loan ceiling on regular operating loans from $100,000 to $200,000, opening the program up to larger borrowers. With the elimination of the EE program, these larger borrowers would now crowd into the regular program, soaking up funds for smaller farms. In one year (from 1984 to 1985), the average operating loan increased by nearly 50 percent.

At the same time, another policy trend became apparent. Concerned with the growing federal deficit and generally inclined to reduce the role of the federal government in the economy, the Reagan administration moved steadily to replace FMHA loans made directly to farmers with loans from private lenders that were guaranteed by FMHA. The lender receives a guarantee from FMHA that should the loan fail, the lender will be compensated by the government for any loss that exceeds 10 percent of the amount borrowed.

Theoretically, both guaranteed loans and those made directly by FMHA serve the same purpose and the same clientele of borrowers. The purpose of the guarantee is to induce the private lender to make loans it would not otherwise make to farmers who deserve a chance to farm. But the reality is that private lenders are not inclined to make loans to low-income, beginning farmers with marginal resources. Instead, they are inclined to use federal guarantees to protect themselves. They prefer to get an FMHA guarantee on loans they make to some of their bigger farm borrowers whose appetite for credit worries them, or whose borrow-and-buy expansionism has already gotten them in trouble. Because the private lender initiates the request for a guarantee from FMHA, it is the key player in determining who gets those loans. It should come as no surprise that the private lender is more interested in protecting itself from potential losses on its big farms than it is in fulfilling a public purpose in helping low-income farmers.

It might be true that those who get the guaranteed loans would not get as much credit from the private lender without the federal guarantee, but it is not because they are just getting started on limited resources and need the helping hand of federal credit to get on their feet.

Guaranteed loans thus tend to go to a different class of borrower than direct loans made by FMHA. They are bigger, more ravenous borrowers. The proof of the pudding is in the eating: guaranteed operating loans consistently average 2.5 to three times larger than similar loans made directly by FMHA, though the eligibility criteria for both is identical. Guaranteed loans increased over thirteenfold from $47.3 million in 1982 to over $623 million in 1985.

This preference for guaranteed loans is often justified on grounds that they cost the government less than direct loans. But for both the cost is only equal to the amount of money the borrowers are unable to repay when it is due. The rate of default therefore tells you how much the program will likely cost the government. Interestingly, direct loans historically have very low rates of default. The guaranteed loans have higher rates. But the guaranteed loans appear to cost the government less only because of a curiosity in the U.S. government's budgeting process. For reasons unknown, the budget treats direct loans as if they were simple expenditures never to be repaid, but assumes that guaranteed loans will all be repaid and will therefore cost the government nothing. No wonder a Congress trying to balance the budget is easily persuaded to replace direct loans with guarantees.

The real effect of shifting to guaranteed loans, whether intentional or not, is that decisions about who gets and who does not get FMHA credit will be made by private lenders who are not bound to serve any public purpose. The public purse will still be at risk. Public credit services will be further extended to larger, riskier borrowers whose principal characteristic is that their private creditors fear their failure. And, since the amount of federal funds available to back up farm credit is finite, the result will be larger loans to fewer borrowers.

There is a pattern to these changes in the direction of farm credit. They consistently serve to open FMHA up to larger, expanding farmers whose thirst for credit seems unquenchable. While these changes appear not to affect the eligibility of traditional borrowers for credit services, they effectively reduce services to those borrowers by throwing them into competition with the larger, expanding borrowers. Ironically, it was these aggressive borrowers whose propensity to soak up private credit created conditions that led to the need for the FMHA. Now, the very federal credit programs designed to offer alternative sources of credit for those forced out of the commercial credit market are drifting into the mainstream of farm lending.

The purpose of FMHA credit seems to have been turned on its head. It once was an agency mandated to provide economic opportunity to the disadvantaged; it now absorbs the risk of expansion for those whose pursuit of growth threatens their own future while denying opportunity to others.

THE TAX GAMBIT

There is no area of public policy with broader implications for the structure of American agriculture than tax policy, no area with cruder or more duplicitous effects, and no area that until recently was so poorly debated.[2]

Before 1986, the U.S. tax code supported a most potent, inequitable, and deceptive growth policy encouraging farmers to expand and nonfarmers to invest in agribusiness ventures. It was potent because it provided powerful incentives to make investments in land and equipment that could not be justified without those incentives. It was inequitable because the effect of these incentives was to give people with wealth an unfair competitive advantage over those with less. And it was deceptive because the way in which these incentives work was rarely understood by those who were victimized by them. The crowning irony of it all is that those most damaged by these unwise tax policies were for a long time among their most ardent supporters. Fortunately, that has largely changed, and so have some of these policies.

In 1986, Congress undertook a major overhaul of the federal tax system. Some of its most troublesome aspects as it affects agriculture were changed for the better. Unfortunately, the change was frequently in degree rather than in basic direction. Many changes did not go far enough and not all the things that needed changing were changed. A few were changed in the wrong direction. Although better for agriculture, the new tax law leaves a lot of reform left to be done.

To understand why change was needed and what further reforms are still needed, it's necessary to understand how tax policy affects business decisions in agriculture, and particularly how the tax rules in effect for most of the past twenty years have distorted farm economics.

None of us likes to pay taxes. Farmers are no different. But either because agriculture has long held a special place in the public's heart or because farm organizations have been especially effective lobbyists, farmers have historically been able to demand and get special tax rules for agriculture that have made tax avoidance even easier in farming than in most other sectors of our economy.

But to qualify for these tax breaks, farmers sometimes have had to make management decisions—especially decisions to invest in capital goods—that they would not otherwise make. Good farm

2. Credit for most of the research for this section goes to Chuck Hassebrook, tax policy analyst at the Center for Rural Affairs.

management then gives way to good tax management. Moreover, while the direct advantage of such strategies is obvious to the individual using them, the indirect disadvantage to the same individual that results from many others doing the same thing (especially those who are able to receive greater benefit from the same tax breaks) is not so obvious. For most farmers, the disadvantages far outweigh the advantages, though they may find it hard to believe.

The political support that many family farmers have given to the tax privileges accorded agriculture is like a fool's gambit in chess. Willing to sacrifice a pawn to gain some apparent larger advantage, the fool sometimes gains less than expected and gives up more than can be afforded. The pawn turns out to have been an undervalued piece, the gambit an overestimated strategy. In the case of tax policy, family farmers have foregone prudent management decisions in order to pursue tax breaks that appear to hold some larger and more immediate return. In the process, many of them have burdened themselves with bad investments and granted an even greater advantage to larger, wealthier farmers and investors.

But if farmers find it difficult to understand the impact of tax policy on agriculture, the rest of us may be genuinely bewildered by it. How can you lose money in farming and still be better off just because of tax breaks? That doesn't seem possible. In fact, the apologist's argument that you can't make money losing money is probably used more often than any other to disarm people who are concerned about unfairness in the tax code. The logic seems compelling, and most of us don't have a clue as to how it could be otherwise.

But the apologist's argument is as thin as the head on stale beer. The key to understanding how tax rules give an advantage to some at the expense of others in agriculture, how they reward inefficiency, and how they foster irrational expansion, is to realize that the rules work to *distort* the taxpayer's real income, making it appear less than it really is. These accounting distortions have nothing to do with the actual profitability of the operation. You can make money *and* get a tax break as well. The tax game in agriculture is played with the delight of a child who can have his cake and eat it too.

The apologist's next line of defense is to insist that the tax rules are fair—after all, the same rules apply to everyone. There isn't one set of rules for farmers, another for nonfarm investors, one for small farmers, another for the big guy.

The rules clearly are the same for everybody in agriculture, but not everyone is in a position to use the tax rules, nor is everyone who can use them equally benefited by them. In the first place, you have to have a taxable income to benefit from a tax rule that distorts your income. It's pretty clear that the chronically poor don't have to distort their income to avoid taxes. You can't have your cake and eat it too, if you never get any cake in the first place.

More important, in a tax system in which the rate of taxation increases as income increases, those in higher income brackets will reap more gain from any device that reduces the amount of income subject to taxation. This was a particularly potent part of the tax rules prior to the 1986 act, because the tax rates were more progressive. The highest tax bracket was 50 percent. That meant that if a tax rule permitted a reduction of $100 in taxable income, that reduction would save $50 in taxes for someone in the highest income group. But for a moderate income person in the 20 percent tax bracket, the same $100 reduction in taxable income would save only $20 in taxes. Simply put, everybody got to take the same deductions, but those deductions weren't worth the same to everybody. The effect was to make the whole system decidedly less progressive than the rates alone made it appear to be. In a progressive tax system, any tax rule that reduces taxable income is regressive—it benefits the rich more than the poor.

Under the 1986 tax law, deductions still have a regressive effect, but that effect is diminished only because the rates are less progressive (hardly a solution to the problem of overall fairness). The top bracket is now 34 percent for corporations, 28 percent for individuals.

Just as important as the regressiveness of tax deductions, not all kinds of investments are treated equally under tax law. For many years, the most attractive tax breaks have been given for investments in capital items like buildings, land, and machinery. If you can afford to invest in new machinery often, even before the old wears out, or if you can muster the funds to build specialized, heavily automated, large-scale buildings, the tax code will treat you well. But if your income from farming is barely adequate to make ends meet, if you maintain and rebuild equipment, or if you remodel older buildings, you are not going to find much comfort in the tax code.

In sum, tax rules reduce some people's tax burden by distorting their taxable income, notwithstanding how profitable their farming operation might be. But not everyone is equally situated to play the game, or to reap an equal windfall of tax breaks. Saying that the same tax rules apply to everyone is like saying laws against sleeping on park benches apply to everyone. They do apply to everyone, but they aren't meant for everyone.

These dynamics have been and remain a powerful part of agricultural tax policy. Let's see how they have worked, and how the 1986 Tax Reform Act has (and has not) responded to them.

Tax Features Spurring Industrial Agribusiness

There are five basic features of a tax code that, when applied to taxpayers with farm income (both farmers who depend on farm income and others who do not), foster the industrialization of agriculture and the demise of family farming.

Corporate tax rates. An incorporated farm can deduct many expenses that would be considered fully taxable income on the unincorporated farm. For example, if the corporate farm owner is also the operator, any salary paid to him as an employee of the corporation is fully deductible, as are fringe benefits such as health insurance. Although that employee-owner must pay taxes on his own income, the corporate structure allows the farm's income to be artificially divided between the corporation and the employee-owner, placing both in lower tax brackets with lower tax rates. By artificially splitting the farm's income in two, the incorporated farm can avoid the progressively higher tax rates in the schedule. The 1986 act makes no significant change in this particular feature, except to lessen its overall effect by reducing the progressivity of the tax rates themselves. This diminishes the advantage of income splitting between the individual and the corporation.

Cash accounting. Most businesses can only deduct expenses for supplies they actually use during the year. The value of the inventory of any supplies purchased but not used must be included as taxable income at the end of the year. But people who report farm income have another option. They can use cash accounting. Under cash accounting, the expense for all inputs is deducted in the year they are purchased, whether used to produce income or not. This can seriously distort the actual income of the taxpayer, especially if large year-end purchases are made. The 1986 act made only a few changes in this area, which we'll discuss later.

Capital gain. Some capital assets that are used to produce income increase in value themselves, over time. When those assets are sold, the owner receives that increase in value, which is called capital gain. Prior to 1986, capital gain was not treated as ordinary taxable income. Instead, only a portion of that gain had to be shown on the tax return as taxable income. Land was the big item that received capital-gain treatment, but breeding stock and milk cows were important examples also. In fact, in agriculture, capital-gain treatment was extended to some capital items kept for very short periods, such as certain breeding stock, and unlike in most other industries, to some items where the cost of acquiring the asset is also immediately deductible as a business expense. In the case of breeding stock, the cost of raising the animal was deductible, but when it was sold, the entire income was treated as capital gain.

Prior to the 1986 act, only 40 percent of capital gain was taxable, which meant that for the high income taxpayer in the 50 percent bracket the effective tax rate on capital gain was only 20 percent (40 percent times 50 percent). Under the new law, all capital gain is taxed as if it is regular income.

Investment tax credit. Before the 1986 act, part of the cost of some capital assets could be credited against the taxes you owed at the end of the year in which you bought those assets. Spend $25,000 on a tractor, pay $2,500 less in taxes. The percentage varied for some kinds of capital items, and only some items were eligible, but the investment tax credit was the clearest subsidy to capital in the tax code. It was eliminated in the 1986 act, except for some minor provisions that affected transition from the old to the new law.

Accelerated depreciation. The full cost of most capital investments can be deducted from taxable income as a business expense, but not all of it in the year the investment is made. That is because the capital item purchased will be used to produce income over several years. In principle, only a portion of the deduction should be taken each year for the entire useful life of the item. If a tractor is expected to last ten years, annual deductions should be stretched out over the full ten years. This is referred to as depreciation and the actual schedule by which investments are allowed to be deducted is called a depreciation schedule. Depreciation schedules are the source of many tax breaks.

In many cases, the taxpayer is allowed to deduct an investment expense in fewer years than the item is expected to keep producing income. In addition, the deductions are not necessarily spread out equally over all the years in the depreciation schedule, but can be taken more than proportionally in the early years. This front-end loading of deductions is called accelerated depreciation.

Accelerated depreciation gives the taxpayer the benefit of the deduction and the use of the tax savings sooner than if the deduction had to be phased out over the full useful life of the item, as good accounting practices would warrant. The absolute amount that can be deducted does not change, but having the tax break now instead of later gives the taxpayer money to use for other purposes.

The value of an accelerated depreciation schedule is therefore equal to the cost of borrowing the same amount of money for the length of time equal to the accelerated deduction schedule. Believe it or not, that can amount to quite a chunk, as some examples will show.

Many kinds of agricultural investments have benefited from accelerated depreciation. In this respect, there is very little difference between the 1986 act and the earlier law. An irrigation system that can easily last fifteen years, for example, could be fully deducted in just five years under the old law. Under the new law, the deduction is stretched out a little to seven years, but is even more front-end loaded. The effective tax breaks are about the same.

How These Tax Features Work

To understand the importance of the 1986 act, it is necessary to appreciate just how powerful these tax rules have been in furthering the industrialization of agriculture. The following examples are straightforward demonstrations of how these tax features worked prior to 1986 and how they disadvantaged average working farmers and benefited nonfarm investors, well-established farmers, and those who sought to expand their operations. The examples are organized to demonstrate the cumulative effect of the pre-1986 rules.

Prior to 1986, incorporating to avoid taxes was one of the simplest techniques used to farm the tax code, but it wasn't for everyone. Smaller farms with low incomes were actually worse off by incorporating, since their income, and therefore their tax rates, were

Table 8. Avoidance of Taxes by Incorporation

	Unincorporated Farm		Incorporated Farm	
	Income	Tax paid	Income	Tax paid
Before tax profit	$34,000	——	$100,000	——
Manager salary	0	0	34,000	$3,971
Deductible, untaxed fringe benefits	0	0	16,000	0
Taxable income	34,000	3,971	50,000	8,250
Total tax		3,971		12,221
Tax rate on before-tax profit		12%		12%

low anyway. Unless you earned about $15,000, the tax rates were actually lower if you weren't incorporated. Between $15,000 and $40,000 of income, the tax advantages of incorporating were not big enough to bother with. But farms with incomes above $40,000 had an incentive to incorporate in order to play tax-accounting games to their advantage. In fact, an incorporated farm with $100,000 in net income might be able to pay no higher percentage of that income in federal income tax than an unincorporated farm earning a third as much.

Consider two farms (table 8). The incorporated farm is a big family farm run by the principal stockholder who hires himself as the corporate farm manager, paying himself a salary of $34,000 a year. On that income, he personally pays $3,971 in taxes, the same as the smaller unincorporated farm with the same total income. But that "hired" manager's salary is deductible from the corporate tax, as are the fringe benefits the corporation pays the manager-owner. These fringe benefits include the use of the "corporate house" as a home, and insurance for home, health, and life. The manager pays no personal tax on these items, because they are fully deductible fringe benefits to him. The unincorporated farmer knows them only as nondeductible living expenses.

As a result of this charade, the corporate farm's taxable income is now only $50,000, and at corporate tax rates, the tax on that is $8,250. By splitting income between the manager and the corporation and masking income as the fringe benefits one pays to the other, the corporate farm with $100,000 in income pays the same tax rate as the unincorporated farm with $34,000 in income—12 percent. Under these rules, income-tax progressivity was a fiction.

But to the incorporated farm, even the $41,750 left in the corporate coffers after taxes presents a kind of Hobson's choice. What is it to do with the funds? If they are paid to the stockholder(s) as dividends, they will be subject to another income tax bite. This is, in effect, double taxation—once as corporate income, and once as stockholder dividend. The best thing to do under the old tax rules was to reinvest the funds in ventures that would themselves receive favored tax treatment, such as land. Once incorporated, the farm was on a treadmill of expansion to avoid double taxation. A well-managed, incorporated family farm paying appropriate salaries and fringe benefits and reinvesting profits could get bigger and bigger while regularly paying a lower tax rate than a nonexpanding farmer with one-third as much income.

The 1986 tax reform alters this environment considerably. It narrows the gap between top and bottom brackets and lowers the top corporate bracket, sharply reducing the relative advantage of splitting income between the corporation and its principal stockholder. There is less advantage to incorporating as a way to lessen tax obligation on most farms.

Using the cash-accounting rules to distort taxable income by deducting the cost of items as soon as you purchase them has also been limited somewhat by the 1986 law. One of the best strategies was to buy cattle and feed late in the year. These large expenditures are immediately deductible from taxable income under cash-accounting rules, and could reduce tax to nothing. This game was best played by nonfarm investors with high incomes looking for a way to offset that income with big—but artificial—farm business losses. The accounting process by which this was done could be very sophisticated, and these deals were regularly packaged by brokers for syndication to "Wall Street cowboys" with high incomes and big tax obligations. By buying cattle and feed each year toward the end of the year, and selling the cattle in the subsequent year, the Wall Street cowboy was able to defer the payment of taxes on that income indefinitely. A simple example shows how it was done prior to the 1986 law.

In September, the investor would pay $16,000 for a load of forty steers ready to be fattened and then would spend another $6,000 on feed for them. The $6,000 was deducted from taxable income that year. If the investor were forced to use standard business accounting, any increase in the value of the animals as a result of feeding them, or any inventory of feed left on hand at the end of the year would be subject to income tax. Not so for the investor using cash accounting. He could deduct the full cost of the feed in the same tax year without showing either the increase in value of the animals or the value of the feed inventory as taxable income.

He would keep the cattle until early the next year. When they were sold they might bring $22,000, a break-even amount, since that is what he paid for the animals and the feed. But since the taxpayer had already deducted the $6,000 in feed costs from the last year's taxable income, the tax rules required him to report a profit of $6,000. This profit would be taxed later, when the new year's taxes were due. In other words, the taxpayer would still owe tax on the $6,000 of income he originally spent on cattle feed, but he would have managed to defer the taxes a full year. In effect, he had succeeded in getting the government to loan him, *interest-free*, the amount of money he would otherwise have owed in taxes on this $6,000. He was thus financing his cattle-feeding venture with an interest-free government loan. This interest-free loan was worth a lot if the cattle-feeding venture was also profitable in its own right, which the investor hoped it would be.

The next fall, the investor would repeat the process, investing enough in cattle feeding to defer taxes another year. The process was then repeated indefinitely. Eventually, the taxpayer could stop the game when it was to his advantage to do so—when he dropped from a higher to a lower tax bracket or when he found a more permanent tax shelter. Then he would pay taxes on the $6,000 at a lower rate. For the super wealthy with the money to hire accountants to manage these portfolios, this cattle feeding was a great way to keep a retirement account from the revenuers.

The numbers in this example have been kept low. The fact is that this game was regularly played in five- and six-digit figures by people for whom a tax deduction of $100,000 produced an income-tax deferral of $50,000 under the old tax brackets.

The cash-accounting gimmick is not limited to cattle feeding. It's use in cattle feeding is particularly attractive to high-income, nonfarm investors however, because cattle cost so much to fatten, and they fatten so quickly. A lot of money can be sheltered in a short time period with cattle feeding.

How did the Tax Reform Act of 1986 affect this kind of tax sheltering? First, the amount that can be deducted for items purchased one year for later use is limited to a third of all expenses in the year in which they are claimed as deductions. This weakens the strategy of prepaying for feed considerably. More important, investors who are not active in the management of the business cannot use cash accounting at all. And finally, if they are not active in the management of the business, they cannot deduct losses in that business from income earned in other ways. These reforms will substantially dampen the appetite for cattle-feeding tax shelters, though the regulations that enforce these reforms will determine their effectiveness. (Ironically, cash accounting is permitted in farming because a foolish myth has persisted that ordinary farmers are too simple to understand more precise accounting methods.)

Dairying offered even more lucrative tax breaks under the old law for some, although you had to be a little more patient. In dairying, every cow is a potential tax shelter. Since the main product of a dairy farm is milk, the cow itself is considered an income-producing asset—a means to an end, not an end in itself. Generally, such an asset must be depreciated, that is, the cost of acquiring it must be deducted gradually, over its full useful life (usually three to four years is the optimum milking life of a cow).

But dairy farmers don't usually buy cows the way you'd buy most capital assets—they raise them from calves in their herd. Under the old rules, the full cost of raising the cow could therefore be deducted immediately as an ordinary business expense. Moreover, because the owner could also use cash accounting, the value the animal would add to the inventory of cows producing milk on the farm would not be considered income either. Since these animals are to be kept three to four years producing milk, these accounting practices seem more reasonable than in the case of the cattle-feeding operation.

But consider the choices these rules presented to the dairy operator. Each year, his cow herd produced a calf crop. The dairy farmer could either sell the calves or raise them to add to his milking herd. If he sold the calves, the income would be taxed. If he added them to the milking herd, cash accounting allowed him to deduct the expenses of raising the calf without paying tax on the value they add to the herd. For someone in a lower tax bracket, that might amount to less than $100 in tax savings per animal added to the herd, but for someone who was in the 50 percent tax bracket, the saving would be more like $250 per animal added to the herd. That's a considerable incentive to expand the herd.

The 1986 law has made one significant change here. It requires farmers who want to deduct preproductive expenses immediately (rather than treat them as a capital expenditure that must be depreciated over many years) to give up the use of accelerated depreciation on all their farm assets.

Cash accounting was only the beginning of tax incentives to expand in dairying under the pre-1986 rules. The benefits of capital gain also applied to dairy cows. Here, basic accounting principles had to be ignored. Under basic principles, if expenses of raising a calf can be deducted immediately instead of depreciated over the animal's useful life (the way capital investments usually must be), then when the animal has been milked for a few years and is sold, the profit above those expenses should be taxed as ordinary income. But this was not so under the pre-1986 rules. Since the animal was regarded as a capital asset intended to produce income from the milk it gave, not the meat it would provide when its milking days were over, the profit from the sale of the animal was not considered ordinary income by the Internal Revenue Service. It was capital gain. Therefore, only 40 percent of the revenue was subject to tax. On a $500 sale, $300 would have been exempt from taxation. For a wealthy individual in the 50 percent tax bracket, the capital-gain exemption on that sale was worth $150. If you were in a lower tax bracket, of course, it was worth much less.

This is the nirvana of tax sheltering—converting ordinary income that is fully taxable into capital gain, only 40 percent of which is taxable. If cash accounting hadn't whetted a farmer's appetite for expanding the dairy herd, the capital-gains exemption should have.

Between the cash accounting and the capital-gain treatment, that new cow in the herd earned hundreds of dollars in tax breaks for the farmer in the 50 percent tax bracket. But what about the farmer in the 20 percent tax bracket? The same cow in his herd was worth only 40 percent as much in tax savings, because his tax rate was 40 percent as high as that of the high-bracket farmer.

What about the investor in dairying who didn't raise his own cows, but bought a dairy cow ready to be milked? Under the old law, he would get an investment tax credit of 10 percent. On a cow that cost $900, that's $90. When the same owner sold the cow, the income was treated as capital gain.

Is it any wonder dairy herds have been expanding? Under the old rules, the incentives were very clear.

But where can you put all the animals in a dairy herd expanding by, say, 10 percent per year? For that you need more buildings and more milking equipment. These capital investments were also favored by the old tax code with a 10 percent investment tax credit and a depreciation schedule that allowed the buildings to be written off as an expense in only five years, despite the fact that their useful life is more like fifteen to twenty years.[3] The 1986 Tax Reform Act ended the investment tax credit, but made only minor changes in the depreciation schedule.

Used to their fullest advantage, these combined tax subsidies go a long way toward explaining why there has been so much expansion in the dairy industry, and especially why there have been so many new, large-scale facilities built in the southeastern and southwestern regions of the country, areas not traditionally known as dairy country. Before 1986, a corporate dairy farm in the 46 percent tax bracket could use the tax rules to garner $170,000 in tax subsidies on a $1.05 million investment in a five-hundred-cow dairy. That's a subsidy of *$340 per cow in the herd.*

In pork production, the same rules have applied in the same way, leading to a revolution in the way pork is produced. Traditionally, the hog has been raised outdoors with a minimum of housing and space. Risk of disease was minimal and the system took advantage of the animal's own marvelous ability to balance its nutritional needs by foraging.

For years, the hog was the beginning farmer's best moneymaker. Older, better established farmers were especially pleased to leave the time-consuming, vigilant job of taking care of pregnant sows and baby pigs to young farmers. The steady income from selling two crops of pigs per year, the minimal investment requirement in facilities, and the efficiency with which the animal converts corn into meat all made the hog an ideal animal for the beginning farmer with time and enthusiasm for the job, but not a lot of money. Many Iowa farms were started on little more than the willing labor of a young farm couple and two dozen sows.

But new technologies to control disease and automate both feed

3. The value of the accelerated-depreciation schedule is the "present" value of having the tax deduction sooner at the accelerated rate rather than later at the normal depreciation rate. This is equal to the interest cost that would be incurred if the taxpayer had to borrow the funds that he receives as a tax savings earlier than he would have received them under an unaccelerated deprecia-

and manure handling have made it possible to produce hogs on a much larger scale in factory-like steel buildings with as many as 480 sows. The main advantage of these hog factories is that they save labor. Two people working in a hog factory can produce many times as many baby pigs as they could on a traditional hog farm. There are disadvantages, of course, such as poorer breeding habits, higher death loss due to crowded facilities, and lower feed efficiency, except in colder climates where the warmth of buildings adds to the pig's ability to gain weight. And the hog factory naturally costs more than simpler buildings to light, heat, and maintain. But the labor efficiency is impressive.

So were the tax breaks under the old law, largely because of the peculiar way specialized livestock buildings were treated. In the early 1970s, Congress and the Internal Revenue Service implemented a series of policy changes that allowed single-purpose livestock buildings to qualify for investment tax credit and accelerated depreciation. A barn that served several useful purposes on a diversified farm, however, continued to get no tax credit and had to be depreciated over eighteen years. An expensive pork palace only capable of producing hogs, or a dairy parlor only good for milking cows, got the full tax-break treatment. The reason, Congress reasoned, is that single-purpose livestock facilities are not buildings at all—they are really specialized equipment, and should be treated as such by the tax system.

Thus, the more money invested in such buildings, the more generous the tax favors. Moreover, the more spent *per sow* in the operation, the greater the tax benefits per pound of pork produced in it. For example, a corporate hog factory using the most modern technology has a substantial investment in precisely the kind of expensive buildings most favored by the old tax code. Prior to 1986, such an operation would have had about $1,000 invested in buildings alone for *each* of its 5,000 sows. By contrast, an established hog farmer with a 100-sow herd and modern, but less expensive facilities would typically have only about $600 invested per

tion schedule. In this and the following examples cited, the calculation assumes an interest rate of 15 percent and is discounted by the taxpayer's tax rate, reflecting the after-tax interest rate he would have to pay. This is an extremely conservative evaluation of the value of the tax break to a high-income individual.

sow. The beginning farmer with older facilities brought up to date by remodeling and capable of housing 40 sows would have had even less—about $375 per sow—invested in buildings.

Tax breaks were therefore distributed in proportion to the capital-intensity of the operation. Assuming that the corporation was in the 46 percent tax bracket, the established farmer in the 30 percent tax bracket, and the beginning farmer in the 20 percent bracket, the corporation would receive nearly twice the tax subsidy per animal produced as the established farmer ($189 per sow versus $104). Likewise, the established farmer would reap nearly twice the subsidy per sow as the beginning farmer ($104 versus $56). *The corporate farm got nearly three and a half times as much tax subsidy as the beginning farmer.*

There may be few economies of size in the market, but there are plenty in the tax code. In pursuit of these phony, politically-contrived economies of size, many farmers invested heavily in the kind of high-cost facilities that put them deeply in debt and in financial trouble. In the "good" years, these tax rules provided an irresistible temptation for many farmers to avoid taxation by expanding their operation. Incorporating the family farm and reinvesting profit to avoid the dividend tax, expanding the dairy herd to convert real income into capital gain, and overbuilding with hog and dairy facilities, all seemed at the time to be better management strategies than they proved to be. Had the tax incentives not been available, far fewer of those farmers would have suffered the notion that bigger is better.

Trading Tax Breaks for Higher Prices

A political breakthrough for American agriculture came in 1986 with the recognition that most farmers would be better off with fewer tax breaks, less tax-motivated production, and higher commodity prices.

Tax-motivated expansion was a major factor in overbuilding the pork and dairy industries. The additional building and animal capacity in these sectors means more pork and more milk being produced, and that means lower producer prices. Moreover, because the investment is in long-term, fixed building costs on which annual mortgage payments must be made whether the building is used or not, these facilities must keep pumping out pork and milk even if it cannot be done profitably. As long as the owner can meet the operating costs and have something left over to apply to the mortgage, he'll keep turning out pork and milk. And, as Congress has observed, single-purpose livestock facilities are not as versatile as general-purpose farm buildings. They were designed to do one thing, whether profitable or not.

Just how much effect the overexpansion in these kinds of facilities has had on prices farmers receive is difficult to say. It is not so difficult to say how much of a price increase it would take to *offset* the tax breaks farmers received for building them.

For example, prior to the 1986 law, a dairy farmer who was in the 50 percent tax bracket would have had to get $.77 more per hundredweight of milk he produced to offset losing the privilege of the capital-gain exemption on his cows. Dairy farmers in the 30 percent and 20 percent bracket would have had to get only $.41 and $.19 more per hundredweight to make up for losing the same privilege. Of course, a dairy farmer with no taxable income would have had nothing to lose. It isn't difficult to say which farmers might be better off trading the tax subsidy for higher prices.

By the same token, not all hog farmers are affected the same by reform. The well-established farmer in the 30 percent bracket with modern facilities would have had to make $.19 more per hundredweight to make up for losing the investment tax credit and $.14 more per hundredweight to offset losing accelerated depreciation. The beginning farmer in the 20 percent bracket with remodeled facilities would have had to get only $.12 and $.06 more per hundredweight, respectively, to offset these changes.

It is not surprising that the higher a farmer's tax bracket, the less eager he might have been to trade the warmth of the tax code for the discipline of the market.

To put these price changes into some perspective, a $.50 increase in hog prices would be about a 1 percent increase. To tighten market supplies enough to raise prices that much, it would take less than a 1 percent decrease in the number of hogs sold. In other words, a 1 percent decrease in the number of hogs produced will raise prices *more than enough* to make up for the tax subsidies the majority of farmers would be sacrificing.

Without the 1986 tax reform, the likelihood was that more hogs would be produced and prices would be lower. In fact, in 1984, six corporations began or announced major hog production expansions that would add over a million hogs to the market annually. That increase in output will eventually cost farmers about $.80 in lower prices. The 1986 reforms were too late to thwart these expansions, but they should dampen others. Unfortunately, the failure to lengthen depreciation schedules significantly in the 1986 act means continuing tax-motivated investment.

The trade-off between tax breaks and commodity prices exists in all sectors of the farm economy. As farmers have realized this, their support for tax breaks for agriculture has waned. Most of them are not in a position to compete in a tax-sheltered industry.

Bad Tax Policy and Bad Land Stewardship

A further effect of the misdirected federal income-tax policy that was in place for many years has been to encourage the development of marginal farmland not ecologically suitable for tillage. The case of irrigation in the Sandhills region of Nebraska is exemplary.

The Sandhills are an ecologically rare, semi-arid region that occupies most of west-central Nebraska. It is a huge expanse of wind-deposited sand, underlaid by the Ogallala aquifer, a water-rich deposit of gravel. Until recently, this land was not considered suitable for farming because the climate was too dry to support crops, the terrain too rough to permit irrigation, and the soil too light to withstand the erosive effects of wind. The Sandhills were ideal for ranching, however, because the Ogallala water was so close to the surface that it created many wetland meadows in which the roots of native grasses were naturally irrigated. These wetland meadows provided bountiful hay crops that supported cattle herds through cold Nebraska winters.

What made farming possible in the Sandhills is the center-pivot irrigation system (discussed in Chapter 6). It can sprinkle water evenly over rough, sandy soil, applying fertilizer and pesticides directly to the crop through irrigation water. But despite these advantages, the risks of farming the Sandhills are considerable. The land is highly susceptible to wind erosion, and without (sometimes even with) careful management, a crop can be lost to the wind, which drives sand through young corn stalks like a knife. And the costs of farming with high rates of fertilizer, pesticide, and irrigation are substantial.

Notwithstanding the effect of federal tax policy, the pivot would have revolutionized agriculture in Nebraska and elsewhere. But tax policies have significantly affected *who* developed irrigation and *where* they developed it. Promoters found out early that to marshall a lot of capital quickly for irrigation development in the Sandhills, it was best to recruit tax-motivated investors.

The center-pivot system was eligible under the old law for investment tax credit and accelerated depreciation, and if the promoter developed parcels for resale to other investors, these tax breaks could be "sold" to an investor. Moreover, if the developer held the land for a year or more and farmed it in the interim, the entire profit he made from the development and sale of the land was not treated as income, but as capital gain. Moreover, if the land was rough—as much of the Sandhills region is—it might require "shaping" before the irrigation system could be installed. Shaping (also known locally as knob-knocking) is a euphemism for carving away steep knolls and filling in low areas. This bulldozer facelift was considered "conservation" in the curious world of the tax code, and its full cost could be deducted from federal taxes as a conservation expense.

Together, the developer and the investor to whom he sold the land could generate a tax subsidy equal to half its initial cost. But the saddest reality is this: since the tax breaks were proportional to the *increase* in the land's value resulting from irrigation development, the developer had a substantial incentive to develop the lowest priced land. And that usually meant irrigating the most ecologically unsuitable parcels first.

The impact of this kind of development on landownership and land-use patterns was revealed in an early study of center-pivot irrigation development in Nebraska. In a seven-county area where development was intense, about one-third of the irrigated land was owned by nonfarm investors or corporations. In the one county where a detailed analysis was made of the types of soils being developed, researchers found that marginal land accounted for two-thirds of the land developed through 1975 by nonfarm investors of the sort best positioned to use tax breaks. Local farmers developed poor soils, too, but only about one-quarter of their developments were on marginal land. As the land boom continued, the situation was destined to get worse. Based on applications for electrical power service to run their irrigation systems, nonfarm investors had plans to nearly double their total development. Eighty-four percent of the land they planned to irrigate was marginal land (Center for Rural Affairs 1976).

Good management of the farm and good stewardship of resources are both victims of unwise tax policies.

The 1986 act went a long way toward correcting these abuses. You can no longer deduct the cost of preparing land for center-pivot irrigation systems. And no deduction can be taken for conservation investments unless they are part of a conservation plan approved by local conservation officials.

Tax Subsidies and Production Policy

The irony of all these tax subsidies is that they attracted capital and encouraged expansion of farm production throughout the 1970s and earlier despite the fact that the chronic issue in the U.S. farm economy was and remains the problem of overproduction. Apart from a very brief period in the mid-1970s when supplies of a few grain crops were short, the underlying problem with which we have grappled unsuccessfully is surpluses.

In many instances, the old tax rules offset or overpowered other farm policies designed to cope with these surpluses. The contradiction was shockingly apparent in the case of a single corporate farm that received $3.5 million worth of commodities from the federal government under the 1983 Payment-In-Kind program in return for *reducing* food production, and in the same year, received an estimated $3.5 million in tax breaks by *expanding* its hog-production capacity by 15,000 sows. On a smaller scale, the same subversion of public purpose has occurred daily on thousands of farms in America.

Consumers, for their part, might be lulled into thinking that these tax breaks are a good idea, since they mean lower milk and bacon prices. It does seem that way. But isn't that a case of being penny-wise, pound-foolish? Every dollar in tax subsidies accorded a high-income farmer is a dollar foregone to the U.S. Treasury, and a dollar that must be paid in taxes by some other taxpayer. We pay for milk and bacon once in the supermarket, and once with our tax return—unless, of course, you're one of the privileged few who get more in tax breaks than you give up.

More important, such tax subsidies lower the overall efficiency of the farm sector, luring capital where it is not needed and depriving other enterprises not adorned with tax favors of the capital investments they need. Tax subsidies therefore lead to a misallocation of economic resources, contributing to the sagging performance of the American economy overall. For nonfarmers, that cannot be a good deal, and especially for those whose income depends on capital-starved industries. Would workers in the struggling industrial regions of our nation trade their jobs for a nickel-a-gallon lower milk prices?

How Much Better Are Things under the 1986 Tax Reform Act?

In summary, the federal tax code has historically produced unwarranted, unintended, and unwanted effects in American farming. Among these effects are:

— overinvestment, more production, lower prices, and less farm income;
— a misallocation of capital investment from where it is needed to where it is not needed;
— a redistribution of farm income from low-income farmers to high-income farmers, nonfarm investors, and corporations that invest in tax-sheltered farming operations;
— development of capital-intensive, inflexible production systems that provide few management options;
— higher indirect food costs in the form of higher taxes for most taxpayers;
— higher asset values, especially land prices, making entry into farming more difficult for anyone not in a position to exploit these tax rules;
— misuse of natural resources.

Things are decidedly better under the 1986 law, though how much better is not yet clear. The law eliminates the investment tax credit. It allows the use of cash accounting by investors only if they are directly involved in the management of the farm. It also prohibits those investors not directly involved in the management of the farm from using farm losses to shelter other income from taxation, and limits the use of prepaid expenses. Perhaps most important, it provides that capital gain be taxed as regular income. Tighter restrictions on investments that qualify as conservation deductions were also important. Overall, the 1986 Tax Reform Act is good for family farming.

It failed, however, to correct the abuses in accelerated depreciation. The depreciation schedule for most farm equipment is still too short. It was raised from five years to only seven for both center-pivot systems and single-purpose livestock buildings, for example, despite an expected life for these items of fifteen years. To make things worse, investors can actually take an even greater portion of the depreciation deduction in the first year of the schedule. The net effect is that the depreciation tax breaks for these items are about as attractive under the 1986 law as previously.

Furthermore, the abuses of cash accounting were not eliminated. Allowing giant corporations with farm sales in the billions to use cash accounting because they can claim to be family farmers as long as their stock is controlled by a few families is reminiscent of the old pork barrel way of doing things in tax policy.

Notwithstanding the critical defects in the 1986 law, we have reached a watershed in farm tax policy. It is significant that many farmers and some farm organizations worked hard to get these reforms passed in Congress. Interestingly, farmers were about the only "special interest group" that pleaded with Congress to take away their tax breaks because, while they might have helped individuals, they were doing far more harm than good for farmers as a whole. The 1986 reforms represented a proud moment for farmers, and a hopeful point for family farm advocates.

BECOMING THE VICTIM

Most of the growth-biased public policies discussed in this chapter were adopted because legislators and others probably believed that they were good for the family farm. Clearly, they were good for some individual family farmers. Raising the payment limitation allowed a few to stand a little longer at the federal trough. Broadening FMHA loan guidelines gave some a chance to borrow more on better terms than they would otherwise have been able to do. Lavish tax subsidies helped those able to use them save money while expanding their farms. In every case, there was a constituency of farmers who proposed, supported, and benefited from these decisions. Others, including other farmers, were silent out of ignorance or the mistaken point of view that these policies were either good for them, too, or did not affect them.

That fact made these decisions good politics if not good policy. Judged solely on the basis of the expressed self-interest of some farmers, each could be defended as "something farmers need if they are to survive." Each could be described as another tool to save the family farm.

But collectively, government policies have constituted a policy of attrition for family farming. By strengthening the already favorable position of a few, the relative position of many is weakened. In a farm economy in which opportunities are limited, these policies foster the concentration of production, the maldistribution of income, and the accumulation of wealth. The process is continuous. As the number of opportunities diminishes, fewer and fewer are able to enjoy the perceived advantages of these policies as they slip back relative to those who are even more privileged. The narrow circle tightens, and those who once were the victors become the victims.

But is it possible to attribute too much to farm policy? What about the basic nature of our economic system, the technologies we use, and the economic values we hold?

8.

The Market Trinity:
Land, Prices, and Technology

$\mathbf{O}$ver the last fifty years, the federal government has tried valiantly to reconcile the wishes of consumers for cheap food with the needs of individual farmers to have adequate incomes. This effort has been complicated by a societal conviction that larger, more industrialized farms will produce more food at a lower cost, reducing food prices for consumers. Such a conviction leads confidently to the conclusion that farmers must expand their farms if, on the one hand, they are to make use of the technology that makes food abundance possible and, on the other hand, they are to earn an adequate income despite lower commodity prices. Naturally, in this circumstance, some farmers (most, eventually) will have to find other occupations, and will earn more income if they do. Farm income will improve, but only for the individual farmers who survive this competition. The others will be forced into a presumably better life elsewhere. That, in a nutshell, is the rationale for most postdepression farm policy.

This policy of attrition for family farmers has rested on the cornerstones described in the previous chapter. They are:

— tax policies that subsidize capital investments in agriculture, especially by expanding, high-income farmers;
— readily available (but not necessarily cheap) credit that makes debt-financed expansion easier and reduces the risk of failure;
— commodity price guarantees designed to provide expanding farmers with confidence that the revenues they receive from

their crops will be adequate to reward their investments in new technologies and land, but not adequate to provide a normal standard of living if they do not expand their operation enough to make full use of those technologies.

These policies promise stability, gradual adjustment, and the eventual tranquility of "equilibrium" (the economist's notion of perfect grace). No doubt, they have accomplished much of the transition they were intended to accomplish and with little public notice. But the farm crisis of the 1980s, mounting evidence of environmental degradation, huge government expenditures on farm programs, and large individual payments to some farms have all provoked public concern about the purpose and performance of farm policy.

Not surprisingly, one of the most enduring policy debates has reemerged. Should the government intervene to raise market prices for commodities to some predetermined level, or, at the other extreme, should government get out (sooner or later, faster or slower) of agriculture altogether?

This familiar debate reached new levels of intensity in the mid-1980s and is likely to persist for some time. It comes and goes with farm crises. I won't try to resolve it here. But I want to enrich the debate by suggesting that it centers too narrowly on a single issue: the level of commodity prices. In doing so, it obscures more fundamental issues involving the economic values implicit in a market economy and, in particular, the relationship between commodity prices, the use of technology, and landownership.

OUTRUNNING THE BEAR: VALUE CONFLICTS IN A MARKET ECONOMY

Most Rev. John McRaith, a Roman Catholic bishop and former executive director of the National Catholic Rural Life Conference, tells a story that sums up the value conflicts inherent in a market economy. Perhaps fittingly, he says he first read it in *Readers Digest*. It goes like this.

Two hikers came upon a hungry bear who sized them up and started ambling down the mountain path toward them, savoring a meal. One hiker deliberately took off his backpack and boots, removed a pair of running shoes from his pack, and calmly started putting them on. The other looked at him in astonishment and protested, "We can't outrun that bear!" The first replied without hesitation: "I don't have to outrun the bear. I just have to outrun you."

Adam Smith, the classical economist who first articulated the nature of a market economy, might not have liked this summary description of it, but he might not have been able to summarize it more effectively either. According to classical economics, a free market works by impartially directing the self-interest of producers toward greater productivity from which everyone benefits. Because there are many producers, the individual behavior of each has no appreciable affect on the market as a whole; neither increases nor reductions in output by one have any impact on the price he or she receives. In order to make a profit, each will therefore seek to produce goods that sell at a price above the cost of producing them, or to lower the cost of production below that of other producers. By pursuing economies of size—by seeking the optimum combination of capital, labor, and management to produce at the lowest cost per unit of production—the producer maximizes his or her own welfare. If others do not follow suit, the enterprising one who achieves the lowest cost will enjoy higher profits. When other competitors learn to emulate his or her efficiency, all will be producing more, market prices will fall, and there will be no profits for any of them until someone learns how to produce at even lower costs. Those who do not make the necessary adjustments toward efficiency will fail because they will continue to produce at a cost of production that is higher than the price they can receive for their product. There will be *more* of everything the enterprising ones produce and lower prices for those who consume those products. After profits fall, the surviving producers will either find new ways to lower costs or new products whose prices exceed the cost at which they can produce them, and the process repeats itself interminably. The miracle of the market is that enterprising producers in pursuit of self-interest produce an economic surplus, and that surplus eventually benefits everyone.

There are two crucial underpinnings to this virtuous, if impersonal, view of the free market. One is the assumption that the cost of production for a commodity can always be lowered by augmenting human labor with technologies. The logic of economies of size is based on this notion and, as discussed in Chapters 5–7, has real but limited value in explaining the continued expansion of family farms.

168

The second analytical underpinning of the free market is its competitive paradigm: competition among those free to enjoy its rewards breeds innovation and enterprise. This dynamic helps to explain the historical development of American agriculture described in Chapters 2 and 3. There are three interacting agents in this process:

Technology is the production factor that enables enterprising producers to capture the advantage over other competitors. Those who adopt new technologies are able to produce more at a lower cost per unit of production. They enjoy higher profits until others match their cunning by adopting the same technologies and methods. As more do so, production multiplies, and prices and profits fall. As technology enables some to expand their farming operations at the expense of others, capital invested in that technology substitutes for labor. In the predatory world of the competitive paradigm, the quest is to substitute "my capital for your labor." Agricultural economist Willard Cochrane distilled the process of technological innovation in agriculture by likening it to a steadily accelerating treadmill off the end of which those who are reluctant to adopt cost-reducing technologies must inevitably fall (Cochrane 1979).[1]

The Entrepreneur is the human factor in competition. The entrepreneur sees opportunities and takes them, welding capital, technology, and labor (his own or others') into productive enterprise in pursuit of profits. The entrepreneur's self-interest drives the system. His special contribution is a willingness to risk falling off the treadmill by stepping up its pace through technological innovation. If the new technologies don't work well, his costs will increase, his productivity will lag, and he will be the victim. If they succeed, he profits.

Land is the limited resource necessary to employ labor and technology. As such, it is competitively sought by those who hope to survive the competition. The success of the survivors is reflected in the growing value of land. Land is therefore both a store of wealth and a claim on future income—the spoils of successful enterprise that accrue to the victors of the competition.

American agriculture accepts (and demonstrates) the logic of

---

1. Cochrane first described the treadmill in *Prices: Myth and Reality* (Minneapolis: University of Minnesota Press, 1958), chapter 5, but the 1979 reference is more accessible and in many ways, more readable.

the competitive paradigm about as well as any sector of our economy. Nowhere do we find such expression of loyalty to the principles of the market, or such devotion to enterprise, productivity, and libertarian freedom. To use a cliché to describe a cliché, I wish I had a dollar for every time I've heard applause from a farm audience in response to empty utterances about the free market and the virtues of competition. Such a fetish is made of competition that one of the most commonly expressed excuses for periodic financial stress among farmers is the ironic statement that "we must preserve the right to fail if we are to have the right to prosper." Those who accept this as wisdom apparently believe that the right to prosper comes only at the expense of those who must fail. Competition is not merely for honor. Outrunning the bear *requires* leaving someone behind to satisfy its appetite.

Humor is one way in which people confess their least admirable character traits, and it is tempting to share some of the many jokes I've heard over the years in which farmers poke fun at their own competitive cannibalism. There is the one about the guy who doesn't want to own all the land, just the land that borders his farm. Or the one about the farmer who proceeded to tell the insurance adjuster how devastating the twister that hit his farm was, until he learned that his neighbors had been hit even harder, which provoked him to reflect, "Maybe it wasn't so bad after all."

THE YEOMAN VERSUS THE ENTREPRENEUR

But there is a paradox in this competitive paradigm: if left unrestrained, the nature of competition is to eliminate itself.

As victors consolidate their gains, they are better able to profit at the expense of others, notwithstanding the willingness of the latter to innovate or to risk investing in cost-reducing technologies. Increasingly, the capacity to compete depends less on ingenuity, industriousness, and competence, and more on the accumulation of financial advantages in the hands of previous victors. Wealth and power become substitutes for skill and effort. Market dominance replaces efficiency in resource management as the principal ingredient of success. It is at this point that the internal logic of competition as an inducement to enterprise, productivity, and increases in real wealth begins to unravel.

Significantly, the means of accomplishing success are transformed as well. Less emphasis is placed on productivity and efficiency and more emphasis is placed on mere speculation—the buying of productive assets in anticipation of a further increase in their value, unrelated to any improvement in their productivity. This unwarranted escalation of asset values actually deprives the economy of the benefits of enterprise. It pushes the cost of assets beyond the purchasing power of efficient producers who can only afford to pay as much for these assets as they will actually earn in productive use.

The natural aversion agrarian communities everywhere seem to have for absentee ownership of land is therefore more than the parochial jealousies of a backward, suspicious people. It is based on their heritage of experience that when land accumulates in the hands of speculators, people who depend on working the land for their living are sure to suffer.

The competitive paradigm therefore does not fully explain the changing structure of American agriculture and its tendency toward concentration of landownership. Many enterprising, productive, efficient farmers are beaten not by more efficient farmers, but by the tendency of competition to degenerate into land speculation. Having embraced the premise of unrestrained competition in a market economy, bolstered by the myth that bigger is necessarily more efficient, many farmers, like the rest of us, mistake the vices of speculation for the virtues of enterprise. In a period like the 1980s, most could not help but become its victims. Profits in farming were simply not sufficient to support investments made on speculation. Nor were there any guarantees that the most predatory would suffer most. To the contrary, as we have seen, it was usually the neophyte investors who speculated late in the boom process who suffered the most. In effect, many of them were victims of economic behavior that reflected their own misplaced value on unearned income from land speculation.

Sadly, rural communities generally seem to have been without the moral strength to resist the speculators during the boom periods that have characterized American agriculture. Prominent local citizens do not publicly or privately chastise farmers who aggressively expand. Clergy rarely give sermons admonishing against predatory greed in the local land market. Local business people are too eager to sell a little more to the expander to worry about the neighbor whose future he or she threatens. Shame casts a short shadow in many rural communities during agricultural boom periods. Too many are caught up in the wonders of a market economy, their faith in it vindicated by the good fortune of a rising tide that seems to lift all boats. Those who protest are quickly branded naysayers.

Some would even defend the behavior of speculators as natural or rational. But there are no immutable economic laws that compel such behavior. It is an expression of a particular set of values, embodied in economic behavior.

Still, there is a strain within American agriculture that rejects these values. Some people value community and neighbors too much to willingly sacrifice them to the market. For them, farming is not merely an occupation or an opportunity, but an identity. Their farming values are not merely economic, but social and cultural as well. For these socially minded farmers, farming in America is like swimming against the tide, but they do it their way because their values require it of them.

This difference in values and their influence on economic behavior was sharply drawn in a study contrasting management practices of farmers in two communities in Illinois. Their agricultural resources were similar, but their ethnic characteristics were distinct (Salamon 1985).

One community had been settled in the 1830s by "old American stock," primarily Yankee emigrants from Kentucky, Indiana, Ohio, and other parts of Illinois. Its farmers were Protestant descendents of old England and they were plainly "entrepreneurial." They managed for business profits, rented land aggressively and were committed to expansion strategies that were limited only by available capital. They borrowed heavily. Their farms were larger than average, and tended to be specialized as cash grain farms. Land was viewed unsentimentally as a commodity to be bought and sold for profit and absentee landowners thrived in this community. The farm was not viewed as a permanent base for the family. Competition between generations was characteristic on these farms. Children were not necessarily expected to farm, and if they wanted to, were expected to set themselves up in farming. As heirs, the children were responsible for acquiring the farm from their parents on the parents' terms.

By contrast, the other community, located only twenty miles away in an area with similar soil types, had been settled in the 1840s by Catholic immigrants from the German province of Westphalia. Their values were more family-centered. Their basic farm management goal was to provide a viable farming unit with at least one farmer from the family in each generation. The farm provided a continuous identity for the family. They borrowed reluctantly, expanded cautiously, and preferred owning land to renting it. To make the best use of family labor, their farms were more diversified with livestock as well as crops. On the whole, their farms were significantly smaller than the entrepreneurs', and there was little absentee ownership. Because the family goal was to preserve the farm as a base for the family, there was more cooperation between generations. Parents retired early in order to help establish the farm heir. These farmers exhibited the values usually associated with the term "yeoman."

The quality of community life was also influenced by these contrasting values and the farm management practices that flowed from them. In the entrepreneurial Yankee community, loyalty was weak and people complained that despite the wealth held by local landowners, too little was invested in local schools, and church life was minimal. On the other hand, the German yeoman community had an ethnic environment that was "vital, integrated, and reinforcing."

According to its author, the study suggests that both the entrepreneurs and the yeomen can be viewed as successful depending on the economic criteria used. If scale of operation is the measure of success, the Yankee approach is best. If long-term persistence of a farming community is the goal, the yeoman approach is better.

The differences between the two also suggest that they behaved differently during the 1970s boom period. The Yankee entrepreneurs borrowed heavily against rising land values to expand. They recognized no upper limit on their success. During the bust, they suffered greatly. In fact, the author reports that one of the more aggressive Yankee farmers, considered successful by his neighbors, failed in the year following the study.

The yeomen, on the other hand, hardly noticed the boom and did not change their operations because of it. In the good years, they were more likely to pay off debt on the farm and less likely to expand than were the entreprenuers. They were content to reach their farm size goal and stop. As a result, they were stabler during hard times. While fewer failed, those who did found it more difficult to accept. For them, losing the farm was not merely a business failure. It was a loss of identity.

Common ground, similar circumstances, but different responses bred by different views of what counts in life. Economists consider all people to have the same values. Everyone wants to earn more, to buy more, to have more. They discount the influence of other values—community, loyalty, love of the land, and continuity, for example. But these values are real, and they are economic values because they influence economic behavior. Sometimes, when it counts the most, they are the values that can be measured most readily.

The boom/bust sequence is itself an expression of values. It is the get-rich-quick, something-for-nothing, winner-take-all attitude in us that first produces the fever-pitched expansion, then the panic-ridden retreat. The entrepreneurial spirit argues "nothing ventured, nothing gained." But it is not the spirit of true competition in which quality of performance determines results. Nor is it a legitimate quest for efficiency. It's just high-stakes poker.

Unrestrained competition can only destroy competition. To protect competition in the farm economy, the predatory tendencies of some family farmers must be restrained, and the yeoman-like tendencies of all must be nourished. But such a step turns primarily on cultural values, not mere public policies. In a democratic society, policy cannot do what the people do not want done.

THE RIGHTS OF PROPERTY AND OPPORTUNITY

As long as the market economy works by rewarding ownership of farmland for its speculative value, those with wealth will accumulate property and reduce opportunities for others. These property interests themselves must be limited if family farming is to flourish. Unless they are, the success of the few will increasingly smother the prospects for the many by restricting access to land. In this respect, saving the family farm requires resolution of one of our society's most profound value conflicts—that between the rights of property and the rights of opportunity.

The conflict between the property rights of landowners and the economic opportunity to farm are manifest in many ways in American agriculture. Clearly, the conflict is intense between the rights of absentee investors who own land and tenant farmers who rent from them. Most people concerned about social justice have no trouble deciding whom they favor in this conflict.

But this conflict exists in microcosm *within* family farms as well.

Most farmers in the United States are both owners and operators, both landlords and tenants. They are pulled by their interests both as landowners and as farm workers, and sometimes they are pulled in opposite directions.

Significantly, not all farmers have equal interests as owners and workers. Which of these interests is of greater importance to a given farmer is a matter of personal financial circumstance, perception, and values. For the most part, American farmers have tended to place greater emphasis on the rights of property. Those who believe themselves to be comparatively well served by their property interests, no matter how slight those interests may be, tend to defend the rights of property with greater enthusiasm than they ought to. Some simply place so much store in property rights that they favor them even if they realize that they are not well served by them. For many, it is only the prospect of outrunning the bear long enough to accumulate considerable property that matters. As long as they have their chance to do so, why worry over whether others do as well? Success is the individual's doing, opportunity is something for society to worry about.

The conflict between unlimited property rights and opportunity is joined in the market place. The market determines the rewards both of farming and of owning land. One of the principal factors in the market for land, however, is the price farmers receive for commodities. In the debate over the proper level of commodity prices and means of regulating them, the conflict between the rights of property and of opportunity becomes sharpest.

THE FAUSTIAN BARGAIN:
TECHNOLOGY AND THE PRICE ISSUE

In a competitive economy, the market price of commodities should reflect the relationship between supply and demand, and supply is a function of (among other things) the technology available to the producer. To restate the competitive paradigm: If technology is available to make two bushels of corn grow where only one has grown before (i.e., to make the cost of producing each bushel of corn lower), then those who use the latest technology will produce larger volumes of corn and the price of corn will fall until those who refuse to use the technology (or can't muster the capital to buy the technology) will be forced out of business, giving up their land

Figure 7. Net Farm Income and Number of Farms

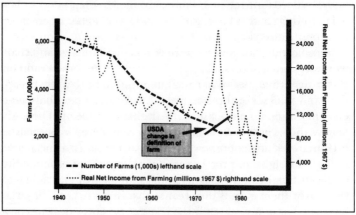

Source: U.S. Department of Agriculture 1987.
Note: Beginning in 1975, USDA excluded from the definition of a farm all operations with farm commodity sales under $1,000.

to those who, in the vernacular of rational economics, are more "progressive." Low commodity prices fuel the competitive process, but technology is the engine that drives it.

If the purpose is to save the family farm, why not strip the competitive process of its principal fuel, low farm prices? There probably isn't a demand more universally appealing to farmers than that of higher commodity prices.

And why not? Intuitively, higher commodity prices mean more income for farmers. As a general rule, farm income and commodity prices do vary directly. But even when commodity prices and farm incomes were relatively high, including the golden years of the 1940s and '70s, farmers continued to leave farming (figure 7). But why? Why, instead, don't more people enter farming when farm income is high?

The answer is that because agriculture operates as a market economy in which the rewards of adopting new technologies are transformed into the accumulation of ever-more-valuable farmland, the relationship between commodity prices and the well-being of farmers is not as simple as it seems. Are farmers well off if they farm successfully, live frugally, and plow every available dollar into more machinery and more farmland? How can such farmers be made better off? Would such farmers be better off with higher commodity prices that make it possible both to buy more land and to live better? Would their neighbors be better off?

There was a time when higher prices meant higher incomes for all farmers, pure and simple. But that was when most people were farmers, when farmers were more or less similar in size and character, when they produced most of the inputs they used right on their own farms, when land was plentiful and relatively cheap, when debt was the exception, not the rule, and when tools were more important than machines and the primary factor of production was still human and animal labor. Because farmers purchased and borrowed little, there were few leaks in the farm financial boat through which to lose the benefits of an increase in commodity prices. If the price of corn went up, the additional money went into the farmer's pocket.

But labor is no longer the chief input farmers provide. They now provide more capital, technology, and management sophistication. And increasingly, they buy, rent, or borrow these inputs from others who, by supplying them, gain a claim on some of the income from farming. Even labor, which farmers increasingly hire, is a cash cost of production. As the industrialization of American agriculture continues, farmers' incomes become increasingly dependent on more than the price of the commodities they receive. Their income also depends on the price they pay for the inputs they use, and on the amount they choose to invest in land, buildings, and machinery. The problem of commodity prices is therefore intertwined with other issues: landownership, land prices, and the proper uses of technology.

While some farm organizations have from time to time argued strenuously for public attention to the commodity-price issue, most have not been so eager to address these related issues, perhaps because they require a critical inward look at the behavior of farmers themselves.

To understand these issues better, consider in more detail how the "cost" of farming has changed over time. Time was, farmers produced most of their own inputs. They raised horses for draft power and the oats with which to feed them. They recycled animal manure as fertilizer, saved seed from one crop to plant the next, and controlled pests by planting in late spring after one crop of weeds had been destroyed, cultivated later weeds, and rotated crops from year to year. They let the crop dry naturally in the field. Land, labor, tools, and some machines were their main inputs. Farming was a matter of hard work, good timing, and knowing how to cooperate with nature.

Technology has changed that. Farmers buy a host of intermediate products—purchased inputs like hybrid seeds that grow bigger crops, chemical fertilizer and pest controls, bigger and more specialized machines. There has been an endless stream of new technologies, many of them, in recent years, by-products of military and space-exploration research. These technologies allow farmers to intercede in biological and chemical processes, to short-circuit nature's constraints on production. By regulating when natural processes occur, they standardize the production process, allowing labor to be routinized. They alter the environment, making it possible to conduct economic activities in climates and under conditions in which they would not naturally occur. They eliminate the balance between predators, making it possible to intensify crop production over vast acreages without diversification or rotation. They influence the pace, scale, location, and character of modern agriculture.

To acquire these powerful technologies, farmers borrow money in large sums and pay interest on the loan, which itself is another input. To use this technology, they rent more land or borrow to buy more land. More interest follows.

The full impact of the post–World War II technological revolution on how farmers spend the money they receive for their crops is evident in table 9. First, note that their gross income—the amount of money they have to spend—has climbed fifteenfold, from $10.8 billion in 1940 to $162.3 billion in 1984 (column 2). Adjusted for inflation, this still represents a doubling of gross income. This doubling reflects a dramatic increase in the *output* of all farm commodities, and it has occurred despite the fact that prices of those commodities have fallen relative to inflation. Between 1950 and 1982, yields per acre for wheat, rice, and cotton have roughly doubled; corn yields have tripled. These yield boosts, coupled with increased acreages of all these crops (except cotton), mean total production has increased even more—171 percent for wheat, 198 percent for corn, and 296 percent for rice. Thus, while prices of these major commodities have fallen in real terms by 40 percent to 60 percent during the same period, gross farm income has doubled because they have had so much more to sell.

How does the picture change when we subtract production ex-

Table 9. Where the Money in Farming Goes ($ millions)

Year (1)	Gross Farm Income (2)	Intermediate Products (3)	Capital Consumption (4)	Business Taxes (5)	Non-Real Est. Int. (6)	Total (7)	Hired Labor (8)	Land Costs		Returns to Operators (11)
								Rent to Landlords (9)	Real Estate Interest (10)	
1940	10,756	3,491	661	382	186	4,720	1,029	672	243	4,092
1950	31,923	10,984	2,301	810	334	14,429	2,811	1,822	225	12,636
1960	36,747	15,940	3,773	1,373	719	21,805	2,754	1,491	549	10,148
1970	55,769	25,188	5,890	2,383	1,618	35,079	3,906	2,360	1,586	12,838
1980	138,675	73,420	17,847	3,607	8,717	103,591	8,270	5,760	6,920	14,134
1984	162,293	75,925	19,233	4,088	10,396	109,642	8,976	5,442	9,879	28,354

Source: U.S. Department of Agriculture, *Economic Indicators of the Farm Sector: National Financial Summary*, 1986, table 4, pp. 13, 14.

penses from this increase in gross income? The rest of table 10 reveals that although farmers have more to spend, they spend much more to earn it, and as a result, have relatively less for themselves.

The portion of gross income kept as net return to all operators (column 11) has declined from 38 percent in 1940 to as low as 10 percent in 1980. In 1984, the net was $28,354 million, which is equivalent to $3,758 million in 1940 dollars. That is 10 percent less than the $4,092 million net that farmers actually received in 1940, despite a real doubling of gross farm income. Where does the money go?

Most of it goes to purchase off-farm inputs. In 1940, these cash operating expenses consumed 44 percent of gross income, but by 1984 took 67 percent (column 7). Intermediate products—seed, fertilizer, and fuel, for example—increased their share from 32 percent to 47 percent of gross income receipts (column 3). Capital consumption (depreciation and damage to buildings, vehicles, and equipment—column 4) doubled its share (from 6 percent to 12 percent), and interest on loans to pay for these items (column 6) tripled its share (from 2 percent to 6 percent). Business taxes (column 5), so often the rhetorical villain, did not significantly change their share of the take of income.

These figures underscore the growing dependence of farming on expensive technology and capital. But they also reveal something more. A Faustian bargain has been made between the user of the technology and the impersonal market. The bargain is this: In return for the splendid increase in production made possible by this technology, the producer must both accept less money for each unit sold, and share the rewards of increased output with those who produce the technologies. The suppliers of the technology that make cheap abundance possible must be paid, and they take an ever-growing share of the rewards while farmers take less. In return for a chance to profit, farmers have condemned themselves to an endless race against their neighbors to outrun the bear.

Although the profits among most farm input suppliers cannot be documented easily, it is safe to say they are substantial. If these profits were added to net farm-income figures, the overall rate of profit from food production would not appear nearly as dismal as it does. The fact that those profits are not farmers' profits reflects the extent to which farmers have paid dearly for the benefits of no longer producing their own horsepower, fertilizer, and weed control.

180

With less net income to spread among farmers, many cannot continue to farm. They go out of business while those who make use of the new technologies expand. In 1940 there were 6.35 million farms. Today, there are about 2.33 million. Over 4 million farms simply failed to outrun others, and were caught by the bear. The remaining 2.33 million are still running.

Because today there are so many fewer of them to share the profits, the *average* return to a farm operator has actually more than doubled, after adjustments for inflation, even though the total real net income to the farm sector as a whole decreased by 10 percent. Of course, we have seen in Chapter 4 what averages hide: this bounty is hardly distributed evenly among farmers. Three-fourths of the net income to farmers is concentrated among the largest 5 percent, the ones who have run fastest to escape the bear.

In effect, the profit in agriculture has not been diminished as much as the presence of thousands of broke farmers suggests. It has merely been redistributed in two ways: from farmers to the companies that sell them inputs, and from smaller farmers to larger farmers.

Will mechanically raising commodity prices change that? Not alone. For while farmers compete with each other vigorously, the firms that supply them with technology do not compete in the same way. As a result, when commodity prices increase, suppliers can raise their prices, too. The benefits of higher commodity prices end up in the pockets of the suppliers, not the farmers.

Input suppliers are better able to reap the gain because there are fewer of them and they are less competitive than the farmer. If there were many input suppliers in competition with each other, a rise in commodity prices would not affect the prices they charge farmers for inputs. Farmers would be able to keep the additional income from a commodity price increase. But there are only three major manufacturers of farm machinery, a handful of highly specialized chemical suppliers, and a rapidly dwindling number of seed companies. While the pricing practices of these and other farm input industries are poorly documented, the evidence is sufficient to support skepticism that competition among them would prevent them from raising their product prices enough to capture at least part of any increase in farm income.

In fact, a 1981 analysis of the major farm-input industries by the staff of the Federal Trade Commission (FTC) (Leibenluft 1981) revealed that none of the four major input industries—fertilizer, chemicals, seed, and machinery—were clearly competitive. The FTC staff analysis suggested that the most competitive was the fertilizer industry, despite the fact that, historically, it has been the subject of a large number of antitrust actions. The nitrogen fertilizer subsector—easily the largest of the fertilizer subsectors—is dominated by natural gas and petrochemical companies. In the other input sectors the level of concentration certainly invites monopoly pricing practices. This is especially so within particular product lines within those sectors.

For example, two companies dominate the market for hybrid seed corn, with the leader holding a third of the market and earning a return on equity as high as 25 percent in 1980. Four companies account for 87.1 percent of the sales of herbicides used on corn, two of them alone producing 92.4 percent of the sales of herbicides used to control grass weeds and the other two producing 76.1 percent of the broadleaf weed herbicides.[2] From 70 to 81 percent of the sales of tractors, plows, and harvesting and haying machinery are controlled by four companies.

Likely, a rise in farm prices would simply encourage these input suppliers to raise the price of their products. That would be particularly true if commodity prices were actually pegged to input prices, so that any increase in input costs to the farmer would automatically be reflected in higher commodity prices. In that case, the farmer would be insulated from the consequences of increases in input costs, but the rest of society would not. There would be little incentive for farmers to conserve on these inputs and the farmer would become officially what he is now unofficially—a passthrough account for these suppliers to charge consumers for their services. Farmers would probably be a little better off, but only because they would be on the same gravy train as the suppliers.

Failing to come to grips with the economic power of these input suppliers has made farmers vulnerable to the unjust uses of their market power. But tying commodity prices to input prices, as many family farm advocates have suggested, would do nothing but let this power loose on society. As it is now, these concentrated industries must moderate their prices enough to allow some profit in

2. A USDA study from about the same period found that the top four corn herbicide companies had 94 percent of the market, the top two 74 percent, and that similar levels of concentration in crop herbicide subsectors existed in most other commodities (Eichers 1980).

182

farming, lest they kill the goose that lays the golden egg. It was revealing that, after the bottom fell out of the farm economy in the 1980s, suppliers lowered prices for fertilizer, chemicals, and tractors, causing some thoughtful farmers to wonder how much they had been overpriced before. If farmers were guaranteed sufficient income to pay these companies whatever they charged, there could be no limit to their profit taking. A concentrated market place is likely to be an unfair market place, but protecting only farmers from the unfairness is not the right solution.

At an even more fundamental level, the issue is whether even a genuinely competitive market, through the mechanism of commodity prices, should be the sole determinant of the technology used in modern agriculture. It is the technology, brilliantly deployed, that has altered the market equation between supply and demand. No amount of quibbling about the greed and inequities at work in the market can overpower this central fact. If we are going to use the full range of technologies available in agriculture without caution or restraint, the price of commodities will continue to fall. The low price that most farmers painfully experience is but a symptom—a revelation—of the power of technology. Ultimately, the issue is not whether to raise farm prices to relieve the stress in farming, but whether the technology that causes the stress should be restrained. If it should not be restrained, then the bargain has been made and farm policy can do little to resolve the difficulties of those farmers who fail to outrun the bear. But if for any reason the technology does not increase the well-being of society as a whole, then it should not be used (or allowed to be used). The price of commodities will then rise to reflect the restraints placed on the unbridled use of technology.

Will it work the other way? Would simply mandating higher commodity prices dissuade farmers from adopting new technologies that are harmful to society? Would higher prices slow down the treadmill? Not likely for long. It is true that those who are not inclined to make new investments in technologies—the old, the satisfied, or the ethical—would be sheltered from lower prices and would survive despite the impact of the technologies. The overall rate of adoption would therefore be retarded. But for the willing, the rewards of adopting new technologies would only be that much greater. They would then produce more and sell at the higher, protected prices. The benefits of technological innovation would thus be concentrated among them. The rest of society would gain nothing. It would, of course, be stuck with whatever social and environmental costs are associated with the new technology.

An alternative is to protect prices by limiting production, thus reducing incentives to produce more even among the willing adopters of new technologies. Of course, limiting production diminishes incentives to adopt any new technology, harmful or not. The technology issue is discussed on its merits in Chapter 9 and mandatory production controls in the section on policy at the conclusion of the book. For now, we are interested only in the relationship between technology and commodity prices. As much as some would like to, you can't have it both ways. Wanting both higher commodity prices and the right to unbridled use of technology is like wanting the coin to come up both heads and tails.

COMMODITY PRICES AND THE LAND QUESTION

The prices of commodities and inputs are the guiding lights of a market economy. They tell the farmer when things are right or wrong and how to change the operation. They tell when too much or too little of something is being produced, or when too much or not enough of something is being used. When hog prices periodically fall, farmers traditionally curb production by reducing their breeding herds until prices rise. When the price of an input rises, farmers adjust in other ways, as when they became more energy conserving during the 1970s.

Not all adjustments are made easily. Fixed investments in capital items make change most difficult, as we saw in Chapter 6. Still, the price of commodities sends a signal to farmers (and others) whether or not to invest in inputs. And that includes land. Higher corn prices mean more investment in land, and therefore higher land prices. It follows as the night follows the day. Commodity prices are a principal factor in land prices.

On the other hand, the cost of land is also a factor in the cost of producing commodities. In fact, it is the largest single cost. In other words, commodity prices and land prices interact powerfully, significantly influencing the well-being of farmers. When land prices are high relative to commodity prices, there will be financial stress, sooner or later (i.e., as soon as bankers begin to worry about whether the income from farming justifies the loans they have made on land). When, on the other hand, commodity prices are high relative to land, profits in agriculture will tempt farmers to expand their landholdings or new investors to buy land, in both instances raising land prices.

This crucial relationship between commodity prices and land prices affects farmers in different financial situations differently. Begin by considering what the cost of land really is. In a theoretical sense, land costs society nothing. As classical economist David Ricardo described it over 170 years ago, it is a free good provided by nature, an "original and indestructable" source of new wealth (Ricardo 1817). What costs is the socially sanctioned right to use land, either by owning it or renting it. It costs one person a sum of money to use land the way he or she wants to, rather than let someone else use it the way they see fit.

These acquisition costs are exacted in two ways. For tenants, the right is secured by rent payments to landlords; for an owner, by interest payments on any debt incurred to buy the land, plus whatever land taxes are imposed and whatever income is given up by not investing the money in something other than land. Whether owner or tenant, the farmer may or may not be able to afford to meet the expense of acquiring the right to use land. What a farmer can afford to pay for the use of farmland is roughly the amount left over from the sale of the crop after all production expenses, including a living wage for the farmer's labor and management services, are paid. This amount, usually referred to in economic shorthand as the residual, therefore varies directly with the price of commodities and the costs of other production inputs. If commodity prices go up or if other costs go down, the residual increases and the amount farmers can afford to pay for land increases. For this reason, economists like to refer to land as the residual claimant. Whoever owns the land can count on keeping all that's left from crop sales after expenses are paid.

This unique role of land as the residual claimant interacts with commodity prices to determine what farmers must pay to use land, whether they are renting or buying it. Commodity prices therefore determine more than farm families' standard of living. They also determine how much farmers can afford to pay to acquire land.

How do changes in commodity prices affect the cost of acquiring land for farmers in different financial situations? And how is the standard of living for various farmers changed when commodity prices change, altering land costs? The answer to both questions depends in large measure on whether farmers rent or own land, and if they own, how much they have borrowed to buy it.

If farmers rent land, their rental payments are either a flat fee for the use of the land, or a share of the crop. What happens to the tenant's well-being with a rise in commodity prices? For the tenant, a rise in commodity prices means more money in the pocket, but only for a short time if it amounts to much money. If prices had previously been so low that the farmer could not even meet production expenses, the increase in income simply goes to pay for unmet expenses. To the extent that the unmet expense is the tenant family's living expenses, they will enjoy an improved standard of living. But that is only so if the landlord realizes that raising the rent to confiscate the additional income may cause a good tenant to move on to another farm. If the increase in the tenant's income is so much that the landlord believes the tenant will be able and willing to pay more rent and still live well enough to stay on the farm, the landlord will raise the rent. He will do this because he knows that another tenant lies in wait, able because of higher commodity prices to pay more rent, and willing to live on what the current tenant will have to live on even after the rent increase.

There are mitigating circumstances. Land rental arrangements are frequently personal between landlord and tenant and bound by tradition and custom. The nature of the personal relationship between landlord and tenant—its duration, and the level of trust and mutual goodwill between them—plays a large role in the calculus of rent. Many landlords would remain loyal to a tenant despite opportunities to raise rents. Some would do so out of fear that a better, more honest tenant could not be found if the current one were driven off. They'd rather accept a little less than the going rate than run the risk of unknown difficulties in the search for a new tenant.

But in most cases, they will accept only a little less, and not for long. The evidence is too clear to conclude otherwise. When farm income increases, so do rents to landlords (figure 8). In the 1970s, rents increased soon after increases in prices and incomes. Later, when prices and incomes fell, rents did too, if somewhat more slowly. It is axiomatic that landlords look for any sign of prosperity among their tenants, and raise the rent to confiscate it. Commodity price increases may keep tenants on the farm earning a decent

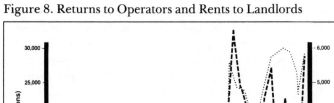

Figure 8. Returns to Operators and Rents to Landlords

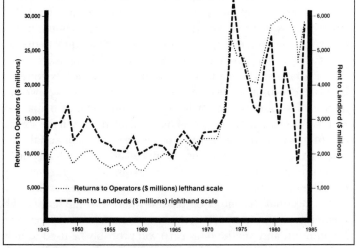

Source: U.S. Department of Agriculture 1987.

wage for their labor and management, but any substantial increase in commodity prices will simply raise the rent. Most of the
benefit of a commodity price increase will go to the landlord eventually, and will probably put an end to any nagging notion he might
have had about selling the land to the tenant. Not surprisingly,
landlords have a real affection for government farm programs
tying commodity price supports to acreage.

If the farmer owns the land rather than rents it, the relationship between commodity prices and the farmer's standard of living is much more complex. For owners, the cost of acquiring land
is more difficult to assess than it is for tenants. Like the tenant, the
owner-operator must pay other production expenses first, but after that, the amount left over is not clearly separated into land rental
payments and family living expenses. There is no landlord to ne-
gotiate with over the proper rent, and the annual land cost does
not vary with fluctuations in the theoretical residual that remains
after family living expenses.

What are an owner's land costs? If the land is debt-free, the
farmer pays nothing for the use of the land (except taxes) and the
residual amounts to a return on investment in farmland. Economists like to think that in this situation it still costs the farmer to

own farmland because he could sell it and invest the money in some other business that would pay a dividend. The income opportunity forsaken by not doing so is his cost of owning farmland. This is a pretty abstract cost. You don't sacrifice bread and butter if farm prices are not high enough to produce a residual equal to the rate of return you might make from some other investment.

For a farmer buying land on credit, the situation is quite different. He owns it only to the extent that he has made a down payment or has built up equity by making additional principal payments. For this owner, the cost of using farmland is both the abstract cost of foregone income on an alternative investment and the real cost of the interest payments he makes to the lender (who, in American agriculture, incidently, is frequently the former owner). The more the farmer owes on the land, the greater the share of the residual that must be paid as interest to the lender. The farmer has little equity from which to earn a return on investment for himself, and any he does earn will probably be used to build equity by making principal payments. If farm prices fall and the residual shrinks to zero, this farmer must choose between family living expenses and interest payments on the land. It's no choice. Failing to make the interest payments means foreclosure in short order. The kids live on beans.

In effect, though land is an input that costs society nothing, the acquisition of land through rent or ownership costs the individual who uses it something. How much it costs varies enormously, depending on how much equity the farmer has in the land.

Ownership of land is therefore a social invention that determines not only who uses land, but who gets to claim the residual from agriculture. Some theorists maintain that the mere ownership of land makes a tangible contribution to food production by placing people in competition for the right to claim the residual. The people who can make the best use of land (i.e., can produce the largest residual) will do so. Ultimately, their competitive success is reflected in the price of land, which should reflect how much they can pay for it by making annual interest and principal payments from the residual.

The unequal distribution of land and the unequal competition for its use are pivotal in determining who benefits from an increase in commodity prices. Those who are heavily indebted to lenders for land purchases are benefited by having more residual from which to make interest and principal payments. If prices had

Table 10. What Happens to Farm Income after Production Expenses ($ billions)

Year (1)	Income Returns to Assets, Optr. Labor, & Mgt. (2)	Cost of Acquiring Assets		Returns to Operators			
		Rent to Landlords (3)	Interest (4)	Labor (5)	Mgt. (6)	Equity (7)	Total (8)
1970	18.4	2.4	3.2	5.3	2.1	5.4	12.8
1971	19.1	2.3	3.4	5.6	2.2	5.7	13.5
1972	24.8	3.5	3.7	5.4	2.5	9.6	17.5
1973	42.0	5.5	4.5	5.5	3.6	23.0	32.1
1974	34.8	4.8	5.5	5.9	3.6	15.0	24.5
1975	33.3	4.7	6.1	5.6	3.8	13.2	22.6
1976	27.8	4.0	7.0	5.2	3.7	7.9	16.8
1977	28.1	4.0	8.1	5.5	3.9	6.5	15.9
1978	37.5	4.6	9.7	5.5	4.6	13.1	23.2
1979	44.7	5.6	12.6	5.8	5.3	15.4	26.5
1980	35.5	5.8	15.6	6.4	5.2	2.5	14.1
1981	47.6	5.8	19.1	7.6	6.0	9.1	22.7
1982	44.2	5.7	20.9	6.7	5.8	5.0	17.5
1983	33.7	4.6	20.5	6.0	5.2	−2.7	8.5
1984	54.1	5.4	20.3	6.4	6.4	15.5	28.3

Source: U.S. Department of Agriculture, *Economic Indicators of the Farm Sector: National Financial Summary,* 1986, from tables 3 and 60.
Note: Numbers rounded off to nearest tenth.

been so low before that there was not enough money left after expenses to make even the interest payments and the lender was on the verge of foreclosing on the loan, the increase in commodity prices would mean keeping the farm. For those who were not so indebted, however, the increase in commodity prices simply would mean a sharp increase in return on their investment in farmland. What they do with this windfall is a matter of some importance, as we will see.

But first, let's examine these relationships in concrete terms. Table 10 shows income left to farm operators for the years 1970–84 (column 2) after all production expenses other than rent, interest, and the operator's family living expenses were paid. Note the sharp increase in income in 1973–75 resulting from world commodity price increases, and again in 1979 and 1984 due principally to government price supports. Columns 3 and 4 show how much it cost the farmer to acquire the use of farm assets—rent paid to landlords and interest on both real estate and non–real estate loans. As we noted in figure 8, the rent payments roughly rise and fall with income. Interest payments, however, simply mushroom, both because the amount of money borrowed by farmers to pay for production expenses and to buy more land at higher prices rose, and because federal monetary policy in the latter stages of the period supported higher interest rates. Taken together, the rent and interest payments—the cost of acquiring the use of farm assets—increased sharply. In 1970 they consumed 30 percent of the income left to farmers after other expenses were paid; in 1984, they consumed 48 percent of that income.

In other words, in just fourteen years the share of farm income after cash expenses that was available to the operator to pay for family living expenses, to save, or to build equity in the farm by making principal payments (primarily on land) shrunk from 70 percent to 52 percent.

We can only guess how farmers actually used that money, and table 10 presents the USDA's breakdown of how much of the operator's return is attributed to family labor and management, and how much is theoretically a return on the operator's equity investment in the farm. The share attributed to labor (column 5), for example, is a calculation of the amount that would be paid to operators if they were paid the average hourly wage. (Note that labor returns are fairly constant over the past fifteen years, revealing that while the amount of operator labor has declined, the average wage rate has risen.) The return to management (column 6) is an arbitrary figure set at 5 percent of the gross value of farm products. It increased because the gross sales of farm products rose during the boom. Together, these two items might be viewed as the wages and salaries of farmers.

Assuming that farmers actually reserved these amounts as wages and salaries to pay for family living expenses, the rest would be a return on their equity investment in the farm. The wild roller-coaster character of those fifteen years can be seen in column 7.

It is very important to recall that these returns are not only uneven from year to year, of course, but are unevenly distributed among farm operators as well. Consequently, the additional revenue from a commodity price increase would not be evenly distributed either. Generally, the larger the farm and the less indebted it is, the greater the share of income that returns to operators for labor, management, and equity and the greater the benefit from an increase in prices.

190

Table 11 shows how returns to operators were distributed among farms of various sizes between 1979 and 1982, the last four-year period during which the USDA published these data. The smallest farms received no net return to operators for either labor, management, or equity. What they were making from farming wasn't enough to pay operating expenses, let alone to live from or make a profit. The largest farms (with over $500,000 in sales) received the lion's share of the residual return due to their sales volume, not necessarily their efficiency.[3]

We do not have precise data on how farm income is distributed among farms of different sizes and levels of indebtedness, but we can understand the relationship from reviewing table 12. We can also see how an increase in commodity prices would affect these farms. The table shows hypothetical data for commercial farms of various sizes—large, medium, and small—at various levels of indebtedness. Each farm is operated efficiently and produces farm sales equal to about 23 percent of the value of the assets being managed by the farm (line 2). Each farm has cash operating expenses equal to 67 percent of gross farm sales (line 3), leaving an income return to pay for the use of farm assets, labor, and management (line 4). This varies directly with farm size.

For simplicity, we assume that each farmer owns or is buying on credit all of the land in the farm. Each has an average interest rate of 12 percent on all indebtedness. The more highly leveraged the farm, therefore, the higher the costs of acquiring assets (line 5), and the lesser the portion of returns that are available to pay for the operator's labor, management, and the return on investment for his equity share of the farm assets. This money is the return to operator (line 6) and can be used for family living expenses, principal payment on loans, savings, or other investments.

Again, *how* this return is actually used by an individual depends on the individual's situation and goals. Some will use it primarily to pay off debt, living as frugally as possible. Some will reinvest in more land. Some will buy certificates of deposit or other relatively safe investments. Some will live royally. But not all have the same options.

3. Figures in column 10, table 11, differ from the totals of columns 5, 6, and 7 in table 10 because of differences in USDA data series. They are theoretically the same. The difference should not alter the distribution illustrated in table 11.

Table 11. Distribution of Returns to Farm Operators ($ billions)

| | | | | | Return to Operators with Sales Of | | | | |
Year (1)	1,000– 4,999 (2)	5,000– 9,999 (3)	10,000– 19,999 (4)	20,000– 39,999 (5)	40,000– 99,999 (6)	100,000– 199,999 (7)	200,000– 499,999 (8)	500,000+ (9)	All Farms (10)
1979	-2.2	-.5	-.1	.7	4.3	5.4	6.0	13.5	27.1
1980	-2.5	-1.0	-.8	-.5	1.0	2.8	3.9	12.5	15.4
1981	-2.7	-1.0	-.7	-.2	1.9	4.0	5.5	16.5	23.3
1982	-2.7	-1.1	-1.0	-.7	.5	2.6	3.8	13.6	15.0

Source: U.S. Department of Agriculture, *Economic Indicators of the Farm Sector: National Financial Summary*, 1986.

Assume for the sake of argument that each farmer chooses to take 5 percent of gross sales as a management fee to himself (line 7) and the equivalent of $6.00 per hour for all family labor (line 8). The family uses that money to meet their living expenses, including a savings fund for the children's education. Not an imprudent strategy. The large farm can justify taking $35,000 for management (5 percent of $700,000 in sales) and $49,920 for four full-time workers (actually, about one-half of this is probably hired labor). The medium farm takes $11,500 (5 percent of its gross sales of $230,000) for management and $24,960 for two full-time family workers. The small commercial farm gets to use $4,600 (5 percent of $92,000) for management and $12,480 for one full-time worker—the farmer.

If this strategy were used, the three farms would clearly have significantly different standards of living and the children significantly unequal chances of going to college. While the larger farmer might live modestly and conserve some of these funds for other purposes, it is doubtful that the smaller farmer would live well enough to buy new shoes for the kids, let alone save for their education.

Nonetheless, assuming that each reserved this level of return for family expenses due their labor and management, the portion of remaining income would be a return on their equity investment (line 9). Clearly, this return to equity is not well distributed. Highly leveraged farms in all size categories are earning negative returns—which is really a way of saying that there is not enough income to allow them to take the amounts we've hypothetically allowed them for labor and management. Highly leveraged big farms would have to reduce family living allowances by $33,920 just to meet operating expenses and the interest cost of acquiring assets. If they failed to do so, their indebtedness would increase by that amount (lender willing) and their return on equity (line 9) would be negative. For highly leveraged medium-sized farms, the damage to their standard of living is even greater. To avoid more indebtedness, $20,560 would have to come out of the family allowance. For even moderately indebted smaller farms, the return to operator is too low to meet family expenses.

Now supposing that commodity prices were increased by government action, so that gross farm sales increased 10 percent without any change in the level of production on each farm (line 11). What would this increase in revenue mean?

Table 12. How Commodity Price Changes Affect Farmers in Various Financial Situations

Line	Item	Large Farms with Debt to Asset Ratio of			Medium Farms with Debt to Asset Ratio of			Small Farms with Debt to Asset Ratio of		
		.1	.3	.5	.1	.3	.5	.1	.3	.5
1	Assets	3,000,000	3,000,000	3,000,000	1,000,000	1,000,000	1,000,000	400,000	400,000	400,000
2	Farm Sales	700,000	700,000	700,000	230,000	230,000	230,000	92,000	92,000	92,000
3	Cash Operating Expenses	469,000	469,000	469,000	154,100	154,100	154,100	61,640	61,640	61,640
4	Income Return to Assets, Labor, Mgt.	231,000	231,000	231,000	75,900	75,900	75,900	30,360	30,360	30,360
5	Cost of Acquiring Assets	36,000	108,000	180,000	12,000	36,000	60,000	4,800	14,400	24,000
6	Return to Operator	195,000	123,000	51,000	63,900	39,900	15,900	25,560	15,960	6,360
7	Return to Mgt.	35,000	35,000	35,000	11,500	11,500	11,500	4,600	4,600	4,600
8	Return to Labor	49,920	49,920	49,920	24,960	24,960	24,960	12,480	12,480	12,480
9	Return to Equity	110,080	38,080	−33,920	27,440	3,440	−20,560	8,480	−1,120	−10,720
10	Rate of Return to Equity	4.1%	1.8%	−2.3%	3.0%	.5%	−4.1%	2.4%	−.4%	−5.4%

Line	Increased Revenue from 10% Price Rise / Return to Equity								
11	Increased Revenue from 10% Price Rise	70,000	70,000	70,000	23,000	23,000	23,000	9,200	9,200	9,200
12	Increased Return to Equity	180,080	108,080	36,080	50,440	26,440	2,440	17,680	8,080	−1,520
13	Increased Rate of Return to Equity	6.7%	5.1%	2.4%	5.6%	3.8%	.5%	4.9%	2.9%	−0.1%

Line	Explanation
1	given
2	.23 × assets (line 1)
3	.67 × sales (line 2)
4	Sales (line 2) – cash operating expenses (line 3)
5	12% interest × assets (line 1) × debt/asset ratio
6	Income return to assets, mgt, labor (line 4) – cost of acquiring assets (line 5)
7	Imputed at 5% × sales (line 2)
8	Imputed as follows: large farm: 4 full-time workers at $6.00/hr., including family labor; medium farm: 2 full-time workers at $6.00/hr., including family labor; small farm: 1 full-time worker at $6.00/hr., family labor
9	Income return (line 4) – cost of acquiring assets (line 5) – return to mgt. (line 7) – return to labor (line 8)
10	Return to equity (line 9) / equity [assets – (assets × debt/asset ratio)]
11	10% × sales (line 2)
12	Return to equity (line 9) + increased revenue (line 11)
13	Increased return (line 12) / equity [assets – (assets × debt/asset ratio)]

Between size categories, the rich would get richer. The largest farms would realize a $70,000 increase in revenue (10 percent of $700,000), the medium farms, $23,000 (10 percent of $230,000), and the smallest farms, $9,200 (10 percent of $92,000). *Within* size categories, those with lower costs of acquiring farm assets (those with less debt) would receive more cash with which to make additional investments while those with higher costs simply get to meet their current obligations and tighten their belt less.

Specifically, most of the small and medium-sized farms would now be able to maintain a subsistence and decent standard of living, respectively. All but the highly leveraged small farms would be able to take their management and labor fees for living expenses and enjoy at least some return on their equity investment above that (line 12). The highly leveraged small farms would still have to tighten their belt a little ($1,520) to avoid going further into debt and reducing their equity in the farm. Nonetheless, most of these hypothetical farms would stay in business, a goal most urgently sought by many family farm advocates.

But what of the large farms? For those that are highly leveraged, the $70,000 increase in revenue means that not only can they maintain an $84,920 standard of living, but they now have a $36,080 return on equity that allows them to make a substantial payment on their principal, or to make further investments in farmland. For the moderately leveraged and low-leveraged big farms, the windfall is even more substantial. Even the moderate farm, if low leveraged, experiences a doubling of its return to equity (from $27,440 to $50,440).

Is this necessarily bad? Maybe society should help the rich in order to salvage the poor. That is certainly the argument of many who support government intervention to raise farm prices as a remedy for farm distress. But what does this approach do to competition in the market for land? How does it affect land prices?

If land and other farm assets were evenly distributed in the first place and the competition for additional land were balanced, an increase in commodity prices might have relatively little effect. But when some realize such a large windfall because of their advantaged position, there is a temptation on their part to acquire more land. Because some of their financially weaker competitors are strengthened by the additional income, however, less land is placed on the market. With some in a strong position to buy land and little land for sale, the result is that any land that is made available will bring a dear price. This was, in fact, the prevalent condition in American agriculture throughout the 1970s. Land prices quadrupled in the farm belt after commodity prices rose sharply in 1973–75 and were supported near those levels by farm programs after that.

Increases in the price of those parcels of land that are sold also affect the perceived value of all similar farmland and make every owner of such land feel "richer," more secure. This increase in farmland value is measured as capital gain. After 1972, capital gain exceeded the total income returns to operators every year until 1981. In effect, those who were making a profit from farming were able to bid up the price of farmland. Their success convinced other investors that they could buy land and charge more rent as it appreciated in value. Even farmers who did not buy more land were encouraged to borrow more against their rising equity in land they already owned to pay other expenses. As a result, they effectively raised the cost of using land they already owned. They felt secure, too.

It was, of course, a false feeling of security. For everyone renting or buying farmland, all this meant higher costs of acquiring the use of farm assets. When the false feeling of security gave way to reality in the early 1980s, everyone whose land cost had grown out of hand (either through higher rent or higher interest payments due to both higher interest rates and higher land prices) was doomed.

The problem was not only that the absolute level of commodity prices gave false security, but that people expected that level to persist over time. Government price guarantees nourished those expectations during the late 1970s, when government loan programs offset the downward pressure on commodity prices and eventually filled government grain bins to overflowing. When the government guarantees a price and does little or nothing to restrain production, two outcomes are certain: the government will end up owning the commodities, and land prices will be unrealistically high.

In sum, the price dilemma is this: When government sets commodity prices, it is not fixing a minimum standard of living for farm families. Instead, it is establishing a minimum return on investment in farmland. The benefits of such a program fall squarely to those who own land, and in direct proportion to the amount they own. Any impact it has on the standard of living of farm people is incidental to that overwhelming fact of life. Those who want to help the family farm by providing a price increase with the intention of improving minimum standards of living for small farms or of helping those who have to pay high interest costs, inevitably if unintentionally provide a disproportionate windfall for larger farms and those who already own the land they farm. And they will use that windfall to tighten their grip on American agriculture.

THE RATCHET EFFECT

There is an additional dilemma for public policy. If the government guarantees a price calculated to equal the cost of producing a commodity—as it was our policy to do in the late 1970s—then how will land costs be factored into the formula as a cost of production? A farmer who owns land now worth $1,000 per acre will argue that his costs are equal to the income he could earn if he sold the land and invested that much in securities, stocks and bonds. A government economist might point out that the farmer only paid $200 per acre for the land twenty years ago, and that his land costs are only equal to the income he could earn if he invested *that* much in securities, stocks, and bonds. A politician will probably settle for a formula that splits the difference.

The issue is critical, however, especially to the beginning farmer. If the price of corn is set at a level that assures a return on investment based on current land prices, he might just break even. If it is set any lower, he might not make it. But for the established farmer who bought land years ago and has paid off most debt, the higher price represents a windfall. And at the higher price—one based on a formula that includes land at its current market value—the established farmer will have no reason not to buy more land, since the higher price guarantees him a return on investment in land at its current value. The established farmer will have additional incentives to buy more land. If he has to outbid the beginning farmer for more land, his bidding will have the effect of raising land values even further. Not to worry, for the higher land values will ultimately be reflected in yet higher commodity price guarantees.

Advocates for commodity price guarantees have been reluctant to acknowledge this ratchet effect of guaranteeing a return on investment in farmland. To do so suggests that controls are needed not only on commodity prices, but on land prices as well. If the government is going to regulate the price (or supply) of commodities, it should be willing to intervene in the land market as well.

There is a clear analogy to the electrical utility industry. Because the utility companies that supply electricity are natural monopolies, government regulators set the price they can charge for electricity at a level calculated to provide their owners with a fair rate of return on their investment. But the government does not allow those utility companies to invest as much as they want in the generation and delivery of electricity. In nearly all situations, the utility must justify the public need for new power plants, transmission facilities, and distribution systems before it can use these investments as an excuse to charge consumers a rate increase. When government regulation of investment is weak, the public gets unneeded power plants and unwanted transmission lines, and unnecessarily high utility bills. Analogously, if commodity prices are to be regulated, so should investment in land (and machinery, for that matter).

MARKET INTERVENTION

Taken together, tables 9–12 indicate that farmers have paid dearly not only for the new technologies but also for the right to own or rent the land on which to use them. This is especially true as farmland ownership becomes more concentrated and as the cost of borrowing money climbs. During boom periods, these relationships are reflected in the rising price of land made dear by unequal competition for it, and in the rising cost of merely acquiring the use of land—rent to landlords and interest on real estate. During busts that follow, they are made clear by the shake out of those whose land costs are too high to compete in a falling commodity market. After the shake out, the winners consolidate their winnings by acquiring the farms once owned by the losers.

Boom-and-bust is thus an integral part of the technological development of American agriculture. Land prices are bid up in a competition to use new technologies. But as commodity prices fall, so eventually do land prices, until land is held in the strong hands of those who first adopted the technology or who have sufficient financial reserves.

But this process is not interminable. When land is sufficiently concentrated, acquiring it will be nearly impossible and new competitors will be locked out of the competition. When that happens, land will be priceless, and landowners will achieve the status of gentry. At that stage of development, agriculture might well lose its dynamic character, resisting new technologies much as many of the mature industrial sectors of the United States became so concentrated that they resisted new technologies. Commodity prices might then be stable and relatively high, but the victory over low prices will have been a Pyrrhic one gained only at the cost of creating monopoly privileges.

Of immediate concern is the fact that the rewards of a market economy aged with unequal competition and a rapidly changing technology base, go increasingly to those who own and less to those who work. Because farmland is not evenly distributed, the rewards of higher prices are not evenly distributed, either. Providing more profit does not correct the basic imbalance, any more than driving a car with unbalanced wheels faster makes it ride smoother.

The unbalancing factors in American agriculture are the growing concentration of wealth and property and the unbridled use of technology. Efforts to redress the grievances of farmers over low commodity prices cannot ignore the inequities in land ownership that new technologies, working through the market, have also generated. Without limits on the accumulation of property, on the right to produce, and on inappropriate uses of technology, setting commodity prices at levels that assure profits will simply feed the process of industrializing American agriculture.

This is not to suggest that commodity prices should be left to the market. To the contrary, market injustices must be remedied by policy measures that address fundamental problems, not merely their most painful symptoms. Land reform and fair competition are full partners with price policy, not its shirt-tail cousins. Those who insist that the singular nature of the farm crisis is low commodity prices are too quick to ignore the land question and the problem of technology. They risk winning the battle against low prices and losing the war to save family farming.

9.

Technology: Getting Control of the Farm

Our society is just beginning to come to grips with the problems of its technology. Before the automobile, the issue was pretty insignificant. But the automobile raised new questions in American society. Its capacity to cause damage to people and property was obvious. That alone prompted an unprecedented level of social control over its use. First, there were simple rules of the road—drive on the right, stop at intersections, signal turns. There were soon limits on speed. Over time, it has become apparent that some of the automobile's most potent impacts are environmental. Those impacts cannot be remedied by imposing controls on the management of the machine by its everyday user. They require regulating the form in which the technology is made available—its very design. We are still wrestling with the problem of how much and what kind of regulation of this machine is desirable.

More broadly, the range of policy questions raised by the environmental movement, from reducing toxic chemicals to remedying acid rain, present even more complex challenges to our reluctance to limit technology. The nuclear bomb issue presents, of course, the ultimate test. It suggests not only regulation of certain uses, but deliberate, selective rejection of some technologies altogether.

We need to give more attention to the industrial technologies used in agriculture, and to consider restraining, rejecting, or replacing some of them. Some farmers are leading the way on their own farms by changing the technologies they use. For many it is a matter of economic survival. They know that the predominant technology base is designed to eliminate farmers. Whether they intend to or not, these pioneers are doing us all a service.

In agriculture, many environmental impacts of technology are subtle and seemingly unconnected. You can smell or see many forms of urban air pollution, you can worry about toxic chemicals in your tap water, and you can certainly identify with the misery of a baby seal clubbed to death on the icy shores of Canada. But it is difficult to grasp the largely invisible erosion of topsoil on good farmland in Iowa. Why should the general public get worked up about soil loss when the bad news seems to be too much food, not too little good land for growing it.

Environmental problems are largely unnoticed in agriculture because most of them occur on or to private land. Unlike air and (for the most part) water, land is not regarded as a public resource that no one has the right to pollute. Though no less essential to human life than air or water, land is a commodity that you can own, and if you wish, willfully destroy. Moreover, most of the environmental destruction in agriculture occurs in relatively unpopulated areas where it doesn't easily offend. When the damage is noticed, it frequently goes unmentioned, since most of the neighborhood may be engaged in more or less the same destructive activities. Perhaps most important, many of the most serious environmental problems of agriculture involve microorganisms, trace minerals, and pollutants that are difficult to measure.

But everyday, the seriousness of environmental damage caused by farm technology becomes more apparent and more difficult to ignore. More of the damage is affecting those off the farm. Moreover, farmers themselves are beginning to recognize that they are on the front line of exposure to many adverse and unanticipated environmental hazards caused by farm technologies.

Gradually, modern farming practices are being recognized as the number one environmental issue in our society. Consider these tell-tale signs:

— If we continue to erode topsoil at current rates for the next fifty years, crop yields will fall enough to equal the loss of 23 million acres of cropland. In the Midwest alone, where two-fifths of the land used for principal row crops is highly erodible, soybean yields on such land would be reduced 15 percent and corn yields 29 percent (National Association of Conservation Districts 1980).

— Drinking-water pollution from farm chemicals is now widespread and officially recognized in farm states. An Iowa state environmental official recently reported that pesticide residues have been found in one third of the state's wells serving 27 percent of the state's population (Stone 1986). In one area of the state, a five-year study indicates that nitrate pollution due to the leaching of fertilizer through the soil into the groundwater has tripled since 1968, leaving the water supply at the threshold of unacceptability under federal pollution standards (Murray 1985). In Nebraska, the situation appears worse. Half of that state's eight hundred municipal water systems are contaminated with farm chemicals (Thomas 1986). Nitrate pollution levels at or above the maximum standard set for drinking water by the Environmental Protection Agency have been found in eighty-six public water systems (Nebraska Department of Environmental Control 1985). The major source of this contamination is fertilizer and livestock waste. In Minnesota, a report by environmental officials says that pollution from farm chemicals and animal feedlots "may be the most serious and complex environmental problem" in the state, and a farmer who serves on the board of the agency that commissioned the report criticized it for making recommendations that rely too much on education and incentives rather than mandatory controls (Ragsdale 1986).

— Underground water supplies are being depleted in eleven states. The water level is declining between six inches and six feet per year beneath over 15 million irrigated acres. Over half the land being irrigated from underground water supplies in those states suffers from groundwater declines (Sloggett 1981).

— Genetically specialized seeds now account for most crop production. Crops grown from these seeds are especially vulnerable to disease because they are genetically uniform (U.S. National Academy of Sciences 1972). They therefore require more disease-preventing chemicals.

— The widespread use of antibiotics commonly used in human medicine to reduce risk of livestock disease and improve the efficiency with which animals convert feed into food has produced strains of bacteria that are dangerous to human health *and* resistant to the antibiotics (Lappé 1982).

Other environmental impacts of agriculture are virtually un-assessed. Soil compaction, which results from the use of heavy equipment, reduces the capacity of soil to absorb water, reducing yield and increasing erosion due to runoff of rainfall. It is recognized as a serious problem, but no comprehensive study of its extent and consequences exists. Similarly, we know that the common practice of producing the same row crops without rotating them with soil-building grasses and small grains and without adding manure reduces organic matter by as much as 66 percent in thirty years (Salter and Green 1933 cited in Sampson 1981). We also know that increasing organic matter from 1.7 percent to 3.6 percent raises corn yields about 25 percent (Lucas, Holtman, and Connor 1977). Yet loss of organic matter in soil has not been systematically measured.

While these environmental impacts make the production of food more expensive, they are rarely linked to the technology that causes them. We do not know, for example, the cost of growing cancer rates among farmers. If we did, we could force farms that use the technologies responsible for these costs to pay for them. There would be less use of these technologies and smaller farms. But so far we have not seriously considered doing so, and the use of the technologies that cause cancer among farmers continues.

Inarguably, the farming methods associated with industrial agribusiness spawn these environmental costs. Large, heavy equipment compacts the soil. Continuous cropping requires heavier use of chemicals to replace depleted nutrients in the soil and to control pests that grow stronger from a steady diet of their favorite crops.

Moreover, many conservation practices don't stand up to the requirements of industrial farming. Terraces that reduce erosion by preventing water from quickly running down long, steep hills are obstacles to large equipment. They require too many turns and create too many small, odd-shaped parcels. The bigger the farm, the bigger the equipment, the fewer the terraces. The same is true of strip cropping (alternate planting of crops that discourage erosion and those that do not) and contour farming (planting rows that follow the natural lay of the land, rather than straight rows that run up and down hills). And, as soil conservationist Neil Sampson points out, the capital requirements of large, industrialized farms steal capital away from investment in long-term conservation practices. Such farms invest in tractors and irrigation, rather than terraces and field windbreaks (Sampson 1981).

In fact, industrial agribusiness thrives on technologies that have the most serious environmental impacts. Consider, for example, the burgeoning business of raising livestock in factory-like operations. Without the technology—climate-controlled buildings, automated feed and waste-handling equipment, and computer-controlled feeding regimes—these operations simply could not exist. Without antibiotics routinely administered within feed, the animals would be vulnerable to diseases that spread easily wherever large numbers of animals are kept in close quarters. Without antibiotics also routinely fed to enhance the animal's conversion of feed to meat, the factories would not be profitable (many are not, anyway). But given these feed additives, animal factories are possible. As a consequence, manure has become a waste-disposal problem and a pollutant instead of the fertilizer resource it was when animals were widely scattered on thousands of farms.

Removing animals from the land for life in the factory has had yet another environmental consequence: land once protected from erosion by grasses grown to maintain herds of grazing livestock is now opened to row crops, and to erosion.

Examples of the dependence of industrial agribusiness on destructive technologies are common. The misuse of the center-pivot irrigation system on ecologically fragile soils in the High Plains, the use of cancer-causing hormones as growth stimulants in cattle, and the continuing battle over regulation of pesticides used on food crops are illustrative.

But a reminder is in order. These technologies and their impacts are certainly not exclusive to large or corporate farms. At fact, some of the worst abuses of these technologies are on family farms trying to compete with industrial agribusinesses. The bigger-is-better myth has driven many family farmers to try to farm bigger than they can farm well, or to farm with technologies meant to be used on larger farms. They cut corners, making compromises with the methods they know should be used. Some, of course, do so gleefully, but most do so to survive. Saying so is not intended to exonerate them. It is meant only to reiterate a theme: The transformation of agriculture from family farming to industrial agribusiness is incremental and pervasive. It captures all but the most conscientiously resistant farmers. Smaller farms engaged in the process may exaggerate the worst features of the industrial agribusiness system, as a boy trying to prove he's a man sometimes exhibits the least admirable characteristics of his gender.

Some environmentalists consider farmers to be little more than petty land abusers and are inclined to discount any social concern over their economic future. They prefer to allow the market to determine technological progress, and then to regulate environmental impacts with scientific precision. This technocratic view prefers the neat prospect of regulating a few large farms over the messy chore of forcing many small, stubborn, independent farmers into line with environmental needs. You can't blame them. Farmers' reputation for blind political resistance to environmental regulation is legendary, and for the most part, well deserved.

But both environmentalists and farmers are wrong to pose the issue as farmer versus environment. The most serious environmental problems in agriculture are those caused by technologies that make large-scale farming possible, and that sever the rewards of farming from the rewards of stewardship and husbandry.

Our need to understand the impact of technology and its interaction with our economic system will become more urgent in the immediate future. We are poised on the edge of a starburst of new technologies that will constitute a revolution as sweeping as those of mechanics and chemicals. The new information and genetic technologies may dwarf the impacts of those of the past. A recent report by a congressional agency identified 150 new agricultural production technologies likely to be available to the public by the year 2000 (U.S. Congress 1986a). One of them, the bovine growth hormone, may increase milk production from a single cow by 20 to 30 percent, and is expected to be widely available by 1990. While some of the boasts about the potential of these technologies may be little more than giddy talk, it's indisputable that the technology base for agriculture is changing rapidly. Whether we have the capacity to choose among these technologies rather than just cope with their adverse consequences, will become more, not less of an issue.

THE PSYCHOLOGY OF FARM TECHNOLOGY

Farm technology gets more than the usual level of devotion from its users. At many county fairs and small town celebrations, the big event is the tractor pull, a competitive test of the available horsepower of a tractor. It's a prideful competition, a demonstration of mechanical prowess. In a like vein, seed companies and commodity groups sponsor competitions for top yields of various commodities. Astronomical yields are possible if fertilizer and pesticides are applied without consideration of their cost. Yields two to three times the typical yields achieved under ordinary conditions are common in these tests. Whether the farmer who wins the tractor pull or the yield contest can make a living using technologies like this is not tested, except, of course, in the market. But the technological fetish is reinforced by the demonstrations, and by the declaration of the winner.

It is reinforced, too, by the powerful cultural images portrayed in the news media and in advertising of the farmer as a manager of complex technological systems. At spring planting time especially, farmers are bombarded with television advertisements aggrandizing them as top managers if they use the right brand-name chemicals, seed, or machinery. Many emphasize masculine ego and play on the male gender's emotional weaknesses. They appeal to aggression (kill this weed dead), power (sentence this pest to death), and envy (how can my field be as weed-free as my neighbor's?). The come-on for many of these ads is plain: use our product and you'll be considered tough, smart, and ahead of the pack, better than your neighbors, the one people turn to for advice. You'll have more time for your family, you'll be less vulnerable to Mother Nature, and you'll pass the farm on to your kids. If you place any store in these ads, farmers don't do anything anymore, save choose the right products. One machinery manufacturer arrogantly brags that its latest model doesn't do *everything* for you—you still have to drive it.

For good measure, many ads add a soft touch of the homespun, portraying the farmer as country laid-back, folksy-smart, and common-sense savvy. One company goes so far as to run image-building advertisements about farmers that are ostensibly aimed at urban people. You can't help but believe, though, that they are intended to cultivate farmer loyalty to the company's products.

These characterizations of the down-home, self-sacrificing farmer are only a cloying appeal to the farmer's deluded self-image of agrarian independence. But the subliminal message is this: You aren't good enough to make it without our products, and you know it.

THE DETERMINISTIC VIEW OF TECHNOLOGY

Because the power of modern technology is not merely physical, but psychological as well, it begins to have a life of its own, a method, a design, a capacity to shape the economic system itself. If technology makes something possible, it not only may be done, but must be done. We seem powerless to resist.

We forget that technology is nothing more than technique—a way of getting something done. It exists to further work and production, to make them easier and more fruitful. Implicitly, technology is neutral with respect to how it is used. It does not tell us how much work or production is needed, or what should be produced, or who should benefit from it. Those issues are resolved by the economic system.

But that economic system does shape the uses of technology, and to the extent that the economic system has a "personality" of its own—a peculiar set of values that influence social behavior—the technology it uses will reflect that personality and those values.

The personality of our industrial system is materialistic. It is designed and expected to produce "more." The production process and the technology it employs conform to this expectation. It requires uniformity. Both diversity and individuality are its enemy. Industrial technology must be freed from the limitations of human ability, and therefore humans must be eliminated from the production process, to the extent possible. Cleverness in the management of complex machines replaces craft in the manipulation of simple tools. Ultimately, even cleverness in the use of machines becomes redundant. By increasing the complexity of machines, the worker can be reduced to robotic movements which the machine commands by signals. People as well as parts become interchangeable and expendable. Industrial technology must be, first and foremost, powerful.

Industrial technology's power derives not only from its capacity to produce products, but from its mystery. Like it or not, most of us do not understand even the household machines we use everyday, and are helpless if they break down, wear out, or malfunction. For many, there is nothing to dislike about this disability. Indeed, for many there has never been a time when it was otherwise. "Things" have always been technologically mysterious. The simple physical phenomenon that provoked Newton's great articulation of the law of gravity—the falling of an apple on his head—seems arcane in a world that routinely enjoys an array of services not even vaguely related to the pushing of the button that activates them. We simply don't understand what makes things work. Who can explain the workings of a common home computer? As important, who can add and subtract without a pocket calculator?

Things have become so complex and mysterious that we are losing our capacity to appreciate the truly simple. Indeed, it may take the innocence of a child to appreciate things once considered plain. This point was poignantly brought home to me by a friend who told about some neighbor boys who visited him one day. They were about eight and twelve years old. As they entered, they heard the melodic tones of a classical seventeenth-century music box he had wound up to play moments before. Impressed by the quality of the tone, they took careful notice of the strange, surprisingly plain box. One noticed that the box was not "plugged in," and asked, "Where's the cord?" The box doesn't plug in at all, he explained, you "wind it up." "What does wind it up mean?" they wanted to know. "Well. . ." He was at a loss for words. It's spring wound, by hand, he tried to explain. They didn't understand or believe him, and commenced a search for the batteries, which by now they were certain were hidden behind one of the carefully crafted wood panels that formed the box. No, he insisted, there were no batteries. To make the point, he produced the crank handle, inserted it into the gear drive, and wound up the three-hundred-year-old music box once again. As it chimed out its crystal-clear notes, one boy turned to the other in amazement and exclaimed: "Well, what'll they think of next?"

The powerful, mysterious technology that fosters industrial agribusiness is directed at immediate materialistic objectives—more food and more profit—with little concern for long-run sustainability. If a new technique can make twice as much corn for one farm or one farmer, it must be used, even if it eventually ruins both the farmer and the farm.

This deterministic view of technology is so common that it is held by both those who approve and those who disapprove of particular technologies. Those comfortable with the technology are simply devoted to it, as a subject loves majesty. On the other hand, those who fear and resent the technology complain that it is impersonal, as if it ever had a heart. Both responses treat technology as a self-determining, independent factor in the economic system.

This is cultural avoidance behavior. It serves to insulate us from responsibility for the uses and misuses of technology. By accepting technology as an autonomous factor, we are also free to accept its most onerous effects fatalistically. But those effects are really the effects of our economic system, its values, and the peculiar technology it fosters. Technology is not deterministic. Only our view of it is.

ONE THING LEADS TO ANOTHER

Of course, technology partisans are quick to chant the familiar refrain that "technology creates problems, technology solves problems." A technical solution to one problem leads to another problem, which itself will be solved by another technical innovation.

A good example of this one-thing-leads-to-another view of technology is the current controversy in rural areas over the offensive odor from many of the large-scale hog factories that now dominate pork production. In a Nebraska case, a corporate farm, National Farms, Inc., built facilities for producing 350,000 hogs per year, instantly placing it second among hog producers nationwide. Modern, mechanized, and temperature-controlled hog buildings make this scale of operation possible. However, the problem of what to do with the mountain (or ocean) of hog waste created by such densely populated hog cities remains largely unsolved.

For National Farms, the problem seemed to be solved by another technology: sprinkler irrigation systems. Why not remove as much solid waste as possible, dilute the remaining slurry, and spread the liquid waste over corn fields through the sprinkler irrigation systems? It would eliminate much of the costly waste-removal problem, and would reduce fertilizer costs.

What are the environmental costs of such a strategy? They are pretty much unknown. But ask one of the farmers who lives in the neighborhood of these waste disposal sites. When the summer clouds hang low or the winds blow, the odor from this indelicate spray is unbearable. A group of neighbors filed a lawsuit against National Farms asking them to find some other way to dispose of their waste. In response, National Farms argued that this was not economically possible. "The sheer quantity would preclude handling it any other way," according to National Farms' manager. "If we couldn't spread it through the irrigation rigs, it would shut us down." (Associated Press, 1986c). In September, 1986, a court ordered the company not to alter its operation, but to pay one farm couple $125,000 for the loss of satisfaction of their home. Technology determines the tolerable level of neighborliness, as well as the scale of the operation.

The problem crops up wherever this particular technology is used. In South Dakota, a hog-confinement complex planned to produce 20,000 pigs per year about eight miles from the state capitol. Area farmers protested before local zoning boards for fear the project would pollute water, ruin recreational fishing, and drive down property values (Associated Press 1986c). In Michigan, Jackson County farmers and nonfarmers have joined in a political movement to restrain corporate hog factories because of odor, fear of groundwater pollution, and other environmental problems. A state environmental official calls it "the hottest environmental issue in the state." (Campbell 1986). These people now recognize that technology does not solve all the problems it creates, not at least without exacting a price from someone.

When should human judgment intervene over market forces to determine technological change? Never, according to technology's partisans. The power of technology to right wrongs will always overpower the damage it does. But most of us are not sure. Why depend on technology to cure us of its own aftermath, when we can decide now whether to accept the consequences of its misuse or curtail it? Why should we passively allow the market place to determine which technologies we will use, and which social and environmental problems we will have to learn to solve? We are reduced to the level of self-control of a dog chasing its tail because that's where the tail leads it. And after all, even a dull dog eventually stops chasing its own tail.

If we do not discriminate between technologies, it is partly because of a world view that obscures the advantages of smaller, simpler, less impressive approaches to problems. I recall an incident when I was helping a friend move. We had to pack my car full of an assortment of odds and ends. We arranged and rearranged, carefully selecting the smallest boxes to protect fragile items so that we could fit them into every available space without jeopardizing them on the long trip. We were down to unpacking clothes that were in boxes too large to be added to the load, and stuffing the clothing into remaining spaces to make use of every square inch. A small tangle of socks tightly wedged between the driver's seat and the side panel finished the chore. As we were admiring our triumph, a neighbor stopped by to help. He surveyed our tightly packed knot of small parcels and shook his head in sympathy. "Why did you bother with all those small boxes?" he asked. "I've got two big ones that would have handled it all." He farms big.

Big boxes have a use, and small boxes have different, sometimes better uses. Any society ought to recognize the difference, learn to discriminate between technologies, and use them appropriately.

PATHS NOT TAKEN

In agriculture, there are alternative paths to technical change, though they have been spurned in favor of the industrial path. These alternatives need to be reconsidered now, and not just in the so-called developing nations. Our own agriculture needs to develop more appropriate technology. For even if it is true that the industrial path made sense at one time, it is time to reevaluate that judgment. We know more now about the limits of our environment and about the technical and social failings of industrial technology.

Unfortunately, the debate between the technologies—"soft," "appropriate," "intermediate," "industrial"—can be dogmatic on all sides. Much of the debate has been like arguing in the dark over whether and how to light the room. But some progress is being made in seriously criticizing technical development in more than ideological ways. The energy crisis helped to persuade some practical but narrow-minded people to drop their defenses against alternative technologies, while forcing theoretical but romantic people to drop some of their pretenses about the virtue of their particular brand of alternatives. The problem is that the energy crisis appears to have gone away for the time being, and we've forgotten a good deal of what it forced us to learn about technology choices.

Nonetheless, some agricultural development theorists have become less rigid in their assumptions about technology. Previously, many considered technology an independent factor, "given" to farmers for their adoption. But some have begun to ask *why* certain technologies are developed, and why those technologies differ from country to country and situation to situation. This important analytical breakthrough makes agricultural research, agricultural scientists, and the technologies they produce active rather than passive parts of the development process. As such, they are also subject to criticism and evaluation.

One of the leading thinkers in this area is Vernon W. Ruttan, an agricultural economist from the University of Minnesota who has written widely on agricultural research policy. He (and various colleagues) has criticized agricultural development theory for failing to recognize how the peculiar resource endowments of a society influence the development of technologies, and how the relative prices of inputs and products shape investments in research that will make the most of those peculiar endowments. Technology, he argues, is a product of the practical constraints within which a people must try to feed themselves. Because the constraints under which different people operate vary according to natural resources, climate, and social systems, the technology that is best suited to them will vary as well. They will choose technologies that make best use of whatever production inputs are relatively plentiful, and therefore cheap, as replacements for other inputs that are relatively hard for them to get and therefore expensive. The character of technical change must be consistent with the resource and cultural endowments of a people. Ruttan suggests that the way to understand why particular technologies are selected in particular societies is to think of them as induced. He calls his model of agricultural development the induced innovation model (Ruttan 1982).

To make the point, Ruttan compares the different paths to agricultural development chosen by Japan and the United States, both advanced industrial societies with productive agricultures. In the United States, labor has been for most of our history relatively scarce compared with seemingly endless supplies of land. Technical development favored mechanical power as a means of spreading labor, the expensive input, over more land, the cheap input. Substituting land and machines for people in precisely the way described by the treadmill model (Chapter 7) made a great deal of sense. Larger, more capital-intensive, labor-saving farms followed.

In Japan, by contrast, land was precious and labor was abundant. There was no opportunity to increase the supply of land, but the supply of labor was growing. As a result, technologies that yield more from land, the limited and expensive input, and require relatively more labor were favored. Biological technologies, especially genetic changes that improved crop response to fertilizer, an input that fell steadily in price, were pursued.

Ruttan argues that his model is reinforced by changes in technology that respond to changes in resource endowments. As the United States eventually ran out of unused land, land prices began to rise relative to the price of either wages or fertilizer. In time, this prompted more interest in the United States in higher-yielding crop varieties and other land-saving technologies that increased yield per acre, such as chemical pest controls. But because land costs in the United States were always lower relative to fertilizer than they were in Japan, increases in fertilizer applications in this country continued to lag behind Japan. Significantly, in recent decades, as wages have risen in Japan and land costs have risen in the United States, there has been a noticeable shift in the agricultural technology mix in the two countries. The Japanese have increased tractor horsepower per acre faster than in the United States, and the United States has increased rates of fertilizer application faster than in Japan.

Implicit in Ruttan's model of agricultural development is the notion that those who engineer new technology—research scientists—must be responsive to the conditions in the resource economy in which they work. Sometimes, research scientists who are out of touch with the conditions under which farmers operate will produce inappropriate technologies. For example, Ruttan concludes that agricultural technology developed by scientists conditioned to think in terms of the rich land and mineral resources of the industrial world is biased against the potential of the underdeveloped world where labor is the key resource. Moreover, he says, "countries that have attempted to rely primarily on borrowed technology have rarely developed the capacity to adapt and manage the borrowed technology in a manner capable of sustaining agricultural development" (Ruttan 1982). They should develop their own research and development institutions to minimize the cultural gap between research scientists and indigenous farmers.

Though fairly theoretical, this model is useful because it emphasizes that our selection of technologies depends on our situation. Some research and extension scientists have begun to think differently about how to shape technologies to fit the conditions in which they will be used. Their concern has been the small farmer, especially in the underdeveloped world, whom technology-driven progress generally passes by. Under the rubric of "farming systems research," these scientists try to understand the multi-faceted context within which farmers farm.

Small farms in the underdeveloped world are family units. It is very important that whole families participate in defining their goals and in working with scientists to develop workable approaches for those families. Constant feedback by the user and adjustment of the research objectives are essential. Significantly, farming systems research conceives the whole farm as an interdependent system, not as a separable scramble of commodity-production activities (Shaner, Philipp, and Schmehl 1982).

The farming systems approach is used minimally in this country, and when it is, it is limited to those farms considered by researchers to be technologically (and perhaps culturally) backward. It's application to commercial family farms has been nearly nonexistent. Possibly, researchers assume there is no cultural gap between farmer and scientist in this country, or that the technological needs of small commercial farmers in the United States, unlike the needs of small farmers in the underdeveloped world, are at odds with the larger needs of society. In any case, farming systems research in this country has had to be justified as a social welfare remedy for farmers left behind by otherwise beneficial technological change, not as a legitimate part of economic development policy aimed at reshaping technical change. Not much of it goes on as a result.

It remains to be seen whether farming systems research is a genuine attempt to redefine the means by which research goals are defined and pursued in a cultural context, or whether it is simply a more effective means of accomplishing traditional research objectives. It is noteworthy that much of the rationale for this new approach derives from the failure of the green revolution to change the lives of many small farmers. In the final analysis, reducing cultural resistance to the adoption of technology by finding the most effective ways to insert the technology into the social system may be enough to satisfy most proponents of farming systems research. If so, it will amount to nothing more than clever social engineering, and it will have done little to empower people to participate consciously in the development of technologies that serve their needs.

Motives aside, both practical farming systems research and Ruttan's theoretical induced innovation model of agricultural development champion the same theme. Technology is a function of societal selection based on perceived needs—social and economic. But still at issue are these questions: Who perceives the needs and shapes the technology? And to whom are they accountable?

While a growing number of agricultural scientists may find these questions appropriate with respect to the third world, not many see them as even remotely relevant to our own situation. The state agricultural universities (known as land grant colleges because the federal government first launched them with grants of federal lands to the states), which conduct the bulk of publicly funded agricultural research in the United States, are well known for their insular, almost defensive resistance to criticism that their research agenda does not serve broad public interests. Numerous critics, have complained about unresponsiveness and unaccountability. Examples stretch from Jim Hightower's strident *Hard Tomatoes, Hard Times,* which found that the agricultural research establishment has "wedded itself to an agribusiness vision of automated, vertically-integrated, and corporatized agriculture" (Hightower 1972), to the more staid National Academy of Science study, which found in agricultural research "an inexcusable amount of mediocre and duplicative research [much of which is] outmoded, pedestrian, and inefficient" (National Research Council 1972).

Sifting through the criticism and the defense against it, it is clear that agricultural research has avoided certain introspective questions about the relationship between scientists themselves, their social values, careers, and institutions, and the kind of research they do.[1] Agricultural research priorities inevitably reflect the political realities of agriculture in the state in which the research university is located. This is because about three-fifths of the agricultural research budget comes from state government appropriations and from various private sources. Only a third comes from the federal government.

Generally, grants from agribusiness sources amount to less than 5 percent or so of the agricultural research budget, but that 5 percent plays a far greater than proportional role in determining research priorities.

Our own study of how researchers at the University of Nebraska Department of Animal Science set their priorities helps to explain how this is (Strange et al. 1982). In 1980, private grants provided only 4 percent of the research funding in that animal science department. Federal funds provided another 11 percent. Appro-

1. The void is not complete. For an important exception that helps prove the rule, see Vernon W. Ruttan's thoughtful book, *Agricultural Research Policy* (1982), especially chapters 11, 12, and 13; and Busch, Lacey, and Sachs (1980).

216

priations from the state made up 28 percent, and the rest—56 percent—came from the sale of experimental animals and their products. This latter account, termed the revolving fund, is an important resource because it constitutes a *renewable* mass of research funding. Access to animals that can be used in research experiments is critical to the advancement of the animal scientist's research program, and to his or her career.

Before a research project is approved by department officials, its impact on the revolving account must be considered. Some research (such as many basic physiology studies) requires the premature sacrifice of animals and would draw down the revolving account. Other research, such as some nutrition studies, may actually generate more income from the sale of animals than it consumes. This fact alone, makes research dependent on the market place to some extent. If hog prices are high and cattle low, swine research earns a dividend, while beef research takes a loss.

Far more important, scientists have different degrees of control over research funds from various sources. Basic support for the scientist—salary, office, clerical help—are provided from state and federal funds over which he or she has little control. The department allocates these among the scientists who see them only as paychecks and institutional services.

The revolving fund, as noted above, is more flexible. The scientist can gain greater access to these resources by expanding his or her research program to include more experiments. How? There are a number of ways. Success in a project might warrant an increase in commitment of revolving funds. Or a change in research design, such as the use of one lot of animals to conduct two or more experiments simultaneously, might justify allocation of more animals and facilities.

But one of the best ways to expand your access to more department resources is to generate more private funding for your work. Scientists have total control over the use of these funds. They can support graduate assistants or technicians, pay for computer time, cover laboratory costs, or any other incidental cost of research. By helping scientists "pay their own way" and support the department's operation, the grants are an important source of clout in administrative decisions. They give the scientist influence over the allocation of public funds. In short, the private grants leverage public funds.

Importantly, the accounting for the use of these private grant funds is so vague that it is impossible to determine precisely how the funds are actually spent. All the private grant funds a particular scientist raises in a general research area are pooled into an account over which that scientist has control. Some of the costs of the actual experiments requested by the grantor are paid from this account, but the rest are absorbed by the university.

Since the cost of experiments are not separately accounted for, no one knows just how much expense is involved. But it is clear that in many cases, the grantor only intends to pay for the cost of the animals and their feed, not the facilities and staff time committed to the project. In fact, the scientist finds it most useful to see to it that the requested research is done with as little expense to the private grant account as possible, because whatever unused balance remains in that account can be used by that scientist to support other research in which he or she is interested. The only stipulation anyone other than the scientist has over the use of those funds is that they must be used to support the broad research program approved by the animal science department.

In effect, by generating private grants for research that is ultimately paid for primarily by public funds, scientists have converted public resources over which they have no discretion into public resources over which they have almost total discretion. It is the best way to build an ambitious research program employing numerous graduate assistants and more than a proportional share of the laboratory services, computer time, experiment facilities, and revolving funds of the department. As a result, scientists find themselves in hot pursuit of small grants that can leverage more public support for their work. It doesn't really matter if the research supported by those grants is scientifically important or even intellectually challenging. The grants expand the resources under the scientists' command, making it possible for them to do more of what they want to do.

There is no corruption in this system. Public funds are not being stolen. Nor is the grantor being fleeced. The research requested is done. Since the grantor knows that the research costs more than the amount of the grant, it is more than satisfied.

But this system for allocating scarce resources has the effect of encouraging scientists to divert significant public research funds into petty, commercial projects in order to enhance their competitive position within the science community. In the Nebraska animal science department, for example, the overwhelming majority of private grant funds analyzed in our study (89 percent) were for testing or developing commercial products or markets for commercial products. Much of the emphasis was on testing the effectiveness of feed additives used to help cattle and hogs convert feed into meat more quickly and efficiently. These grants came from pharmaceutical companies interested in securing clearances for the sale of their feed additives from the U.S. Food and Drug Administration, which requires tests by independent laboratories. The companies only offer drugs for testing that they have already patented and believe will prove effective. This work, which the scientists themselves politely refer to as contract research, barely deserves to be called research at all.

This system can lead research astray, as demonstrated in the case of the high-fat pig diet. In the 1960s, a research project was established in the Nebraska animal science department to determine the best sources of energy and protein in the diet of very young (preweaned) pigs. Early investigations focused on the problems newborn pigs have digesting plant sources of protein, which are less expensive than animal sources. Bakery by-products, high-lysine corn, wheat, alfalfa meal, and other plant sources of protein were tested.

In 1974, the research program took a sharp turn when an industry-sponsored research foundation, the Fats and Protein Research Foundation, took an interest in it. The foundation's interest was related to the potential uses of tallow (fat rendered from slaughtered cattle and sheep) as an animal feed. Could rendered fat be added to pigs' feed, the foundation wondered? Not a surprising question, considering that about seven hundred companies in the business of processing by-products from slaughtered animals support the foundation.

The project accommodated. Citing growing competition between people and animals for protein (remember the world food shortage of 1974?), the project's research plan was revised to look into alternative sources of protein. The following year, the Fats and Protein Research Foundation tripled its previously modest grant support for the project, and soon after, public funds from state and federal sources spiraled upward as well.

For the next six years, the project devoted itself to the noble quest for a high-fat diet for pigs. In that period, the project consumed $959,799 worth of research, with less than 6 percent of those funds coming from the foundation. The rest was public funds. Average annual use of the revolving fund more than doubled compared to the previous seven years. Among active projects in the animal science department in 1981, it ranked second in lifetime funding. Results gushed forth—two masters' theses, three abstracts presented at professional meetings, two manuscripts presented to a scientific journal. Five of six publications authored by the project's leading scientist during those six years were about fat in the swine diet.

The summary conclusion of all this research? Animal fat does, indeed, enhance fattening of adult hogs, but it is impractical for either farmers or commercial feed mixers to handle tallow as a feed additive. Further, although tallow in the mother's feed could also help baby pigs survive infancy, the level at which it would have to be fed to the sow in order to do so was "probably not practical" (Moser, Boyd, and Cast 1978). About the only farming operations likely to find the approach even interesting are hog factories that can afford to add expensive new facilities for handling tallow. Only one feed company now exerts any serious effort to market a feed with animal fat and it began doing so in 1974, without the benefit of any public research on the subject. Its formula is, of course, a trade secret.

By 1980, with corn prices plummeting and the attractiveness of animal fat as a source of energy or protein in feed waning, the research project turned its attention back to improved plant sources of protein and energy, and the Fats and Protein Research Foundation stopped making grants to the project.

Would this research into what for all practical purposes is a technology suited best to industrial farming operations have been undertaken without the inspiration of a relatively minor commitment of private funds from a commercially interested foundation? How might nearly a million dollars of public research funds have been spent otherwise had they not been used to chase this peculiar dream? Quibbling aside over the merits of this individual project, the research selection process it demonstrates makes publicly funded scientific inquiry the handmaiden of private interests. It reduces scientists to grantsmanship opportunists. Most important, it thwarts complete discussion of the public interest in choosing among alternative paths to technical development.

Farm technology in the United States has been shaped by an assessment that natural resources are plentiful and labor is dear, as noted earlier. But does that assessment remain accurate? If it doesn't, then it is time for us to reconsider our technology base.

Of course, it was never true that natural resources were inexhaustible, as all the tell-tale environmental signs at the beginning of this chapter suggest. Consider the most vital inputs for industrialized agriculture—oil and natural gas. It's hard to exaggerate the extent of our continuing dependence on these particular fuels to power machinery, to control weeds and other pests, to supplement fertility on soils stressed by repeated planting of the same crops, to dry those crops after harvest, and to heat animal factories. For some of these uses, there are clear alternatives. Solar grain drying and space heating are well proven, for example.

But our technological dependence on oil and natural gas as unique sources of energy is nearly complete. A study by the Complex Systems Research Center at the University of New Hampshire concluded that by 2020, domestic supplies of both oil and gas will be depleted, and that if agriculture's technological base does not shift, 10 percent of the oil and 60 percent of the natural gas consumed in the United States soon after that will be used in food production. The problem is compounded because the technologies on which agriculture has been built use oil and natural gas and cannot economically consume coal, the fuel alternative cited most often as the successor to oil and gas (Gever et al. 1986). A farming system so dependent on fossil fuels can't last forever—not even for long.

It is also appropriate to ask whether the social objective our farm technology is designed to accomplish—to produce ever more food with fewer people—is still relevant. The rationale for this objective is that if people can be freed from the burdens of working to produce their own food, they will be able to contribute to other economic development objectives. That is the fundamental development premise of modern society.

In our society, only about 1 percent of the population is directly involved in commercial food production and they supply nearly all the food we eat, plus half again that much for export. A further reduction of the labor force in agriculture is not going to contribute much to increased economic development in our own nation.

Unemployment and poverty, not food shortages, are the social problems in America.

Moreover, other nations have undertaken agricultural development with an intensity we might not have expected just a decade or two ago. In the 1970s, as we engaged in a massive buildup of agricultural production capacity to feed a hungry world, that world was fast going about the process of improving its own food output. As a result, world demand for our food is simply not as strong as predicted. China was once viewed condescendingly as a gigantic open mouth, waiting for the American farmer to shovel grain into it. China is now the world's largest grain producer, a net exporter of grain. Six Third World nations—Mexico, Brazil, China, India, South Korea, and Indonesia—have nearly half the world's population and have increased agricultural production faster than their population since 1970 (U.S. Department of Agriculture 1984b). More and more countries once considered prime targets for American exports don't seem to want our grain. The problem of world hunger is still real, because in most of these countries the poor have no access to the increased output of food. But the solution surely is not—and should not be—dependence on American agriculture.

If a market for boundless U.S. production is not to be found in the rest of the world, the prospect of finding it at home is even more remote. Overfed for decades, America is on a societal diet, cutting out most of the rich foods American agriculture has become specialized to produce—red meat, milk, and eggs. Per-capita consumption of all has fallen sharply. Between 1976 and 1985, Americans trimmed beef consumption an average of 16 percent. We began cutting out milk and eggs even earlier, per-capita consumption falling by 16 percent and 18 percent respectively between 1970 and 1985.[2]

With such a small part of our population engaged in food production as it is, with diminished expectations of what we might be able to sell in the world market, and with excessive eating becom-

2. All food consumption data are from the USDA. Milk consumption data is for fluid milk and cream only. If butter and cheese are included, the decline is 19 percent per capita between 1970 and 1981, after which a significant increase in cheese production reversed the trend. Betweeen 1981 and 1985, per-capita milk consumption has increased 10 percent, due entirely to increased cheese consumption.

ing a health menace at home, there is little need for more food output from American agriculture.

In short, our assessment of both our resource endowments and our social objectives needs to be overhauled. Capital and resources are increasingly scarce, whereas people willing to farm are plentiful. More food is not needed, but less resource destruction is. Based on this reassessment, a farm technology employing people and conserving natural resources is more appropriate to our needs than one that economically dislocates people from the farm to the cities and in the process, squanders soil, water, oil, and other natural resources. The innovations we need from agricultural science are those that recognize this fundamental reassessment of our needs.

We might also view this reformation as a necessary change in our strategy for improving productivity. Productivity is not a measure of how much we produce (though many people seem to think it is), but of how much we produce per unit of input we consume in doing so. Productivity can therefore be improved either by increasing output or by reducing input, since in either case the ratio of output to input improves. In light of a diminishing resource base, the best strategy for improving productivity is one that conserves inputs and sustains natural resources. The greatest gains in productivity can be achieved by maintaining current production levels while reducing input use. Resourcefulness—the capacity to make the best long-term use of what we have—must become the measure of technology choices in agriculture. In fact, we only kid ourselves to believe that productivity can escape the test of resourcefulness.

The challenge for agricultural colleges was laid out in a speech by William E. Marshall, president of the Microbial Genetics Division of Pioneer Hi-Bred International, Inc., one of the leading seed-corn producers in the world, and chair of a prominent USDA advisory committee on agricultural research. Marshall said the colleges should "develop research and extension programs to decrease input costs while holding or increasing production. . . . Profitability should be achieved by decreasing the costs of farming while maintaining or increasing yields." He used the case of biotechnology, the generic term for genetic engineering, as an example.

Citing the research of Dr. Robert Kalter of Cornell University,

Marshall contrasted the economics of bovine growth hormone (BGH), a drug used to achieve staggering increases in milk output, with that of selecting natural microorganisms to improve the efficiency with which cows convert silage to milk. Using BGH, a farmer with 100 cows would spend $4,000 a year on the drug plus $9,000 per year on the additional feedstuffs necessary to make the drugged cow yield more milk. If current milk prices were maintained, this additional investment of $13,000 would produce enough extra milk per cow to generate $17,000 in additional income. That is about a 30 percent return on investment. But it is based on the spurious assumption that the world can use and will pay as much for that much additional milk.

By contrast, if research were directed at selecting natural microorganisms that would improve the cow's digestion of silage, the same farmer with 100 cows would have to spend about $600 for the organisms, increasing milk production enough to generate $2,400 more in revenue while reducing feed costs. That is about a 400 percent return on a minimal investment that will have far less negative impact on milk prices.

Moreover, as Marshall pointed out, the microorganisms are a technology that requires no great management sophistication, no great investment, and no great change in the farming operation. The BGH approach requires additional investments in veterinarian services, other management changes, and significant new cash costs, all of which make it less appealing to smaller farmers, and less cost-effective to society (Marshall 1986).

The choices are there for us to make.

GETTING BACK CONTROL

How do we regain control of the technology we use in American agriculture?[3] It will require a fresh approach to problem solving, one that places greater emphasis on know-how, and less emphasis on technical devices. Technology should become the servant, not the master of good farming.

Is that a realistic goal? Are there practical alternatives for most farmers trying to make a living on the land? The work of Nebraska farmers and my colleagues at the Center for Rural Affairs (1980)

3. This section draws heavily on the work of my colleagues at the Small Farm Resources Project, especially Dennis Demmel, Ron Krupicka, and Rob Aiken.

has demonstrated that there are real technological choices in agriculture, and that they can help small commercial farmers.

In 1976, as oil prices spiraled upward and threatened the existence of many farmers, we set out to show that farmers could turn the energy crisis into an economic opportunity. Rather than help farmers cope with a worsening situation, we proposed to change the relationship between farming and energy. There were three complementary strategies: to conserve purchased energy supplies, to produce new sources of energy, and to use energy in different ways. The new sources and uses of energy on the farm were what is usually described as appropriate technology.

Over three years, we worked with 48 farmers testing new ideas in energy use. These were small commercial farmers with average sales of about $36,000 and average net farm incomes of only $3,400. Most were diversified crop and livestock farms averaging 357 acres, small by Nebraska standards. They were full-time, mud-on-their-boots farmers, however, with little or no off-farm income. Leading agricultural advisors in the state warned us that they were also conservative, reluctant to change, doomed by their own resistance to new technology.

One-half of the group undertook conservation measures—insulation, caulking, and simple practices, such as painting fuel tanks white to reduce evaporation of fuel in the summer—and experimented with new energy conservation practices on their farms. The other half agreed not to do anything they would not have done anyway to conserve energy. Both groups kept careful records of their energy use and expenditures and farm production. The goal was to see if the innovators could reduce energy expenditures while maintaining production levels, improving their farm income by doing so. The project provided some information about alternative energy sources and some modest funds for cost-sharing on innovations.

These farmers were, indeed, conservative. Some made very few changes. But all participated in educational programs, listened to speakers describe possible projects, and worked with the project staff in designing innovations for their farms. The most popular were solar devices to heat homes and livestock buildings, to heat water for use in dairy barns, and to dry grain. But there were less exotic offerings as well—composting of animal manure to improve its use as a fertilizer and soil conditioner, for example. Numerous designs were rendered, each tailored to the farm and the farmer. Gradually, after some initial reluctance to take the plunge was softened by a hands-on workshop in which most cooperators built a simple solar collector, some of these designs were undertaken on the farm.

With few exceptions, the projects were successful, and many cooperators quickly moved on to additional ideas. Dozens of projects were built in the second year. By the concluding third year of the project, the difference in the two groups was startling. The farmers had made one-time investments of $29,699 of their own money in 148 major and minor innovations that reduced their energy consumption. That year alone, these innovators consumed 13 percent less energy and spent $27,312 (17 percent) less money on energy than the noninnovators. In effect, they had saved almost enough in one year to pay for their long-term investment in alternative energy. In one energy use category—heating of farm buildings—the innovators decreased energy expenditures by 15 percent while the others suffered an increase of 15 percent.

Moreover, there was no difference in the amount of food produced on the two types of farms. Both groups increased output by the same amount. As a result, the innovators enjoyed an average improvement in farm income of $1,138—about one-third of their average farm income at the beginning of the project. And they did it with innovations requiring minimal investment of their scarce capital resources.

Of course, not all the farmers did as well as the average. About one-third of the innovators did little more than implement basic conservation practices. Another third undertook at least one minor alternative energy project as well as the conservation measures. The other third undertook one or more major innovations. For them, the project was a particular success. They consumed much less, produced as much, and were better off for it.

This project did more than demonstrate that farmers could save energy and make money doing so. It demonstrated that farmers were rational decision makers capable of selecting among technologies that were not all equally suited to their farms. At the conclusion of the project, our analysis showed that the most popular innovations proved to be the most cost-effective as well. For the most part, farmers selected the technologies that did the most good for them and gave them the greatest return on their limited financial investment. They were not "conservative" or resistant to change. They were simply careful with the limited resources at their disposal. Significantly, seven years after the project ended (among the worst years financially in American agricultural history) *all* of these innovative small farmers were still farming, a remarkable survival rate. It says more about the farmers, of course, than it does about the project.

As rational decision makers with limited resources, what these farmers needed most was not alternative energy *devices* designed by researchers or other experts with high engineering performance standards. They needed alternative energy *skills* they could apply on their own terms to their own farms. As variations on successful solar designs proliferated, we became acutely aware that appropriate technology is custom-made by its user to its user's needs. Instead of standard design rigidly imposed on farms, the farmers were producing site-specific applications of energy principles tailored to meet the needs of their farms.

The appropriateness of a particular innovation therefore depended partly on whether it permitted a change in the use of energy that was compatible with the way other resources on the farm were being used. For example, farmers had to cope with the fact that they had substantial investments in harvesting equipment and storage facilities that required them to dry the crop with fossil fuels that were rapidly increasing in cost. There was too much money already invested in grain-handling equipment and storage facilities to abandon them. Yet this equipment and these facilities made it impossible to harvest and store the grain in the ear (still on the cob, for the city folks), a grain-handling method that would not require artificial drying. The best energy solution—storing corn in the ear—was economically impractical.

Given this limitation, the next best solution was to build a solar collector around the surface of the storage bin. The collector minimized the farm's vulnerability to the rising cost of operating drying equipment. The best technological solution depends on the circumstance.

Perhaps the most important lesson we derived from the project, however, was that the energy crisis is far more than a technological crisis. Technology alone, therefore, is not the solution to it. At the conclusion of the project, we tried to determine exactly how the farmers had managed to save on energy. To our chagrin, we discovered that only 6 percent of the total energy savings could reasonably be attributed to alternative energy devices that we had helped the farmers design and construct. Even more startling, basic conservation measures such as insulation and caulking, could only account for another 25 percent. The remaining 69 percent was purely the product of changes in behavior on the part of the farm families. As one farmer explained to us, the family felt "responsible" for the success or failure of the solar collector they had built themselves, and took steps to conserve fuel in other ways as well, so the collector would "look good." Were they "freezing in the dark?" we asked. No, they assured us, they simply became more conscious of energy savings, closing off rooms not being used during the daytime. They also became more conscientious in other areas: shutting off the tractor when they went to the house for coffee on cold winter mornings, coordinating family trips to town, turning off unnecessary lights in the barn. When farm families gained a sense of responsibility, of ownership and control over their technology, they behaved in a more resource-conserving manner in all areas of their farm life.

Careful distinctions are in order. The point here is not simply that "alternative" technology is better than "conventional" technology, that solar is superior to oil. The point is that when people understand and make rational choices about the technology they use, when they adapt the technology to their needs, they behave more responsibly in its use. I have no doubt that had we simply purchased and installed the "best" commercial solar devices, the results would have been disappointing. The farmers would not have understood these new machines and would not have cared if they worked well—as long as they could enforce any warranty claim against the manufacturer. More energy might have been produced by the manufactured collectors, but I'm confident not nearly as much would have been saved by the families in other ways. Direct involvement in the technology and its use produced ripple effects that outweighed the performance of the devices themselves. The process, more than the product, was the source of success.

What those farmers and we learned is that the energy crisis is not a crisis of technology, but one of culture. These farm families were reasserting cultural values long since overpowered by industrial technologies.

As the project matured and public interest in it grew, these farmers were asked to host tours of their alternative energy farms. During these tours, we were stunned by two obvious developments. First, some of the cooperating farmers who had been quite shy began to speak out forcefully about the things they were trying to do on their farms—not just the energy innovations, but the cropping patterns, the livestock management, the family goals. Second, whereas they had joined the project with apprehension because its title—the *Small* Farm Energy Project—labeled them pejoratively as small farmers, they were now eager to defend the virtues of their farm's smallness, pointing out that being small gave them the flexibility to adopt energy-saving practices that would not be possible on larger, less versatile farms. They advertised how advantageous it was to be a small farmer if one intended to use the kind of technology they were demonstrating. What they were really demonstrating, of course, was not technology at all, but pride in taking back control over a part of their lives that had only recently seemed entirely out of their control. If the project was about skills rather than devices, it was also about power—human power—rather than energy.

Out of the experiences of these farmers evolved an understanding of appropriate technology. At the beginning, we weren't sure we knew what that was, but as we worked with farmers on these approaches, our understanding of what it meant became clearer. For us, appropriate technology

— is low-cost, within the financial means of small commercial farmers
— can be built, operated, and maintained with common materials, common tools and common skills
— will produce or conserve sufficient economic resources to pay for itself within its useful lifetime
— fits the management, financial, and other existing constraints of the farm, enabling it to change its technological base at a pace which is affordable and manageable

Technology cannot be evaluated by such purely technical criteria alone, however. Technology is shaped by cultural values, and the way it is used reflects the way we treat each other. What is technologically appropriate therefore has cultural as well as technical meaning. It depends on more than mere engineering and economic performance. It depends, too, on how the use of the technology affects the relationships among people and between people and the rest of the natural world. Some technologies that are appropriate by engineering standards are inappropriate because of the destructive, anti-social behavior they encourage or the exploitive relationships they reinforce. Appropriate technology brings out the best in us, and opposes our worst.

Most important in this social dimension of technology is whether it lends itself to concentrations of power and control, and therefore tempts the abusive use of that power. Take, for example, the splendid accomplishments of Eli Whitney, the erstwhile Yankee mechanical genius who invented the cotton gin in 1793. Southern planters were desperate for a machine that would separate the cotton lint from its seed. Earlier machines had been clumsy and ineffective, leaving broken seed bits in the lint and giving American cotton a reputation for inferiority in the important British market. Whitney's genius was to perceive that the problem was not to squeeze the seed from the lint wound tightly around it, as earlier machines had done, but to comb the lint from the seed with a series of wire brushes.

His machine was simple and effective. It was inexpensive to build, could be made from easily available materials, and was easy to operate and repair. It revolutionized southern agriculture. Cotton became king in the South almost overnight, and a robust export trade brought in generous revenues.

But Whitney spent much of the rest of his life unsuccessfully trying to capitalize on his patent rights to the gin. First he attempted to monopolize ginning by operating and licensing custom services, and then to profit from the manufacture and sale of the gins. But both efforts were futile. The device was so simple that once anyone saw one, everyone had one, so to speak. Eventually, the state of South Carolina provided a token payment to Whitney in recognition of the gin's contribution to the state's economic development, but that barely offset the legal fees he had incurred trying to defend his patent. Toward the end, with all hope of substantial gain lost, Whitney summarized the lesson to be learned from the cotton gin: "An invention can be so valuable as to be worthless to the inventor" (Green 1956). That's still the best one-sentence definition of appropriate technology I've heard.

But there was another lesson in the cotton gin as well. Offered into an economic system built on certain moral deficiencies, it was used to help justify the enslavement of a race of people because the machine made it convenient for the rich and the powerful to exploit their forced labor. We are all still paying for the consequences of this sorry misuse of an otherwise appropriate technical device. The machine empowered people to do more, but it made them no wiser, and it brought out the worst in their character. There is no technology that frees us from the moral responsibility to treat each other well.

A RESURGENT AGRICULTURE

Thousands of American farmers are demonstrating that there are practical alternatives to the technological treadmill. They are leading the way with private decisions about how they farm. Out of the malaise of American agriculture has emerged a growing commitment among many farmers to farm differently in order to survive. The old values of frugality, diversity, resourcefulness, and flexibility in farming systems are reappearing in commercial agriculture. These changes are taking place in many shapes and forms, in greater or lesser degree on farms across the nation. Reduced chemical usage, integrated pest management, alternative cropping systems, new ways of marketing—all herald an awakening among practical farmers. Importantly, this awakening is partly driven by a parallel consumer movement toward more wholesome, locally produced, fresh foods. A few years ago, the nascent trends in these directions were written off as token efforts on the periphery of commercial agriculture. Today, the periphery has grown to include thousands of once-conventional, cash-crop farmers looking for economic salvation. In a sense, agriculture is resurging from its root values.

The evidence of this resurgent agriculture is everywhere. And to a large degree, its development is consumer-driven. At first centered on the West Coast, the movement has spread nationwide. It is best known in heavily populated farm states like California, where opportunities to serve the exotic tastes of the beautiful people has long sheltered the most unorthodox farming and marketing practices. But now organic vegetables are airlifted daily from California farms to ritzy restaurants in New York City. Concern over the healthfulness and quality of food has lead to a nationwide boom in "natural" food sales. From 1970 to 1982, health and natural food stores increased in number from 1,000 to 8,000 and in sales from $140 million to over $2 billion (Price and Brown 1984).

Several supermarket chains now feature organic food products, including "natural" beef. Specialized suppliers now market beef that they not only certify has "technically and analytically nondetectable" residues of farm chemicals, but that they grade into one of four categories depending on caloric value, cholesterol levels, and mineral content (Gauger 1986).

States eager to tap these new markets have established certification programs to encourage consumer confidence that the organic foods are genuine. Half a dozen states have some kind of official standards, and they are being considered in many others. Dozens of producer groups have established certification standards and a growing number of food processors hoping to establish a reputation for quality are adopting their own as well.

But this movement is not merely for the rich or the pure. In some states like Massachusetts, where agriculture has been on the decline for a century, an agricultural renaissance of sorts is occurring. Rooted in consumer preference for locally grown products—whether organic or not—and in a public desire to preserve open space, that state has embarked on a deliberate program to rebuild agriculture. It has purchased development rights to farmland to prevent conversion to nonfarm uses, promoted locally grown foods with television ads, food fairs, and farmers' markets, lent $200 million to 37 food-processing companies, and put another $600,000 into research on nonchemical pest-control methods (Muhm 1987). The objective is to become less dependent on food imported from other states and nations, to develop economic opportunities on the farm, and to use the state's limited land resources to their fullest potential. Bouyed by a strong nonfarm economy and a firm public commitment, the effort has been remarkably successful. As the farm crisis deepened in the Midwest, the Massachusetts farm economy grew. Since 1970, the number of commercial farms in Massachusetts has actually increased and sales of farm products have more than doubled (Massachussetts Department of Food and Agriculture 1985).

Nor is resurgent agriculture limited to the most populous regions of the nation. It is in the Midwest, as well, where fundamentalist attitudes about the efficacy of chemicals are giving way to "practical farming." Most midwestern states now have organic, alternative, or sustainable farming organizations. Their memberships are bulging with conventional chemical farmers looking for alternatives. The University of Nebraska proudly boasts that it has been conducting alternative agriculture research, comparing cropping systems with and without chemicals since the late 1970s. Agricultural universities in fifteen states now have sustainable agriculture research programs (Haney, Krome, and Stevenson 1986).

232

Local direct-marketing associations that link farmers and consumers have also sprung up like bindweed in July. Their efforts help to market new food crops from farms that once depended on cash grains. Agriculture agencies in nineteen states have formed direct-marketing assistance programs (Northdurft 1986). Perhaps most significant, one of the nation's leading farm magazines, *Successful Farming*, as orthodox as any farm magazine in the nation, recently sponsored a conference on alternative cropping featuring over one hundred unconventional ways of diversifying the farm. Thousands of farmers attended. Even the USDA has formed an Alternative Farming Systems Information Center in its National Agricultural Library.

Many farmers are searching for practical ways to reduce chemical usage on their farms. Their motives are many, and sometimes mixed. Some are concerned about cutting costs. Others are concerned about the impact of chemical farming practices on their family's health. Some are environmentalists in a larger sense who worry about the chemicals' wider impact. These farmers are willing to take chances on their own farms. They are not waiting for a public policy decision to save family farming.

It is difficult to measure the growth of this quest for a change in farming systems, but there is little doubt that it is significant. In the heart of conventional agriculture there is doom and despair. On the periphery, where change emerges, there is hope and ambition. In 1986, I spoke to about five hundred organic farmers at a national eco-farming conference. Whereas the farm crisis and the problem of coping with disaster had dominated the talk at other meetings of conventional farming I had attended that year, the alternative farmers were bubbling with enthusiasm over the challenges and opportunities ahead. They were sympathetic, but more curious than outraged as I described the financial and political problems of conventional agriculture. They understood, however, when I told them that they were to conventional agriculture what the Renaissance was to the Dark Ages.

As you might expect, there is no unanimity with respect to what the best alternative to conventional farming methods is. This frustrates some farmers, but it should not. Instead, it should reinforce our conviction that the path to better farming is uncharted and unknown, and not the predetermined plan of vested interests.

While there is no settled path, many have been recommended. Each of the alternative approaches to conventional agriculture has its devoted adherents. There is "organic," "sustainable," "biological," "regenerative," "ecological," "natural," and even "low-input" farming. Some of these concepts are methodologically rigid, others more versatile. Some are ideologically refined, others sufficiently vague to be politically coy. No point is served in trying to define or refine their meaning here. They are all part of the movement to revise the way we think farming ought to be done.

In fact, there are no formula solutions to the survival problems of individual farms. There are practical problems with the adoption of any farming system that eschews the use of conventional farming technologies. For real farmers, two generations removed from farming without relying on chemicals for pest control, and farming in a world of insects and weeds that have grown genetically tough through competition against potent chemicals, switching to chemical-free farming is no small step. They need ways and means, practical measures, halfway steps. The purist attitude that runs through some alternative-agriculture cults doesn't help. In fact, it is part of what retards the wider adoption of alternatives. For some, the quest for a less environmentally destructive agriculture is on a level with the quest for the Holy Grail. Most of us don't have a heart as pure as Sir Gallahad's.

All the words describing various approaches to alternative agriculture are somewhat ethereal, coined by proponents of particular theories of what makes good farming. As ideologies, they are bewildering to practical people who are only looking for a way out. In a way, they are words in search of meaning, part of a competition among ideas. That is at least intellectually healthy. But what gives these ideas an invaluable unity of meaning is that they all represent a tacit rejection of the status quo in farming systems. They all suggest that farming has strayed far from its fundamental purpose, which is to produce food in a way that can be done year after year, generation after generation. The search for a practical and environmentally gentle way of producing food has barely begun, and is in great need of more ideas.

The best ideas will come from practical farmers like Gary and Delores Young of McLean, Nebraska. The Youngs have farmed all their lives, for many years as conventionally as anyone. With 320 acres and 40 cows, their farm is considered by the experts to be too small. A few years back, the Youngs reassessed their situation and decided that the experts were not right, but that if they kept farming the way bigger farms do, they weren't going to make it. Economics weren't the only issue, either. The Youngs were suspicious of the quality of the water on their farm and had it tested for chemical contamination. The tests showed low levels of contamination for a dozen farm chemicals. Concerned about the health of their daughters (they now have six) and about the possibility that the cows' milk would eventually reflect the contamination, the Youngs decided to make changes.

This was not an emotional decision, and the Youngs have never considered themselves to be ideologically antichemical. They were not part of any movement or attached to any cause. They still shy away from the term "organic," though they use few chemicals. Ten years ago, they were without a map or a compass, seeking a new direction for the survival of their farm and the health of their family.

They began by deciding to reduce the cost of tillage operations. They invested in some minimum-tillage equipment designed to conserve soil and reduce the number of trips across the field in planting the crop. But unlike most conventional farmers shifting to minimum tillage, the Youngs decided not to control weeds by increasing pesticide use. Instead, they instituted a rigorous nine-year crop rotation plan including corn, milo, corn, soybeans, corn, oats, and three years of alfalfa. The rotation helps control insect diseases while maintaining fertility.

Gary cultivates the row crops twice, which costs a little more in fuel than most herbicide-using farmers, and his fields aren't weed-free, the way some of the neighbors' are. He's also not a purist. He uses herbicides once in the nine-year rotation, to kill the alfalfa before planting it to corn. But the bottom line is what counts, according to the Youngs, and their field costs are lower than they used to be (Center for Rural Affairs 1982).

The innovation didn't stop there. The Youngs began experimenting in other ways. They built a solar collector to heat the dairy barn and another portable one that serves double duty drying their grain and heating their home. The portable collector was so well designed and so inexpensively built that it won recognition and warranted a special report from the USDA (Heid 1981).

The Youngs also began experimenting with various cropping alternatives. They're growing lupins, a legume similar to soybeans but which, unlike soybeans, does not need to be processed before it can be fed to farm animals. They are overseeding rye in their corn and milo to control weeds, add fertility, conserve moisture by reducing rainfall runoff, and reduce winter erosion. To give their soybean land more protection from erosion, the Youngs are alternating strips of corn and soybeans planted in narrow rows. This should help reduce wind velocity and trap snow much as a snow fence does. When the snow melts in the spring, the extra moisture will help the crop. They're also trying a new crop, triticale—a small, high-protein grain that resists drought better than corn. And for long-range plans, they've planted nut-bearing trees that will produce a new source of income in the future.

Biological pest controls are also receiving practical tests on the Young mini-lab. Musk-thistle weevils have been imported to help control the musk thistle, one of Nebraska's worst pasture weeds. The weevil lays its eggs at the base of the plant's seed head, and when the larvae hatch, they make their first meal of the weed's seed. They also are trying to control weeds by including grain sorghum in their crop rotation. Grain sorghum is believed to have an allelopathic affect on weeds—chemically inhibiting their growth.

To increase the fertility of their soil as well as its ability to retain moisture, the Youngs compost the manure from their dairy herd. During composting, bacteria break down the manure, stabilizing nutrients and minimizing the amount of nutrient that is lost to the atmosphere when the compost is spread on the field. Composting also reduces the volume of the manure, making it easier and less expensive to handle. And heat naturally generated during composting kills weed seeds that otherwise might sprout in the field.

When it's haying time on the Young farm, they use a device called a refractometer to measure the sugar content of their hay crop so it can be harvested at just the right time for optimum feed value. And they have adopted a very sophisticated pasture management system. They divide the pasture into small paddocks and move animals from paddock to paddock at precisely the opportune moment to harvest the grasses and legumes at peak nutritional value.

Which of these and other experiments on the Young farm prove to be of benefit and which ones they abandon remains to be seen. But one thing is for sure: they have broken faith with the myth that bigger is better. Gary and Delores Young simply aren't being told how to farm by the chemical companies and the machine dealers anymore. They have accepted responsibility for the way they farm, and they are looking for ways that give them a future on the land. They are off the high-tech, high-production treadmill. They've stopped trying to do more, and have started trying to do better.

That is true of thousands of small commercial farmers across the United States who represent a commercial counterculture in American agriculture. They intend to survive, and they know they can't survive by farming conventionally in a farm economy geared for bigness.

I believe future generations will look back on the period following the Second World War as a quaint and somewhat curious period during which agricultural technology became preoccupied with the many uses of oil, and during which agricultural science suspended inquiry into solutions to farm problems that were not based on use of that resource. Farmers like Gary and Delores Young, who have led the way in search of other solutions during this era, will be regarded as pioneers. Public policy can encourage alternative agriculture, but only farmers experimenting and adopting it to their own farms can make it become the conventional farming of tomorrow. These private policies may, in the long run, be as important as any public policies in determining the fate of family farming.

10.

Within Family Farming

O ne Christmas Eve, a couple I know drove to an overnight family gathering in their old but reliable Ford. When they arrived, they were taken aback by the sharp contrast between that old Ford and the newer cars being driven by others of their generation in the family. They had given most of their professional lives to things they believe in, serving as Peace Corps volunteers, teaching, and practicing antipoverty law. They were approaching midcareer and had two children soon to be in need of a higher education. The shiny new cars stood out sharply as a metaphor for the material things they had denied themselves and their children as they had pursued other values. It had never seemed so obvious before. For them, it was a sobering Christmas Eve, filled with doubt and introspection.

But on Christmas morning the Nebraska winter graced them with a chilling twenty-five degrees below zero . . . and with the opportunity to crank up that old Ford and jump start each and every one of those newer cars.

Some things in life are enduring, and though old Fords really aren't, the story serves to remind us that basic values are. In essence, American agriculture is stalled in the chilling values of industrial society. It badly needs a jump start from some old agrarian values.

But who has the jumper cables? Where will that jump start come from? Farm politics is a wasteland of eroded institutions, droughty

238

ideas, and barren philosophies. It is too crowded with narrow commodity interests and disregard for social justice.

In farm politics, you can justify any position by invoking the family farm. That rhetoric is largely a front to avoid talking about the basic human values that are reflected in farm policy. We don't like to talk directly about economic values, especially if the discussion forces us to be critical of ourselves or of others we don't want to offend. It's no fun to consider how our behavior falls short of what we claim to believe in, especially if that behavior is self-destructive. We need to lose our fear of discussing economic values, and with it, our fear of finding out what's wrong with American agriculture.

It is all right, for example, to admit that farmers don't live up to their agrarian image. We can't understand why they don't if we aren't willing to admit that they don't. And some of us who are most committed to saving the family farm haven't been. Admitting that farmers fall short of our agrarian expectations also helps us evaluate the reasonableness of those expectations.

We'd like to believe that farmers are an uncomplicated, homogeneous group of individuals whose rights have been trampled on. More important, we prefer to think of them not only as victims, but as victims worthy of being saved. They are thought to be hard working, independent, industrious, honest, noble—the little guys stacked up against the system. This sympathetic image of the family farmer is held deeply in our society, even by those who have never met a farmer. We simply prefer to see the virtuous yeoman, and to overlook the scheming entrepreneur. We want to consider the miserable troubles of individual farmers today as a matter of broad social injustice.

The affection some of us feel for the family farm is about as deep as our affection for the unspoiled Garden of Eden. We're sure that it must have been a pleasant place, but most of us aren't sure we'd really like to have lived there. As long as we don't have to make that choice, of course, there is no point in criticizing our idyllic image of family farming. Likewise, many who would save the family farm are chasing an agrarian myth they would just as soon not catch, and are comforted in believing they never will, anyway. This is not intended as a criticism of people who want to save the family farm. It is intended to suggest that our analysis of the values at stake needs to be refined. Our loyalty to farmers needs to become more discriminating.

In truth, the agrarian myth persists because it suggests that farmers are, as a group, different from the rest of us, and that suggestion has some foundation in reality. Farm people really are different from the rest of us. At least that seemed clear only a generation or two ago. But when it was clear, the difference was the source of cultural derision. Farmers were too simple, too naive, for those of us who were on the fast track toward chic and clever. Sophistication was more desirable, if not more virtuous, than simplicity. Farmers, and especially farm children, were socially bland. They couldn't participate in things—they lived too far from town and always seemed to have too many chores to do. They didn't have money for the good things in life, either. They stayed home nights. Their homespun and gingham ways were a little bit embarrassing. The "better" ones we urged to move on to better things. From virtuous yeoman to country bumpkin is only a mood swing away for most of us.

It shouldn't surprise us then that the very attributes that distinguish the family farm of agrarian myth from the rest of contemporary urban society are the ones most threatened today. As agriculture industrializes, farmers become less frugal, more profligate, less productive, more consumptive, less independent, more vulnerable, less satisfied with labor, more enamored of machines. In doing so, they are merely meeting the expectations of society. If people think farming is an inferior occupation because farmers never get to go on vacations, then specializing in corn and soybeans and spending the winter in Florida proves they are wrong.

The family farm's persistence as a cause is a reflection of its deep roots in the American experience, right to the political rationale for our war for independence. According to the visionaries of our revolution, the virtuous, independent farmer was to be democracy's foundation. The yeoman was industrious and self-reliant and wanted to be free of despotic restraints on his productivity. Once free, he could and would carry his own opinions into political action. Thomas Jefferson made a habit of elevating the farmer to the status of a civic demigod, but his political adversary, John Adams did, too, and so did their mutual patriarch, George Washington. Both the federalist and republican strains of our revolutionary heritage proclaimed the farmer's indispensable democratic qualities.

Central to this agrarian rationale for democracy was the fundamental belief that the farmer placed public values above private interests. As historian Tamara Plakins Thornton puts it:

> Americans of the early republic attached tremendous symbolic significance to the yeoman farmer and to agriculture. Contemporary political theory held that republics were fragile things, able to exist only so long as their citizens placed the public good above private gain. Just this sort of public virtue, it was held, was the natural attribute of the propertied husbandman. The yeoman farmer, then, was the guarantor of public virtue and, thus, of the continuance of the republic (Thornton 1986).

Farming was, of course, the common occupation of early America, and it would have been difficult to lay the theoretical foundation for American democracy without placing a good deal of faith in the public capacity of our most numerous citizens.

Harmonizing the private and public interests in democratic theory was consistent with the harmonizing assumptions of another emerging theory—that of the market economy. Just as private pursuit of individual political interests by farmers would suitably fashion the public interest in a democracy, individual pursuit of private economic interests would serve the collective good in a free market. In the view of early America, there was no tension—politically or economically—between the individual interests of family farmers and the public interest in maintaining a system of family farming. The coincidence of private and public interests was an essential feature of both the democratic rationale and the competitive market paradigm.

Today, farming is not the common occupation and the private interests of individual farmers are not necessarily harmonious with the public interest. In fact, they are quite often in open conflict. From the time we ran out of free land, the property interests of farmers began to run up against the interests of the landless. And, as agriculture becomes more concentrated, more technologically sophisticated, more capital-intensive, and more competitively predatory, the conflict grows.

For contemporary farmers, the conflict between private interests and the public interest is especially acute. To preserve their vested interests, family farmers frequently find themselves supporting public policies that benefit themselves while limiting opportunities for others to become farmers. In fact, a policy of attrition among farmers is rationalized largely on the basis that it serves the private interests of those who survive. Naturally, many family farmers prefer responses to the farm crisis that salvage those who have expanded rather than restore those who were squeezed out by them. When they talk about saving the family farm, they're talking about their own farm. This self-serving political posture is a tribute to deeply held economic values in our society that elevate self-interest to a state of inherent virtue.

Those who would save the family farm only to serve the private vested interests of those who are family farmers (or worse, who now own farmland), do a disservice to the agrarian tradition as well as to the public. The accumulated private interests of thousands of family farmers isn't an adequate political foundation for family farming as we have defined it. Larger public values are at stake. To save family farming, we must go beyond private interests vested in the family farm.

GIVING SUBSTANCE TO THE AGRARIAN MYTH

The problem is that there is no consensus about what constitutes the public interest in farm policy. Essentially missing from the rationale for today's farm policies are clearly defined public interests that supersede the private interests of individual consumers and farmers.

Soil conservation, for example, is usually an afterthought in farm policy debate, an amenity that must accommodate itself to the production objectives of commodity programs. When commodity market prices are high, conservation programs wither in the heat of full production. I served on a local soil and water conservation board in the mid-1970s when the boom was in full swing. Conservation was expendable. Following the surge in corn prices in 1973, we watched helplessly as forty years of publicly sponsored conservation efforts in northeast Nebraska fell to the plow in a matter of months. On the other hand, when prices are low, conservation becomes a convenient excuse to pay farmers to remove land from production. The test of the substantial commitment to soil conservation made in the 1985 farm bill will not be met until farm prices recover and the public interest in conservation again conflicts with the perceived self-interests of farmers who want to make money farming highly erodible land. Which will abide?

Or consider, for example, the often praised but never served beginning farmer. Everyone loves the beginning farmer, an abstraction of our future. For many, the beginning farmer's problems offer a concrete demonstration of how rigid the barriers to entry in capital-intensive agriculture have become. Being a good farmer is not enough. You've got to be born rich—inherit or marry the farm, as the saying goes. But as a society we are not willing to do anything meaningful to help beginning farmers. In the "good" years, with prices high and land prices rising, we are told that the public cost of subsidizing a beginning farmer is too high and their prospects of success too low. In the bad years, with land values falling and the costs of entry reduced, we are told that the government ought not to help beginning farmers when so many established farmers need saving. While it may be convenient now and then to conserve soil, it is never really convenient to help new people into farming. Would-be farmers are not a vested interest, and encouraging them is not consistent with a policy of attrition.

Because of this public-interest gap in farm policy, most of us may continue to support the family farm philosophically without knowing why. Some offer platitudes about caring for the land, operating efficiently, providing a stable community life. Our confidence in family farming might be rational, but mostly, it is just what we want to believe. Or perhaps we fear what the alternative, which in many people's minds is corporate farming, might bring. It is Hamlet's dilemma: we'd rather bear those family farm ills we have than fly on to others that we know not of. Apart from that, there seems to be little rationale for family farming in the minds of most Americans, and even less rationale for farm policy altogether. Farm policy lives in a benign vacuum of public understanding.

Indeed, there are no easy solutions if we want to preserve a family farming system that opens opportunities to those of modest means. Those who argue that the solutions are simple—raise commodity prices, end tax-loss farming, prohibit corporate farming, regulate chemicals—are kidding themselves and misleading others. The power of technology and the values of industrial agriculture are too potent to be countered by such narrow reactions.

The greatest obstacle to defining the public interest in farm policy is the political uncertainty and ambiguity of farmers themselves. Many accept the fundamentalist ideology of the unrestrained market, pausing only during hard times to protest its consequences for them. Unless farmers decide that public policy must change, not for their own good individually, but for the general welfare of society, it's unlikely that nonfarmers will take much interest. What is at stake is not only the fate of a couple million individuals who willingly wear the mantle of family farmer. A system of agriculture now and in the future that sustains public values hangs in the balance. If we are to save family farming, farmers, first and foremost, must give substance to the agrarian myth.

TWO CHALLENGES

That may be too much to ask. Why should farmers place the public interest above their own interests when no one else does? Are only farmers expected to be altruistic in a self-serving society?

Of course not. Farmers should not suffer in order to promote agricultural policies that serve society. That, in fact, is what has happened to many farmers in the past thirty years. But the individual farmer should be willing to give up the right to pursue self-interest to the point that it jeopardizes the general ability of farmers to make a living. In order to secure the limited right for many, including himself, to earn a good living by farming well, he must give up the unlimited right to prosper (and to fail) at the expense of others.

In essence, mine is nothing more than a call to reconcile farm policy with its historic rural values. There is nothing wrong with the values commonly associated with the traditional family farm—self-reliance, frugality, ingenuity, stewardship, humility, family, neighborhood, and community. Just because they are agrarian does not make them less important to contemporary society. These values have been depreciated but not yet fully rejected by our industrial society.

They are, in fact, some of the values reflected in the environmental movement, the urban neighborhood movement, the enthusiasm for entrepreneurship that is sweeping the nation, and even in the fiscal conservatism in politics during the past decade. In many ways, post-industrial values offer a dimly reflected mirror image of agrarian values. The irony is that as society embraces agrarian-like post-industrial values, agriculture forsakes them in pursuit of worn-out industrial values, with their misplaced emphasis on size, power, consumption, and material output. It is as if agriculture insists on entering the industrial age just as it is coming to an end. The challenge of farm policy now is to reconcile itself with its historic values, salvaging as many opportunities for expression of those values in the future as possible.

To lead the public in this policy direction, farmers need to meet two political and personal challenges that have been implicitly posed throughout this book. In capsule form, they are:

Accept More Responsibility for Each Other

Farmers, like many other economic groups, have defined their self-interest individually, in the context of the values embodied in the competitive paradigm. They have been lured into favoring tax and commodity policies that appear to favor them individually while actually favoring only those with superior access to capital. Farmers' collective self-interest is better served by policies that encourage rather than discourage the weaker competitors. Professional sports understands the importance of fostering competition by assuring that the weaker teams get to choose new players first each year. Without similar policies, competition degenerates, the quality of play suffers as unevenly matched teams lose their incentive to play each other, and the fans lose interest in lopsided games. The teams recognize that it is in their collective self-interest to encourage competition by strengthening the weaker teams. Farm policy has been the athletic equivalent of giving the championship team first pick in the new player draft each year.

In considering policies affecting competition, it is particularly important to recognize that farm policy is not neutral with respect to its impact on competition within agriculture. Seeking farm policies that affect all farmers in the same way, regardless of their size, level of specialization, market situation, and technological base is futile. More important, it is not the obligation of public policy to be neutral; its obligation is to preserve competition by counterbalancing the forces against it. The public interest in preserving competition far outweighs the private interest in individual reward. Think of it this way: there wouldn't be many bowling leagues if it weren't for handicaps.

Agriculture is rich in its history of cooperation, sharing, and neighborliness, and the remnants of that tradition are alive, if not well. In recent years, the farm crisis has stimulated the caring and pride in community that once were the dominant themes of frontier life. From barn raising to threshing bees to farm crisis response councils, the spirit that says "we are all in this together" still shines in rural America. That spirit rejects the contradiction that progress must produce victims, and argues that if it does produce victims, it isn't progress.

Mutuality extends beyond the limits of farming as an occupation, of course. It is present as the basic theme of Midwestern farm communities that try to minimize class differences. Distinctions between those who own and those who do not are discouraged and grossly unequal distribution of wealth is not socially approved. People are either worthy in character or not, whatever they own.

I recall an incident that revealed to me just how much alive this ethic is in rural America. I was attending a small meeting of farmers in which one participant launched into an extended complaint about farm workers "going too far" by organizing to demand higher wages, more benefits, and improved sanitation facilities in the field. He concluded by saying that these malcontents would all be replaced by machines if they kept up their agitation. "They'll have to choose between accepting a lower standard of living or getting out of agriculture," he said.

Another farmer listened to this diatribe with a deepening furrow in his brow. When it was over, he waited in silence with the others for a moment, then said: "Hmmm . . . accept a lower standard of living or get out of agriculture. That's not a choice I want to make for myself or a choice I want my children to have to make for themselves. And it isn't a choice I'd wish on anyone else." It was a simple, powerful reaffirmation of the golden rule. That farmer held his values up like a beacon that day, just high enough to cast a long shadow of shame on those who would let their economic self-interest destroy what they claim to stand for.

Accepting mutual responsibility requires that we disapprove of behavior that destroys our communities, and that we accept whatever sanctions are necessary to prevent it. Too frequently, tolerance of self-serving behavior in rural society has been its Achilles heel.

Too much of the rationale for farm policy avoids these simple moral standards. Instead, it is couched in terms of false pride and petty technical notions of efficiency. Public intervention on behalf of farmers is justified on the grounds that others alone are to blame for the sorry economic conditions in agriculture. As a result, farm policy aims at redressing inequities between agriculture and the rest of the economy, but conveniently downplays the inequities within agriculture. While there *is* plenty of reason for genuine pride and while there *are* pernicious outside forces in agriculture that must be countered, it is also true that the self-serving behavior of too many farmers living without regard for the well-being of neighbors has been a big part of the problem as well. Farmers (as well as the rest of us) should care more for their neighbors, and farm policy should be designed to advance the cause of social justice among farmers.

Accept More Responsibility for How We Farm

An appreciation for doing things well is one of the most important agrarian values. There is no greater or more genuine source of pride than that found in the careful craft of farming. It is more than that which derives from abundant production; it is the pride that comes from knowing how to work the land. Robert Frost, in his poem *The Death of the Hired Man*, captured the essence of this pride in his description of how the lowly hired man, Silas, builds a load of hay:

> 'I know that's Silas' one accomplishment.
> He bundles every forkful in its place,
> And tags and numbers it for future reference,
> So he can find and easily dislodge it
> In the unloading. Silas does that well.
> He takes it out in bunches like big birds' nests.
> You never see him standing on the hay
> He's trying to lift, straining to lift himself.'
> (Frost 1962).

American agriculture has plainly built a bad load of hay and is now caught straining to lift itself, burdened with excessive debt and overcommitted to production. In the course of things, farmers are increasingly aware that they are not farming as well as they would like to farm. But as long as the ugly notion persists that it is more valuable to do things big and fast than it is to do them well, we'll go from one bad load of hay to another.

The mood, behavior, policies, and values expressed in American agriculture in the 1970s made a particularly bad load of hay. They should be repudiated. Politicians of both major parties baited the trap with high inflation, relatively lower interest rates, tax inducements to invest, and commodity programs that encouraged production of a narrow range of export crops. Farmers and investors too willingly took the bait. Land prices spiraled way out of line with earning power as a wave of debt-financed expansion took place. People who now complain that their net worth has been "cut in half" in the past five years by falling land values are living a myth. In real economic terms they were never worth as much as they thought they were, and in human terms, they are worth a lot more today than they fear they are. The value of a farmer is not determined by the price of the land he or she farms, though the 1970s encouraged us to think that it is.

Dreams born and empires built in such an unrealistic and unfair environment should not be rescued by public intervention. Only intervention to redeem those who have been victimized by these policies and behavior so that they might start over is appropriate.

But there is more to accepting responsibility for farming well than being proud of a job well done. It is also a matter of the tenure of the farmer. The economic rights of ownership should be attached to the social responsibility of using land well. If we want land to be farmed well, the privilege of making decisions and the chore of carrying them out should be in the hands of the people who own the land, or who one day will. This truth is as enduring as any in agriculture. A thoughtful insurance company executive, concerned about growing ownership of farmland by nonfarmers, including insurance companies, told me that "the only way the land will ever be taken care of is by having the owner of the land living upon it, for he is the only person with the good sense to keep it from blowing away beneath his boots." Confucius said it more poetically: "The best fertilizer is the footsteps of the landowner." Public policy should make ownership the just reward of good land use, and good land use the obligation of owners.

A NEW MANDATE FOR FARM POLICY

Farmers who accept these challenges can lead America in a new mandate for farm policy. That mandate will provide for sufficient public intervention in the farm economy to assure bountiful supplies of food, careful stewardship of resources, and a meaningful opportunity for farmers to earn a decent income from their work. In such a balancing of priorities a few sacred cows will be lost, especially farmers' cherished right to operate free of government constraints and their right to benefit from public farm programs regardless of individual need. Most important, a new mandate for farm policy must be based on two premises: that maintaining a healthy, competitive farm economy requires restraining the forces of economic concentration; and that the public interest in conserving natural resources exceeds any private right to their use.

A new mandate for farm policy should really be stated as a modern economic and environmental land ethic. It can be summed up in a few sentences:

— A farmer should be able to pay for farmland by farming it well.
— A farmer should have to farm it well.
— A farmer should have to pay for land by farming it, and by no other means.
— There should be no motive for owning farmland other than to make a living by farming it well.

No society can measure up to such a pure standard. But we can try. No society should be without standards that challenge its members to live up to what they profess to believe.

Many changes in current public policies are needed to fulfill this mandate. For openers, five broad policy changes should be pursued with vigor now.

First, the array of subsidies to capital investment in agriculture should be ended. They distort basic underlying economic values, depreciate natural resources, and encourage unwarranted expansion in farm size.

Second, we need to manage production more sensibly. Current commodity programs only encourage expansion and overproduction, misuse of land and overuse of chemical inputs. And they are very costly. Good land use, resource conservation, and a deep concern for the distribution of farm income should drive farm policy.

Third, we should develop a national land policy to prevent concentration in farmland ownership and to make land more available to those with the ability and eagerness to use it well. Barriers to entry in agriculture should be reduced by programs aimed at financing those with minimal capital, taxes should discourage accumulation of land, and if necessary, new forms of land tenure involving public investment in owner-operated farms should be developed.

Fourth, agribusiness companies who sell to and buy from farmers should be subject to greater federal regulation to prevent unfair trade practices that reduce competition and discriminate against smaller farms.

Fifth, agricultural research and the development of new technologies should be guided by a greater concern for social and environmental effects. More effective ways of anticipating and controlling the adverse consequences of technology are needed, and more important, new approaches to defining technical needs and solving technical problems are needed. The market is not the proper forum for these decisions, because the self-interest of consumers of farm technology (i.e., farmers) is not an adequate foundation for protecting the public interest in either a clean environment or a resource-conserving food system.

Specific proposals for implementing these five policy directions are discussed in a special section that follows the main body of this book. They are separated from the rest of the book because they are politically timely, and likely to be outdated far more quickly than the basic policy directions themselves.

CAVEATS

Such a mandate would provide a clear direction to U.S. farm policy. But some caveats are in order.

First, there are limits to what we can expect farm policy to accomplish. Public policy cannot make us do individually what we do not believe in as a society. Alone, public policy cannot alter the values that govern human relationships. If we have truly given up on the notion that those who work the land should own it, no policy change can arrest the trend toward separation of people from the land. Likewise, if the values, behavior, and character of farmers do not support family farming, neither can public policy. Falsehearted commitments to family farming will only produce political platitudes and ineffective legislation. We have forty years of farm program history to support that conclusion.

Second, agriculture can't live up to a public standard of moral purity that is higher than that expected of the rest of our society. If farmers are expected to steward natural resources even when doing so is not in their immediate self-interest, the rest of us must be willing to sacrifice the immediate benefits of cheap food for the long-range benefits of a sustainable food system. If we expect farmers to conserve resources without providing sufficient economic reward for doing so, we only shift an impossible burden onto

250

their shoulders. Farmers should not have the right to exploit land, but cannot resist the market forces that encourage them to do so without the support of the rest of us. The market alone should not determine the use of resources, and it alone should not determine the economic fate of farmers, either. Public funds must be committed to support conservation.

Third, even good farm policy cannot resist larger national policies that work against it. Agriculture in now integrated into the rest of the economy. Capital-intensive, world-market oriented, and dependent on manufactured inputs, agriculture is vulnerable to changes in major market conditions, and therefore to major macroeconomic changes in this country and in the world. That's why the notion that agriculture can compete in a free market is so impractical, and why people who think that the government ought to get out of agriculture are living in an ideological time capsule.

These caveats shouldn't be used as excuses to abandon farm policy. Instead, they should be recognized for what they imply: farm policy must be comprehensive, internally consistent, and relevant to the policy needs of the nation as a whole. An industrial nation with a well-developed agriculture cannot afford to be without a farm policy.

TOWARD UNCERTAIN ENDS

This is a pretty broad agenda for change. Some will say that family farming isn't worth all the fuss, that it is a transient institution that has outlived its usefulness, that going beyond the private interest of family farmers in order to save family farming is both illogical and irrelevant. The most cynical will say good riddance to small-scale agriculture.

In some ways, it might not matter. If we succeed in restoring economic opportunity in the farm economy but continue to economically disenfranchise other working Americans, we haven't gained much by way of economic democracy. If we improve the economic health of people who farm for a living and allow hunger to continue to grow, we are a less just society than before. If we save the soil and spoil the air, we will only be closer to extinction.

But what happens in agriculture *is* very important. Agriculture constitutes the last vestige of small-scale enterprise and widespread ownership of productive assets in our society. It offers our best and most important opportunity for environmental improvement, because we know how to produce food in far less destructive ways than we now do. And at the bottom of the farm crisis, with broken pieces of the farm economy laying at our collective feet, we have the chance to pick things up and rebuild the way we want—stronger, truer, and fairer. In agriculture we now have a good chance to do things right. We have choices.

Just as important as choosing the right course for rural America is the need to prove as a society that we can accept the responsibility of choosing. Of course, we can't always have what we choose, but we should know what we want and why, and we should work for it.

That burden is shared by all of us, but the weight is heaviest on rural Americans themselves who must be on the leading edge of any change in the direction of agriculture. Many of us who live in rural America don't really know what we want in agriculture, but we know we don't want industrial agribusiness. Where we are headed is almost universally disliked.

But many of us have given in to it as inevitable. We may resent it, but we accept it. Ultimately, we risk the greatest corruption of the human spirit—loving power because we cannot resist it.

Maybe there is a lesson in the literature of the urban industrial revolution. One of the best chroniclers of that era was Charles Dickens whose books and stories capture the full impact on the masses of a rapidly changing society. Most of us have either read his perennial favorite, *A Christmas Carol,* or seen it on television. Those who have read it appreciate the excruciatingly long passage in which the Spirit of Christmas-Yet-To-Come leads the terrorized Ebenezer Scrooge to a desolate graveyard. There, overgrown with weeds and littered with windswept debris, unattended and unremembered, stone-cold, and singularly unloved, is Scrooge's own marker. It is a monument to his miserable, petty, unredeemed life of commercial avarice.

But he is human, and as Scrooge sobs in regret over the vision before him, we sympathize with him and wonder if he can't do something to avoid this fate. Finally, he asks the Spirit the crucial question we have been agonizing over ourselves: "Before I draw nearer to that stone to which you point," said Scrooge, "answer me one question. Are these the shadows of the things that Will be, or are they shadows of the things that May be only? Men's courses will foreshadow certain ends, to which, if persevered in, they must lead," said Scrooge. "But, if the courses be departed from, the ends must change. Say it is thus with what you show me!" (Dickens 1983).

The Spirit does not answer, and in that void lies the magic of the story. We do not know if community spiritedness, generosity, and humility will have their reward. Nor do we know if the things we do will make a difference in our fate or for those who come after us. But we must live as though they do. That, ultimately, is the human condition.

That is also what compels us to care about how our food is produced, who produces it, and how the bounty is shared. The kind of agriculture we have is not a matter of fate. It is a matter of caring. Throughout rural America, people do still care. It is evident in the pioneer farming methods of Gary and Delores Young, in the firm commitment to conservation of John and Teresa Fleming, and in the deep sense of fairness that moved that farmer to defend the rights of farm workers to seek a better life in agriculture for themselves.

More and more farmers realize that there is no place for them in industrial agribusiness. The farm crisis has given us a glimpse of the future, and it is not pleasant for rural America. Scrooge, for his part, changed his life. We in rural America can, too.

What Can Be Done? Policy Choices

The main body of this book sets out a rationale for policies supporting family farming, without offering a package of political proposals. That is because what has been missing in American farm politics is not legislative initiatives, but clarity of purpose. Nonetheless, it is helpful to describe some ideas for reform, for those who might doubt that anything can be done about the industrialization of agriculture.

Public policy cannot do everything necessary to sustain family farming but it can help nourish it. What measures are possible?

It is appropriate to split the issue into two parts. The first addresses the immediate financial crisis that imperils many family farm operations. The second addresses the long-term issues of landownership and tenure, resource use, and the economic structure of agriculture. It is necessary to divide the issue this way to keep the different and sometimes competing objectives of both parts clear. The long term issues need especially to be considered in a deliberate, careful manner, something that crisis doesn't always encourage.

CRISIS POLICIES

We face two crises, one of danger and one of opportunity. The danger is that so many family farmers will be victimized that the farm economy will have lost forever its potential for being owner-operated. For thousands of family farmers, it is already too late.

254

The opportunity is there for those who can now acquire land at less prohibitive prices, or who can refinance their farming operations under more reasonable conditions once the burden of excessive debt is lifted. Such opportunities may seem slight for those struggling to salvage even a small portion of their farm.

The public policy dilemma is such that actions to save some may foreclose opportunity for others. In concrete terms, if land prices are buoyed intentionally to prevent further deterioration in the financial condition of farmers, people trying to buy their first piece of land to start farming, or trying to reenter farming may be denied that chance. On the other hand, if land prices fall to rock bottom, wealthy investors will probably snap up most of the bargains, because they have the resources and the flexibility to respond quickly to opportunity, and because they can frequently pay cash, without having to finance their investment by borrowing.

Intervention is justified for a number of reasons. First, as we have seen, the responsibility for these conditions is privately and publicly shared. If land prices in the 1970s rose to irrationally high levels in part because of careless public policy, then land price declines to irrationally low levels can be partly averted by careful public policies. Moreover, the deterioration of the farm economy is causing disorderly and in some cases unnecessary liquidation of farm assets. This is especially true of farm homesteads, which constitute the base of operations for a farm and are of limited financial value to anyone other than the incumbent farmer. Disorderly and unnecessary liquidation of farm assets also destabilizes rural communities by depriving them not only of a business base, but also by robbing them of their human capital. Some farms being dismantled are among the most efficient and could be restored with very modest measures.

The objectives of intervention should, indeed, be modest. The immediate objectives should be to arrest the financial deterioration, stabilize both lenders and viable farming operations, provide for an orderly liquidation of capital when necessary and for a sharing of losses among responsible parties—borrowers, lenders, and the public. Longer-term objectives should maximize opportunities for farmers to start over and for new farming operations to be established on a financially firm footing. The underlying purpose of these objectives, in other words, should be to avoid any further concentration in landownership as a result of the crisis and to position people to participate in an agricultural recovery.

It should be emphasized that the purpose of intervention is not to protect the property interests of the family, but to secure for them a chance to recover those interests. The cause is rebuilding family farms, not preserving them in the condition they were in at the peak of the boom.

In fashioning public intervention, the borrower, the lender, the federal government, and the state government each has a role. Unifying the interests of these participants must be the principle that *losses must be shared*. For the borrower, most of the losses have already occurred in the form of land devaluation. Additional losses, including giving up ownership of some land, are also likely. Lenders must be willing to restructure farm loans so that orderly repayment is possible for normally well-managed farms. Writing down the loan principal to the current value of the property is important. Lenders should also reduce interest rates, and the state and federal governments should offset part of that cost to the lender. These principles (except for the government interest offset) were embodied by Congress in the family farm bankruptcy code (frequently referred to as Chapter 12) passed in 1986. They should be more widely adopted as guiding principles for all farm debt negotiations, so that the expensive and agonizing process of bankruptcy can be avoided.

Lenders should also help reestablish liquidated farms by leasing land back to farmers who have turned it over to the lender to satisfy a debt, or to beginning farmers who have never had land. Lenders could also offer liquidating farmers a chance to match the highest bid on their land—termed the right of first refusal. If they are not willing to do so, state law should require it.

State government's primary role should be to overhaul long outdated debt-collection laws. Most of these laws were written by lenders and are designed only to protect their interest. They give borrowers few options in settling debts and once debt-collection procedures are set in motion, they are locked in step toward total liquidation of the farm. In many states, for example, a borrower declared by the creditor to be in default does not have the right to bring the loan current by paying only the amount overdue. Such a borrower is at the mercy of the lender. Other states offer a "right to cure default," but only with respect to land loans, not farm operating loans. This refusal to permit recovery is truly Gothic.

Another example of needed state debt-collection reforms involves a borrower's option to buy back a portion of the farm when faced with foreclosure of the entire farm. Under a buy-back option the borrower satisfies the debt by turning over only enough land or other assets to cover it, or by coming up with enough cash to refinance only that part of it he or she can afford. This right to partition the farm is particularly suitable to the current situation because many troubled farm loans were used to finance piecemeal expansion of farms that ought to be scaled down anyway. Fittingly, this strategy is referred to in legal vernacular as partial redemption, and is frequently described in popular terms as homestead protection because the portion redeemed by the borrower usually must include the farm home. This approach is also implicitly progressive, because the more modest the farm home (i.e., the lower its market value), the more likely that the borrower will be able to save it by refinancing. Partial redemption is an option that allows financially troubled farmers to salvage a home base from which to start over. It denies the lender nothing except the opportunity to profit by unnecessary liquidation. In 1986, state legislatures in Colorado, Iowa, Minnesota, and Nebraska adopted versions of this plan.

State legislatures can also change the environment in which debt collection negotiations take place. They can assure that such negotiations do take place at an early point in a deteriorating financial situation. Some states now require that creditors and debtors participate in mediation prior to foreclosure proceedings.

In all these cases, the lenders are not being asked to accept less than they are entitled to. They are only restrained from acting unilaterally to get it by wholesale liquidation of the farm.

Why should lenders be willing to make these concessions? In return, government actions can help stabilize them financially. The federal government can undertake a number of actions to soften the blow of the farm crisis on local banks. It can guarantee private bank loans when a bank refinances a borrower or leases back land to a liquidated or qualified beginning farmer. It can buy down interest rates by offering to pay up to half (or some lesser share) of an interest rate reduction offered the borrower.

The federally chartered farm credit banks are locally organized cooperatives that fund loans to farmers by selling bonds. Here, the government could infuse capital where necessary to encourage these institutions to make concessions to their borrowers. Of course, these institutions should also be permitted to discount their bonds, paying back less than they promised to the investors who bought them. The government could then guarantee investors that future bonds will receive a full payback. These investors should share in the system's losses as well as farmers, particularly since it was their bond buying that financed the lion's share of the speculative boom of the 1970s.

Perhaps most helpful, the federal government could purchase land and troubled loans from lenders at near market value. Farm credit banks have already been aided by such a mechanism (known as the Capital Corporation), providing them with a place to dump bad loans. The problem is that it operates like a liquidation agency only, without any policy with respect to the future of American agriculture. It simply makes it easier for farm credit banks to liquidate troubled loans, and it sells land acquired by foreclosure to the highest cash bidder.

It would be better for the federal government to offer to buy all lenders' inventory of farmland and to offer that land to reentry and beginning farmers under favorable loan arrangements—little down, moderate interest, long terms. This would get the federal financial relief to the lenders who need it the most (i.e., most relief would go to those who have had to acquire substantial amounts of land). It would also protect land values by making it possible for those who could not otherwise buy land to acquire the lender inventory land, removing it from the market.

The danger in all these measures is that their public purpose will be lost or confused. In most debt-relief measures now being seriously discussed, emphasis is on protecting lenders and those who provide them with funds. The farmer-borrower is secondary. Congressional promises to infuse capital into the farm credit banks, for example, have been made to assure wealthy bondholders that they will suffer no losses. But those promises have not been accompanied by any commitment to use those federal funds to strengthen the condition of farm borrowers. To the contrary, federal protection against financial collapse has only made the farm credit banks bolder in collecting debts.

Both federal and state programs to aid financially troubled farmers should be carefully targeted to small and modest-sized farmers. Public funds should be widely distributed and not used to prop up farms that have grown too big too fast by excessive borrowing. This means that if the government is to offset losses to lenders who reduce interest rates to farmers, limits must be placed on the amount of interest reduction to which any farmer is entitled.

In the final analysis, the most effective credit program would maximize the potential for farmers to refinance their farms under terms that make repayment feasible. But with farm income declining and capital costs of farming growing, some people are inclined to abandon the notion that individual owner-operators can ever reasonably afford to pay off farm mortgages. Instead, many experts are now saying that individual farmers can best retain control of a farming operation if they sell the land to silent partners whose investment is sufficient to finance the operation with a minimum of debt. The premise of such a plan is that long-run return on investment in land in the form of capital gain is sufficient to lure investors. In the bargain, they accept a rental payment that is less than the interest payment the farmer would have to make on a land loan. The arrangement assumes that high-income investors can take better advantage of tax breaks associated with farmland investment than can working farmers. In effect, farmers sell their tax breaks.

Such equity-financing proposals are controversial because they introduce the specter of large-scale, organized, absentee investment. One grand design offered by the Continental Illinois National Bank would have channeled pension funds into land purchases. Another group of investors proposed trading shares in their partnership to farmers in exchange for title to their land. The land would be leased back to the former owner. The group artfully named their plan Consolidated Family Farms.[1] In 1985, Forbes magazine championed the widespread use of equity financing in agriculture, suggesting the formation of landowning mutual funds (McGough 1985).

So far, such plans have not been widely implemented. Those that have reached the stage of practical operation have provoked alarm among family farm advocates, and after running into securities-law difficulties or state bans on corporate farming, each has been scuttled by their sponsors, at least temporarily.

Nonetheless, large-scale, equity-financing proposals surface regularly as promoters search for ways to make a bargain in the

1. Not to be confused with an identically named proposal that surfaced later to create a land trust among commercial farmers.

troubled farm economy and as farmers look for ways out of their financial problems.

As a crisis solution, equity-financing proposals are cloying because they represent the instant-miracle infusion of capital into a farm that is about to be lost to creditors anyway. They usually offer the golden promise of "buy-back"—letting the seller buy back the land sometime in the future. This presents the image of benign assistance to help the family farmer back on his financial feet. But when analyzed carefully, these provisions usually only reveal the plans for what they really are. For the terms of the repurchase are rarely such that the farmer has a reasonable chance of accomplishing the buy-back. Instead of a plan to save owner-operators, most equity-financing proposals portend a permanent radical change in land tenure that would convert owner-operators into managers-without-tenure of corporate farms.

The federal government could, however, offer a form of equity financing that might genuinely serve the emergency needs of agriculture. It could offer farmers what amounts to equity investments in their farms without taking title to the land. It could do so by making what are called shared appreciation loans.

Under a shared appreciation loan, the lender would accept a very low interest rate in return for a share of the increase in value of those assets that secure the loan (a share in the appreciation). Such loans are not usual, but are sometimes made where appreciation is rapid and where many buyers cannot afford conventional financing on such large amounts of principal, as, for example, in some urban housing markets. Commercial lenders won't make such loans, however, unless they are pretty certain of ample appreciation, something that cannot be assured in the current farm-land market. But in order to serve the public interest, the federal government could make shared appreciation loans to qualified farmers for up to ten years. The loans could be used to retire existing debt, according to a prearranged plan agreed to by farmers and their creditors that would maximize the potential for farms to repay their remaining debt to the private lenders. Over the life of the loan, the farmer would pay only a minimal annual interest payment —say, 5 percent—plus whatever else he or she would be able to pay on the principal. In the meantime, the government would earn a share of any appreciation in land values, in proportion to the contribution its loan would make to the farm's equity if it were an investment instead of a loan. At the end of the loan period, the farmer would be expected to repay the entire loan, plus the appreciation share, by conventional refinancing.

Such a program could be carefully targeted to people who actually live and work on the farm and get their main income from farming it. Loans would not be made for farms that are larger than typical farms in the area. A limit could be placed on the total asset value of a farm qualifying for these loans, as well as a lid on the amount of a loan.

The federal agency authorized to make these loans could be a publicly owned corporation chartered for this emergency purpose only and designed to go out of business when its loans are repaid. Although the initial capital would come from the U.S. Treasury, the corporation could raise additional capital by selling securities to private investors as well.

The corporation could also help redistribute land already held by lenders or government agencies. For example, it could offer beginning or reentry farmers a shared appreciation loan to make a large down payment on a farm. This would encourage lenders to sell land to its former owners or beginning farmers under manageable terms. The corporation could also directly acquire land held by lenders and lease that land to such farmers.

This crisis plan recognizes that many farms as currently constituted and financed cannot and should not be saved from reorganization. The issue is whether losses will be shared equitably and whether land will be redistributed to working farmers or allowed to accumulate in the hands of investors and well-established farmers.

Crisis intervention should not try to prop up the unrealistic financial expectations of the 1970s or spare either lenders or borrowers at the expense of the other. But it can help redeem agriculture from the '70s and rebuild family farms. Those are worthy and realistic goals.

POLICIES FOR THE FUTURE

Beyond the immediate crisis lies the larger problem of weaving a tapestry of public policies that could nourish family farming, care for natural resources, and provide food security. No single legislative solution is possible. Although simple, doctrinaire solutions have long been popular in American agriculture—higher prices, more exports, new uses for farm products—no miracle cure will remedy the decline of family farming and the diminution of natural resources. For those public values embedded in family farming to prevail, a consistent webbing of political reinforcement is needed in all areas of policy-making.

In simplest terms, the policy objectives must be:

— to encourage entry into farming
— to protect competition by limiting its excesses
— to redress inequities among farmers by favoring the have-nots
— to guide technology and land-use decisions to protect the future common good.

These objectives require a different kind of public involvement in agriculture than we have been comfortable with in the past. But they do not require as much public expenditure as we have recently made in farm programs, nor as much crisis intervention as we now face because food production has already become dominated by industrial organizations, methods, and values.

In some cases, all that needs to be done is to end farm policies that needlessly push agriculture toward industrial agribusiness. A great deal can be accomplished by simply abandoning certain tax, credit, and commodity policies.

If a public commitment is made, it is possible to have the kind of agriculture most of us want—dynamic, productive, efficient, economically fair, and environmentally sound. Specifically, five broad strategies for agricultural reform are needed if we are to accomplish these purposes.

End Subsidies to Capital

Because we believe that bigger is better and that machines do things more efficiently than people, we blindly promote capital investment as a farm development strategy. The consequence is irrational, debt-financed growth on the part of all farms, less efficiency due to the unwarranted substitution of capital for labor, and a transfer of income and wealth from the poorer to the richer. Further, subsidies to capital hasten the adoption of technologies that are unproven and have unintended and unwanted side effects. If there was a time when artificial government incentives were needed to encourage risk taking and capital formation in agriculture, that time has long since passed. It passed with the development of chronic excess capacity and a deteriorating agricultural environment.

These subsidies to capital come in many shapes and sizes. The most obvious are tax subsidies. The 1986 Tax Reform Act went a long way, though not far enough to correct the abuses outlined in Chapter 6. We still need to further reduce the tax incentives for the wealthy to invest in agriculture. We need to make both farmers and investors stretch out deductions for capital investments over their true useful life. And we need to limit the practice of allowing even family farm corporations to deduct salaries and benefits paid to major stockholders in order to reduce the overall tax liability of the owners.

Commodity programs that make benefits proportional to a farm's output and base them on prices received for particular commodities also subsidize capital. Encouraging excess investment, specialization, and overproduction of the favored commodities, such a policy places less heavily capitalized, diversified farms at a disadvantage (more on this later).

Another form of capital subsidy that cannot be justified is the federal investment in irrigation projects in the Western states. Making the desert bloom with crops in surplus is both expensive and wasteful. Many of these mistakes can't be undone, but no more should be made. No more pork-barrel water projects should bubble their way through Congress.

Similarly, credit offered by state and federal governments should not be used by larger operations to insure against the risk of investing in additional land, machinery, and technologies. It should be carefully limited to the purpose of helping farmers establish minimum-sized viable farming operations. In short, breaking down barriers to new farmers is a suitable use of public credit; encouraging farm expansion is not.

Any new farm program should also be evaluated on the basis of whether or not it subsidizes capital. If it does, it should be rejected unless it is clearly shown that more capital investments would improve the performance of agriculture, and that subsidies are the best way to encourage them. Such a standard would be hard to meet for the foreseeable future.

By the same token, policies that penalize self-employed farm labor should be eliminated. For example, farmers should be allowed to deduct all their health-insurance premiums from their taxable income, not just one-half, as is the case now. Businesses are allowed to fully deduct health-insurance premiums and employees in those businesses do not have to report those premiums as income. On the other hand, agribusinesses that hire labor should be required to provide that labor with the normal benefits required elsewhere in our society. Exempting agricultural employers from the requirement of providing workers' compensation and unemployment insurance is inexcusable. Such policies merely subsidize large-scale farm businesses that run on hired labor, treat agricultural workers unfairly and disadvantage family farmers who must insure themselves.

If subsidies to capital are removed, we can expect farming to become less specialized, more diversified, more evenly competitive, smaller in scale, and more resilient.

Manage Production

Current commodity programs work against themselves. They encourage production of crops in surplus and offer only anemic voluntary incentives to curtail production. Yet they allow free-riders who do not participate in the cutbacks to benefit from the higher prices that result. These programs further reward expansion because their benefits are tied to the volume of commodities a farm produces and to the amount of land in the farm. They help the biggest farms the most and protect unwise investments in land.

In addition, the regulatory regime governing the commodity programs is so riddled with contradictions and loopholes that it makes liars and cheaters out of ordinary people trying to beat the rules so they can produce more than the programs are designed to permit.

Commodity programs as we know them are ineffective because they have been misdirected to benefit *farms*. They should be replaced with a *farmer* program rewarding good farming practices and pegging benefits to the people who farm rather than to the commodities they produce. Such a program would allow commodity markets to do the one thing they do best—tell when too much or too little of something is being produced—while leaving more important matters such as conserving natural resources, protecting competition, and stabilizing the income of farmers to government regulation.

In such a program, the level of production needed to protect the public interest would be encouraged. There are at least two approaches to such a program. One would impose mandatory limits on the supply of products allowed to reach the market. The other would separate the benefits of farm programs from the market price for commodities so that only the needed level of production benefits from government action. Let's consider each approach in some detail.

Mandatory controls. Mandatory production controls have been widely promoted in recent years by grassroots farm groups, but they are not a new idea. In fact, they have been used for years in specialty crops such as tobacco and peanuts, and variations of mandatory controls have also been used in some of the staples, especially wheat.

One clear advantage of mandatory as compared to voluntary programs is that the limitations imposed on each farm—quotas—can be expressed in quantities of production (bushels of wheat, for example) rather than in numbers of acres that can be used to grow the crop. This is more effective for two reasons. First, it prevents farmers from complying with the program by removing their worst land from production while increasing production on their remaining acres by intensifying fertilizer use and other inputs. Quantity controls mean that farmers can actually reduce the inputs that are most economical to reduce, whether it is low-quality land, chemicals, or other expensive inputs. In many cases, the farmer will choose to keep land in production, since it is a fixed cost that has to be paid whether it's used or not, and reduce the use of other inputs. Second, quantity controls lessen enforcement problems: instead of monitoring actual production, controls can be enforced by issuing certificates authorizing farmers to sell no more than their quota. They can produce more, but without the certificate, they can't sell it.

There are both practical and ideological difficulties with this kind of public intervention in the farm economy. Its purpose can easily be reduced to a single objective: to raise commodity prices by restricting food supply. This means that the cost of farm programs ultimately shifts from the taxpayer to the consumer in the form of higher food prices. Implicitly, this kind of supply management imposes a sales tax on food. The one-fifth of our population with the lowest income will pay even more than the 39 percent of their income they now spend on food (Blaylock and Smallwood 1986). Such a program raises serious social-justice issues.

Mandatory production controls raise important issues within agriculture as well. How comprehensive should the controls be? Usually, they are imposed only on a single crop and at the discretion of the producers of that crop. In other words, they are legalized collusion to raise prices by limiting output of particular commodities. Those producers may be asked nothing in return and are free to divert the land and other resources withheld from production of the controlled crop into the production of any other crops, worsening the oversupply of those crops.

The problem is particularly vexing with respect to livestock. Mandatory controls on crops that can be used to feed animals can have serious adverse affects on livestock producers because it raises their feed costs. If livestock feeders reduce their own production in response to higher feed costs, the price of their products will rise as well, but those who supply them with feeder cattle and feeder pigs will suffer lower demand—and lower prices for their products. There is therefore substantial resistance from nearly all livestock-producer groups to mandatory controls on feed grains. This problem has become particularly severe as large-scale animal factories have increased their domination of meat production. For them, cheap corn is a blessing because they purchase nearly all their feed, and the thought of controlling its production is almost as chilling as the thought of regulating their own.

But by far the largest problem with mandatory controls is how to decide who gets to produce how much. This is ticklish because it confronts the love/hate affair American farmers have with the market. The very demand for quotas and mandatory controls means rejecting the market as determiner of the fate of farmers. It was the market, after all, that generated the overproduction and low prices by inducing technological change and encouraging expansion. It is the market that must be tamed by government intervention to control production, raise prices, and improve farm income.

But the market has also generated a heavy concentration in landownership and production. In controlling production by quotas, should the government ignore those market-induced inequities or counter them by reallocating land and production rights? Specifically, should everyone be required to cut back production in proportion to their previous output, or should cutbacks be allocated by some formula that takes into account other factors as well and, in effect, redistributes production rights?

If quotas were set according to the amount an individual had produced just before the controls were imposed, the quota system would simply lock in place the inequalities of the market, rewarding those who had expanded the most, or who had contributed most to overproduction. Furthermore, if only the main field crops (corn, soybeans, cotton, and wheat) are included in mandatory controls, quotas based on previous production of those crops would be particularly rewarding to those who contributed most to their oversupply. Farmers who practiced good conservation, rotated those crops with hay and small grains, and refrained from converting potentially erosive land into cropland would be penalized. They would have a history of low production of the controlled crops and therefore, a proportionately low quota.

In fact, the feed-grain quota on many diversified farms might not be high enough to support the level of livestock production they have traditionally maintained in order to make full use of their pasture and range land. They would be especially disadvantaged.

On the other hand, the exploiters who long ago either rid their own farms of livestock or purchased other land in order to convert pasture into row crops would have a bloated production record for controlled crops that would be rewarded with a proportionally bloated quota. Those who contributed most to the problem would be rewarded most by the solution.

A closely related issue is whether the quota could be sold by one farmer to another. Who would own it? If the quota could be transferred for a price, it would really represent a negotiable right to farm, and the benefits of the quota would ultimately be reflected in its purchase price. This problem would be further complicated if the quota were attached to a specific piece of land and could be transferred with the land. The value of the quota would then also be reflected in the land price. If the quota had a price—either directly or indirectly woven into land prices—it would represent an opportunity to farm that would be allocated among farmers or would-be farmers on the basis of ability to pay. The market would still determine who could farm, not by forcing people out of farming through competition and low commodity prices, but by placing the right to farm (and to benefit from the higher commodity prices resulting from production cutbacks) on a bid basis that would exclude those with limited resources. Consumers would pay more for food, not to save family farming, but to sanction a closed farming system.

Such a system now exists in tobacco production. The federal government allots acreage and distributes a marketing quota among people who produce tobacco. To be eligible, a farm has to have a tobacco production history that dates to the time when allotments and quotas were first issued in the 1930s. If you own such a quota or allotment, you cannot sell it outright, but you can transfer it when you sell or bequeath the land. Or you can lease it to another farmer who in effect pays you for the right to raise tobacco.

The General Accounting Office reviewed the ownership and use of these production rights in major tobacco-producing counties in 1982, nearly fifty years after they were first issued. It found that most owners rent or lease their quota to others, and that two-thirds of the tobacco is actually produced under such arrangements. In fact, only 26 percent of the quota owners actually grow tobacco, and only 40 percent farm at all. The typical cost of a leased or rented tobacco quota is from 25 to 90 cents per pound of tobacco covered by the quota. The benefit of the quota is also reflected in the value of land on farms that raise tobacco, even though not all the land in the farm is covered by the quota. The GAO cited evidence from academic studies indicating that in the case of burley tobacco, the value of a farm increases $3.50 for every pound in the quota. And another study cited by the investigating agency indicated that in one county, cropland with a tobacco quota increased nearly twice as fast as other land during the land boom period of 1974–80 (General Accounting Office 1982).

There are two kinds of winners in a quota program in which the quota or the land to which it is attached can be rented or sold. Those family farmers who rent or sell their quota (or their quota-enriched land) may well be able to sell their farm for more than they might otherwise be able to get. Of course, with higher commodity prices, they might not sell out, preferring to keep the land in family hands long after any family members still want to farm. They become wealthier, not because they farm, but because they own land and a quota. Secondly, those who are financially strong enough to buy quotas can use machinery more fully on an enlarged land base. They gain by operating on a much more profitable basis than they would with lower commodity prices. In neither case has the cause of family farming been advanced.

To the extent that a mandatory production-control system ties quotas to the market—the market for commodities, land, or for the quota itself—it will reinforce the inequities produced by the market that led to the need for the quotas in the first place. If commodity prices are protected by a quota, but the use of the technology is not restrained and the quota is transferable, both the quota and eventually the land will end up in the hands of those financially equipped to buy both in order to use the technology profitably. The higher commodity and land prices that result may mean the preservation of family finances for those farmers who choose to sell out or who choose (perhaps in later generations) to become landlords, but it does not mean the preservation of family farming. This is an inescapable dilemma that some proponents of mandatory controls would rather not address.

Quotas do not have to be allocated in such a way, however. The alternative is to allocate nontransferable quotas covering all major commodities. The economic needs of the farm and the conservation requirements of the land would determine the size of the quota. Farmers with a small production history for whom maintaining production would be essential to providing a minimum family income or who did not expand production during the boom period could produce their accustomed volume or even more. Others could bear the burden of reductions. When a farmer quit farming or for any reason gave up a quota, it would return to a pool for reallocation to beginning farmers or to those whose quotas were too small to support a viable farm.

Quotas would only reflect the volume of production possible from the land in a farm if it were used in accordance with good conservation practices, no matter how it had been used in the past. And no quota would be assigned to a farmer to produce crops on land not ecologically suited to crop production. Mandatory production controls should never validate bad conservation practices. Mandatory conservation is part of the price farmers should be willing to pay for mandatory controls.

The problem is that this is social and economic planning of the first order, requiring us to think explicitly about allocating shared economic opportunities on the basis of socially approved behavior and economic need. It is doubtful if contemporary America is willing to make the ideological shift to such a program. Nonetheless, halfway quota measures that duck these issues and only protect vested production interests while denying any need to redress the inequities in the market place are wrong.

Separating Income Support from Market Structure. The second means of managing production in the public interest involves separating government farm support from the price structure of commodities. This approach would still use a quota system, but without mandatory production or marketing controls. Instead, the federal government would secure the nation's food supply by requesting each farmer to supply a share—a quota—of the crops needed by the nation, guaranteeing a minimum income for that volume only. Any farmer could still, with no guaranteed price or market, produce as much as he or she chose.

The market could do what it does best—send signals when too much (or too little) of a commodity is being produced, too much (or too little) has been invested, and too much (or too little) is being spent on inputs to produce it. Freed from this function, public policy could better address issues involving both equity and efficiency.

Such an approach has been suggested by the Center for Rural Affairs (1985). The proposal received little attention in 1985 as the farm bill debate centered on ideological differences between the Reagan administration's free-market doctrine and the demands of grass-roots farm groups for higher prices through mandatory production controls.

Under this proposal, the amount needed for the nation's food supply would be calculated by adding 1) domestic consumption of major crops, 2) a reserve in case of crop failure in subsequent years, 3) food aid, and 4) farm export commitments solidified by written agreements with the purchasing nation. This total would be adjusted for any surplus in storage from previous years' production. Farmers wishing to participate in producing this total would receive a quota. For that amount only, companies buying commodities from farmers would be required to pay a premium in addition to the regular market price. The premium would vary by region and would be based on the full cost of production on an average farm—including the farmer's labor and management. Later, the government would reimburse the purchaser for the premium. In essence, the government would be offering a premium for that portion of a farmer's productive capacity needed by the nation.

Farmers could produce as much or as little as they wanted. For each farmer, however, production beyond the quota would be rewarded by the market price only—no premium. Anyone who produced more than their share of what was needed would be in the hands of the market for the surplus amount. Since no farm would receive a quota covering its full production capacity, any farm that produced as much as it could would receive no more than the market price for at least some of that output. In that way, no one would have any incentive to contribute to overproduction.

Quotas would be allocated among farmers on the basis of their economic needs and the conservation requirements of their farms, and premiums would be calculated in a way that would not encourage overproduction of crops already in surplus. Since much of our current production is on marginal land that should not be farmed for conservation reasons, a farm's production history alone would not determine its quota. Instead, a farm's agronomic potential for producing the crops covered by the farm program using best conservation practices would determine the quota. Quotas would not be issued and premiums would not be paid for any crops produced on farms abusing the land.

This is not a sharp departure from current policy. The 1985 farm bill contains a provision prohibiting farm-program benefits to any farmer who fails to implement a conservation plan for the farm, but the provision does not become effective until 1990.

A farm's quota would further reward conservation by counting good cropland converted to noncrop uses such as hay, pasture, and trees as if it were still in crop production. Farmers who converted land to these conserving uses would therefore not be penalized with a lower quota. Further, farmers who used good conservation practices on land that was suitable for farming but needed special care to prevent erosion would be rewarded with an additional conservation premium.

To take into account varying economic needs, farms would receive a quota for a proportionately smaller share of their capacity as their capacity increased. Very large farms would therefore receive a quota covering a smaller portion of their production than would small farms. How much the farm family depends on farm income would also be considered. Small farms that are only a hobby for the owner would receive a smaller quota than similar farms in which the family depended on the farm for its living.

Two key features of this proposal prevent it from working against itself to encourage overproduction of particular commodities. First, quotas are issued for the aggregate production of all crops produced on a farm, not for each crop separately. Second, premiums are paid on the basis of the difference between the average price received for all crops and the average cost of producing all crops.

This requires converting each commodity from its traditional measurement unit—bushels, bales, and pounds—into "standard production units" so that all commodities can be blended together to determine their average cost and average market price. A standard production unit of any crop is the amount of that crop that can be produced using the same economic resources necessary to produce one unit of a base commodity, say corn. If it takes $3.00 in economic resources to produce a bushel of corn, and $1.50 in resources to produce a bushel of oats, then there are two bushels of oats in a standard production unit (or, if you prefer, a bushel of oats is equal to half a standard production unit).

Shifting to standard production units allows the program to accomplish important objectives. Farmers would be free to fill their quotas with whatever crop or crops they want to produce. All farmers would get the same premium—the difference between average cost and average price of all crops—for each standard production unit in their quota, regardless of the actual market price for the particular crop or crops produced. If they produced a crop that was in relative surplus and therefore had a comparatively lower market price than other crops, they would receive the same premium for each standard production unit as other farmers who produced a crop in relative shortage and therefore received a comparatively higher market price. The farmer who shifted to the crop in relative shortage would be better off than the one who did not. In this way, the premium would not interfere with the market's message to reduce production of some crops relative to others. By contrast, current farm programs guarantee a price for each commodity, no matter how low its market price falls. This only ensures that the greater the overproduction of that crop, the larger the payment to the farmer.

There are some weaknesses to this alternative approach. First, nothing prevents aggregate overproduction other than the aggregate decline in prices that would result. The program therefore doesn't fully correct the inadequacies of markets. It does moderate their adverse effects on most farmers, however. But its greatest weakness is political. Its complex and sure-to-be-controversial formula for allocating farm-program benefits among commodities runs squarely against the interests of powerful commodity groups.

But its strengths are significant. The government does not tell the farmer what to produce and does not expose itself to greater expenditures by encouraging excess production. The system's built-in regulators control its costs. In the first place, the more overproduction of a crop, the worse off its producers will be compared to their neighbors who produce crops in relative shortage. Moreover, the greater the overproduction of crops, the lower the government expenditures in subsequent years, because the amount carried over in storage will reduce the total volume of crops needed in those years, lowering the quota to be distributed to farms. Benefits of the program can be carefully targeted to family farmers according to their conservation practices and economic needs. And commodity policy can be reconciled with trade policy through international trade agreements which determine the extent of federal commitment to producers of export crops.

Intervene in the Land Market

A number of measures are needed to prevent further land concentration and to enable those who know how to farm to acquire land on the basis of their ability to use it well.

Today, we have a splendid opportunity to make land widely available to those who are willing and able to use it. We could begin with the inventory of land now in the hands of federal agencies and other lenders, and the substantial volume of land poised to be placed on the market. That land could be sold or leased on favorable terms to newly established farmers—including those starting over after having lost farms. Low down payments, long-term repayment schedules, and variable interest rates pegged to changes in farm income would be the keys to successful loans to buy this land. Shared appreciation loans, a short-term emergency measure in the case of financially troubled farms, could become a permanent feature of farm-credit programs for a limited number of borrowers qualified by their skills but financially unable to buy their first farm. In addition, the traditional interest-subsidized loan programs of the federal government should be revived and carefully directed to farmers who need help getting started.

But helping farmers with scarce resources acquire farmland is only one part of what must be done. The government must intervene in the land market in more direct and forceful ways to discourage accumulation of property. In warning the new American republic against the unequal distribution of land that had brought France to the brink of revolution, Thomas Jefferson argued that "the consequences of this enormous inequality producing so much misery to the bulk of mankind, legislators cannot invent too many devices for subdividing property" (Padover 1939). That was good advice then, and it is good advice now.

Jefferson proposed a progressive property tax to discourage land concentration. A progressive property tax would increase the rate of taxation on farmland as the amount owned increased. This would be a state government policy. As of 1987, only Minnesota has a progressive property tax, and a modest one at that.

Though inventive ways can be found to mask large individual holdings by artificially subdividing them to avoid the higher rates, equally inventive ways can be found to prevent such tactics. Who would have thought a century ago that a federal income tax could be effectively administered? And certainly not every tax evasion is caught. But the tax collectors are effective, and today, no one seriously suggests that income tax be abandoned owing to administrative difficulty. In matters of taxation, where there is a will, there is a way.

Taxes on inherited wealth are another effective tool for preventing land concentration and restoring family farming. If one generation can pass on a substantial farmland holding free of taxes, the next generation will use that financial head start to outbid less fortunate but equally skilled neighbors for farmland. As discussed in Chapter 3, the object of taxing inherited wealth is not to deprive the child of a stake from the family farm, but to require that child to earn the larger share of the farm by farming it. The skills, dedication, and values that earned the farm for the parents are, in many cases, the child's most valuable inheritance.

The best way to tax inherited wealth is to impose taxes at the time the land is transferred to the next generation. Public loan funds could be made available to the heir, if necessary, to make the tax payments at affordable terms. To further owner-operatorship, heirs who do not farm should be taxed more heavily than those who do.

There are three policy tools in this area—federal estate taxes, state inheritance taxes, and the income tax on capital gain.

The federal estate tax is levied against the estate before it is distributed to the heirs. While the tax rate is substantial, a considerable amount of property can be exempted from it. Each spouse can pass on up to $600,000 in property to heirs without taxation. In addition, prior to death, each spouse can give up to $10,000 per year to each heir without suffering a tax. For farm estates there is a further estate tax break. Land in the farm is valued for estate tax purposes at its agricultural use value, not the higher value it might have for residential or commercial development. Taken together, these exemptions allow a well-planned estate potentially worth millions of dollars to be passed on tax-free from one generation to the next.

As a result, the estate tax is meaningless on most farm estates. Moreover, since the estate tax is levied on the estate, not the heirs, it is regressive in its effect on competition in the land market. The fewer the number of heirs and the greater the value of the estate per heir, the less the impact of the tax on the heirs' ability to leverage additional land purchases from the estate. A lower exemption could make the tax on large farm estates meaningful. At the same time, it would be good to upgrade the generally mild inheritance taxes imposed by states on heirs. If the inheritance tax were made progressive by the states so that larger inheritances were taxed at a higher rate, the competition would be leveled among heirs of greater and lesser fortune.

The Internal Revenue Service now generally turns its head the other way when heirs inherit substantial farmland assets. It taxes no one for the capital gain realized through land price appreciation since the land's purchase. When the original buyer dies, those capital gains (adjusted for inflation) should be taxed as regular income to the estate. That alone would significantly reduce the level of unearned income from land speculation passed on from one generation to another.

A reminder is in order here. Making every generation of farmers pay for the land can only be realized if it is possible to pay for land by farming it. Land must be within the purchasing power of people who produce food from it. The objective of these policies is therefore both to place more land on the market implicitly by requiring heirs to refinance the land they inherit, and to level the competition among heirs and others by mitigating the advantage some gain by being born with a silver spoon in their mouths. With these tax strategies, land prices would be lower than if advantaged heirs could use their inheritance to leverage additional land purchases. If land prices were still too high in relation to commodity prices, additional measures would be needed to lower land prices further or to raise commodity prices. Estate taxes coupled with farm programs should make it harder to inherit but easier to earn a farm.

The states can also intervene in the land market by outlawing the use of some business organizational forms that give nonfarm investors an unfair advantage over working farmers. Most major midwestern farm states restrict the use of corporations and limited partnerships in farming. The corporation—a form of business sanctioned by state law—provides certain privileges to those who use it, and limiting the use of those privileges is essential to the revitalization of family farming.

In a corporation, the owners are protected from full liability for losses incurred by the corporation, and they enjoy tax advantages. Because risk in agriculture is great and because tax-motivated investments constitute unfair competition for working farmers, these states have simply written laws that restrict the use of corporations in agriculture. Nonfarm individuals who might want to buy farmland still can, but they must accept full risk, without corporate tax breaks. That's enough to discourage many nonfarm investors.

In the final analysis, however, new forms of land tenure, rather than policy incentives and disincentives, may provide the real future for family farms. Ideas once considered radical, like land trusts, land banks, and even forms of public ownership, are now openly discussed among practical people concerned about commercial agriculture. All try to respond to the fundamental dilemma: As farmland value increases relative to the purchasing power of commodities, the farmer cannot pay the cost of owning farmland from the income it generates. Rather than fight the rising disparity between land and commodity prices, and rather than succumb to the easy alternative—corporate ownership—these proposals offer individual opportunity to farm by providing farmers with long-term leases to land owned by communal or public entities. In such proposals, the fundamental character of family farm agriculture—owner-operatorship—is preserved, but what the farmer owns is not the land, but the long-term right to use it.

These proposals are not unlike, in principle, the equity financing proposals discussed earlier in this chapter, except that they substitute public objectives for private ones, and provide real security for the farm operator.

Some of these approaches are quite old, a few are tried. Most do not meet with much success if measured on the scale of national landownership trends. Some that border on the conventional—that is, that preserve the greatest degree of private ownership—have been incorporated into state law. For example, in some urban states, legislatures have authorized the state to take what amounts to an ownership interest in farmland by purchasing the right to develop the land from the owner. The owner gets the cash, pays lower property taxes because he or she no longer owns all the rights to the land, and keeps the land as a farm base. The purpose is to preserve farmland by preventing nonfarmers from buying it for condominiums, parking lots, and hotels. A half dozen or so eastern states concerned with haphazard development and loss of open space have adopted such programs in recent years. Obviously, this minitrend, next to nonexistent in farm country, does not constitute a national movement toward public ownership of land. But it reflects a growing public awareness that some forms of group ownership, other than corporate, are needed to preserve farming on a family scale.

Such awareness is reaching farm country as well. It's no longer taboo to talk about forms of public ownership of prime agricultural land. Ronald L. Hullinger, a professor of veterinary medicine at Purdue University and a native Iowan, recently got editorial space in *Agri Finance*, an established farm trade journal, to argue for a national farmland trust. Under such a system, the federal government would buy farmland and provide life-time leases to qualified, licensed farmers. When the farmer stopped farming, the lease would be returned to the trust or passed on to an heir if the heir planned to farm. The plan would "help keep non-farmers from dominating agriculture by manipulating and exchanging land for profit," and make it a "bit easier for young people to enter farming." Significantly, Hullinger argued that while farmers would continue to have the right to buy land, the national land trust would be designed to "remove any incentive to do so" (Hullinger 1986). This proposal comes from a midwestern scientist at perhaps the most conservative agricultural institution in the nation writing for the readers of a publication that is a bastion of the conservative farm press.

A less radical, but perhaps more complex proposal would involve public investments in individually owned farms. The investment could be made in return for a variety of payoffs. The government could purchase the right to determine certain land uses on a farm, not only to prevent conversion of farmland to nonfarm uses, but to require conservation practices by the owner or to prohibit erosive crops. This would amount to a mild extension of current conservation programs of the USDA that provide cost-sharing investments in certain conservation features, such as terraces. If current programs required landowners who benefited from cost-sharing to sign a covenant that bound them and future landowners to maintain the terraces or repay the cost-sharing plus interest, the same purpose would be accomplished.

A public entity could also purchase outright equity shares in individual farms. For this, a new legal form of land title might be needed to record the public equity interest in the farm. Public equity shares could be paid an annual dividend by the farmer based on the actual income-earning potential of the land under current commodity prices and input costs, and could also be paid "in-kind" with mandatory conservation and other favorable management practices. By carefully describing the kinds of farms eligible for public equity investments—beginning farms, diversified crop and livestock farms, organic farms—and by maintaining some public control over who would be an eligible purchaser of the land, the equity financing could both reward good farming practices and create economic opportunities.

We can expect many other forms of alternative landownership to emerge in the years ahead—public, private, and community. Whether these forms contribute to the decline of family farming and the solidification of industrial agribusiness depends on the forces and values that shape them. If the natural forces of commerce are allowed to work their will, some form of corporate ownership will most likely dominate. Perhaps it will be some exotic variety of pooled equity financing, such as that made available by pension funds, in which the ownership interest in a large-scale farmland venture will be widely spread and diluted. The result will be centralized decision making emphasizing capital-intensive operations conducted uniformly on a large scale, using hired labor or tenants without job security. In a word, the full flowering of industrial agribusiness. With it will come the inefficiency, instability, and vulnerability to ecological mistakes described in this book.

If, on the other hand, public values firmly rooted in the spirit of individual opportunity and responsibility infuse the emerging forms of landownership, the alternative will be independent farmers farming for profit, secure in the right to use the land, in return for which they will be required to use it well and constrained from irrational expansion and land speculation. The result will be widespread individual ownership of farming operations, dispersed management by owner-operators, and a diversity of farms operated to maximize return to labor and management on a limited land base. With it will come effective protection of the public interest in soil and water conservation, efficient use of resources by enterprising producers, and rural stability.

Regulate Competition in Input Industries and Commodity Markets

The consolidation and merger taking place in most U.S. industries is reducing competition, which affects farmers both as consumers of products sold by noncompetitive industries and as producers of products sold to noncompetitive industries. It gives some firms with which farmers do business market power—the ability to dictate price, delivery date, premiums or discounts for products of variable quality and for larger or smaller orders, and minimum purchase amounts. The result, as the old adage goes, is that "farmers buy retail and sell wholesale, and pay the freight both ways."

Part of the problem is agriculture's spatial dimensions. It is difficult to maintain diverse distribution and purchasing units for farmers to do business with in every local community. In most market towns in the Midwest, there is no more than one grain elevator, and fewer than three packing-house buyers regularly bid at most local livestock auctions. The distances and shipping costs required to market effectively beyond these limits is prohibitive for most farmers. What might be gained in a fairer price is lost in the cost of a longer haul.

By the same token, though local seed, fertilizer, and chemical dealers may be plentiful, the number of companies they represent is not. Moreover, mergers between the chemical and seed companies in particular raise warning flags about the future competitiveness of those sectors. And in machinery, both the number of local dealers and the number of competing brand names in major product lines is sharply reduced.

Market forces. The market power of large agribusiness companies is attributable to two factors. First, because there are so few, there is little competition among them. With less competition, they are relatively immune from the discipline of the free market. Be-

yond this market concentration, these companies have another
potential advantage. Their sheer size and financial might permits
input suppliers and processors to compete with farmers in the actual production of food, even if they are less efficient than farmers. The reason is simple. They have the advantage of providing
their own inputs and securing their own markets under favorable
terms. In fact, because they are engaged in more than one stage of
production and processing of a product—called vertical integration—firms with market power at one of those stages can dominate competition in another stage.

Some of the best examples are in livestock production. Grain
and feed companies have been involved in both production and
marketing, first integrating broiler chicken production (before
losing control of that industry to other corporations) and more recently buying cattle feedlots and, in several cases, even meat processing facilities. These companies gain an additional market for
their grain and feed products. From the other end of the food
chain, meat packing houses have long engaged in the feeding of
cattle and hogs. They don't want to feed a lot of their own cattle
and hogs—just enough to be able to reduce their purchases from
farmers when cattle and hog prices are high. This depresses the
market price. In recent years, packer feeding of cattle has fluctuated between 5 and 8 percent, though in some states such as
Washington, where nearly 30 percent of the cattle were fed by
packers in 1977, it is much higher (U.S. Department of Agriculture 1979a).

Packers can also act as agents for wealthy investors who hire the
packing house to buy, feed, and sell cattle for them on a contract
basis. The packing house thus gains control over the marketing
decisions for large herds without actually investing a penny in the
animals themselves. A federal prohibition against this practice was
lifted in 1982.

The impact of market power. Agricultural economists have concluded that these market forces are a significant factor in American agriculture. The level of concentration is quite high in meat
packing, especially in local markets, which given the cost of trans-
porting live animals, is all that counts to the farmer. In the seven
leading cattle-feeding states that together produce about three-
fourths of the cattle, the top packing house accounted for over one-
fifth of the cattle buying in 1977, the top four, nearly three-fifths
(U.S. Department of Agriculture 1979a). Just a few years later, the

280

USDA reported that the top buyer of cattle alone in the two major cattle-feeding regions of the country purchased from a quarter to a third of the cattle (Anthan 1982). The situation is no better with hogs. In the fourteen leading hog-producing states that produce three-fourths of the pork, the top packer bought almost one-third of the hogs in 1977; the top four packers took over three-fourths (U.S. Department of Agriculture 1979a).

The impact of such concentration is severe. A study at the University of Wisconsin concluded that for every 10 percent increase in the market share held by the top four packers, prices will be depressed $.10 per hundredweight of cattle. At that rate, the increase in packer concentration that occurred during 1971 to 1980 lowered market prices an average of $.19 for every hundred pounds of beef marketed—about $2.00 per animal. This would have cost farmers $45.2 million in 1980 alone (Quail et al. 1986). In hogs, one study estimated losses to hog producers of as much as $140 million in 1978 due to concentration among hog buyers (Miller and Harris n.d.).

In local markets, the situation can be much worse. The Wisconsin study found that when the largest meat packer of all—IBP—was in the market, the price fell by $.44 per hundredweight or close to $5.00 per animal. For a medium-sized farmer-feeder, the loss could be as high as $25,000 per year, the difference between a decent living and poverty.

A similar effect results from vertical integration. A study by the federal government found that packer involvement in cattle feeding had the effect of reducing prices paid to farmers at local markets by $.25 to $.50 per hundredweight. Significantly, this decline was not simply attributable to the fact that there were more cattle on the market as the result of the packer feeding operation. The study found that a given quantity of cattle shipped to the market from a packer's feedlots caused prices to drop ten times as much as a similar increase in cattle from other feedlots (Aspelin and Engelman 1966). The packer was obviously using its own cattle marketing as a strategy to reduce prices it paid to cattle feeders. With such a strategy in place, it doesn't take many cattle under the packer's control to have a significant impact on the market.

The most advanced case of vertical integration is the poultry industry, where both broiler and egg production are controlled by a handful of processing companies that contract with individual "farmers" (to the extent that the word "farmer" implies independent decision-making, these producers aren't farmers at all). The companies supply the birds, the feed, and the management scheme. The farmers own the buildings and are paid on a piece rate at levels that don't cover their labor costs, let alone a return on investment. Poultry integration has been known for a generation as a form of peonage on the farm.

Market power hurts smaller farms most. This imbalance of power between farmers and agribusiness companies is not equally disadvantageous for all farmers. The smaller the farmer, the more these disadvantages sting. The Wisconsin study mentioned above showed that cattle prices were most depressed where the primary cattle feeders were small farmer-feeders. Larger feeders have more power, and may get buyers to send representatives directly to the farm to line up purchases. They deal directly, without going through local markets. The meager output of the smaller operator doesn't carry much weight, no matter what the quality of his or her cattle. By the same token, seed companies frequently give discounts to farmers who buy large volumes of seed, and even make the large farmers their local dealers, giving them a price break on their seed in return for peddling it to neighbors. Larger farmers find this strategy inviting, since a significant portion of their sales requirement can be met with the seed they buy themselves. Smaller operators don't have that kind of muscle. In a hundred ways, the advantages of size are reflected in unfair terms of trade that disadvantage smaller farms.

Alternatives to market power. None of these problems is new in agriculture. They are as old as farm protests. There have been several responses, some of which have public policy implications we can only briefly review here.

One of the earliest and most effective responses among farmers was the cooperative movement. Farmers banded together to produce and sell to members such products as seed, fertilizer, chemicals, fuel, and other basic inputs, including the most basic input—credit. To a lesser degree, cooperatives have also been formed to market farm products, especially milk and, minimally, grain.

Unfortunately, too many of these farmer cooperatives have either been ineffective or have lost sight of their mission. Those that have done well seem to have internalized the management strategies of the corporate world, using their gains to expand rather than to pay dividends to their member-owners. Over the years, the result has been superpower farmer cooperatives that are listed among the Fortune 500. They treat their members like customers and charge the going price for their services. Some advocate that cooperatives behave more like corporations. They urge cooperatives to recruit large farms as members by charging them less than others for services, to abandon the one-member, one-vote cooperative principal in favor of giving more votes to members who do more business with the cooperative, and even to close membership to others. Perhaps it is true that we tend to become like what we hate too much.

Public policy can help reform the farmer-cooperative movement in a number of ways. Most important, measures that restore the integrity of the guiding principle of cooperatives—one member, one vote, regardless of number of shares—need to be enacted, as do steps to reduce the power and influence of management. Less emphasis should be placed on accumulating earnings and expanding, and more on reducing costs and returning dividends to members. By the same token, public policy can favor cooperatives in their competition with agribusiness corporations. Grain and milk products used as foreign food aid could be purchased by the government from farmer-owned cooperatives only, and foreign trade agreements could give federally funded discounts to nations who buy from farmer-owned cooperatives.

A closely related response to the cooperative movement has been the collective-bargaining movement. Probably no strategy has more ardent supporters than collective bargaining. The National Farmers Organization is the true pioneer of this movement and has persisted against all manner of discouragement to prove that farmers can achieve higher market prices by marketing their products together at a negotiated price, withholding products from the market, if necessary, to get that price. But they have repeatedly faced the paradox of success. As soon as NFO bargaining boosts prices a little, too many farmers abandon the strategy and sell enough to break the market back down. These free-riders exhibit the meanest characteristics of a market economy: a willingness to place immediate self-interest above the long-term interest of the group. However, little needs to be done to protect farmers in their right to bargain collectively. Federal laws in place for sixty years have given them the protection they need.

In recent years, the explosion of new information technologies has brightened the prospect that farmers might buy and sell in their homes using computers hooked into electronic markets. Various electronic marketing schemes have been proposed in the past twenty-five years and some have been tried, with particular success in livestock marketing. In principle, the purpose is to level the playing field between buyers and sellers and among buyers. Electronic markets do this by eliminating the need for buyers and sellers to be physically present at the same time and place, and by assuring that everyone has the same information at the same time. The more successful electronic markets are the ones organized and run by farmers' own marketing associations. These associations can pool members' livestock and offer them for sale electronically, using an inverted bidding system that starts at a high price and works down every few seconds until a buyer "pushes the button" on the computer, indicating he'll buy at that price. Since no one can offer a higher bid after that, the buyers are in the position of having to confirm a sale at as high a price as they can tolerate or risk losing the sale to a more eager buyer. The farmer has the further advantage of being able to sell the product without moving it from the farm, making the option of refusing to sell at today's price a far more reasonable one. This system has been most successfully used to market hogs in Canada and has been discussed for use in cattle marketing in this country (Johnson 1972).

Electronic markets have some potential to counterbalance market power in many areas other than livestock. However, like all technologies, these systems depend on the human institutions that surround them. Unless farmers can pool their product in seller associations, the system will probably be too costly for individuals to use. Without standards that allow the buyer to bid confidently on a product without being able to visually inspect it, the risk of getting poor quality will be reflected in lower prices. Without the inverted bidding system, the buyers are still in a price-dictating situation. And perhaps most important, unless sellers are required by law to market through the system (or forced to pay for the cost of such a system whether they use it or not—in which case they probably will), the buyers will undercut its advantages by offering better prices on the traditional market until the electronic market is strangled.

But while all these strategies have their appeal, the compelling fact is that a strong dose of trust busting is needed in farm markets, both input and output. Most forms of vertical integration should be prohibited or much more carefully regulated to prevent noncompetitive pricing. Packers should not be allowed to feed cattle or hogs, either for themselves or as custom feeders for others.

284

Feed suppliers should not be allowed to own livestock feeding operations. The level of concentration that now dominates major grain and livestock markets cannot be tolerated, either. Federal agencies responsible for overseeing competition in the economy should act to prohibit mergers that reduce competition and to prevent misuses of market power. Without significant new commitments to break up such concentration of economic power, most efforts to remedy its negative effect in individual markets will not be very successful.

Guide Public Agricultural Research and Technology

Agricultural technology should be more deliberately selected for its impact on economic and environmental conditions. To do so, we will have to become more circumspect in our use of knowledge and more comfortable with regulating commercial applications of knowledge.

In conflicts between technology and the environment, the burden of proof must shift from those who want to protect the environment to those who want to use the technology. The rapid rate of change in agricultural technology and the sheer power of the technologies being developed make the need for restraint even greater because our capacity to correct mistakes diminishes with each new wave of faster, more potent technologies.

Unfortunately, changes in the institutional framework of agricultural research are moving us in precisely the opposite direction. Until recently, most farm research produced little by way of patentable property rights to attract investments from the private sector. Private companies gladly deferred to publicly supported universities to do agricultural research. As research became more product-oriented in the chemical and pharmaceutical age, private research became more prevalent, albeit only in those areas where proprietary rights to a product were expected to result.

With the advent of biotechnology, however, conditions have changed sharply. Passage of the Plant Variety Protection Act in 1970 for the first time made sexually reproducible plant life patentable. More recently, a landmark U.S. Supreme Court decision (*Diamond* v. *Chakrabarty*, in 1980) found that a patent could not be denied on an invention merely because it was alive. In effect, these decisions extend the concept of property to life itself. This convergence of legislative policy and judicial opinion has made agricultural research a commodity worth investing in.

The cutting edge of agricultural research is now largely in the field of biotechnology carried out by the private sector alone or in collaboration with public universities. There seems to be a nearly infinite variety of relationships between profit-motivated agribusiness companies and publicly supported universities and scientists. There are retainers and consultancies and contracts and grants and, more recently, complex joint ventures involving profit-making subsidiaries in the public sector.

Michigan State University, for example, has created Neogen, a venture-capital fund to market inventions that flow from university research. The university sells patents it receives to Neogen which musters private investors into limited partnerships to develop and market products derived from these patents. Neogen in turn gives the faculty-inventor either a 15 percent royalty or a stock option in Neogen (U.S. Congress 1986a). By offering faculty entrepreneurial research opportunities in the university, this arrangement, and similar ones in place in many public universities, is supposed to keep faculty from turning to the private sector for more lucrative jobs.

This privatization of publicly developed knowledge has serious policy implications extending far beyond the issue of appropriate uses of technology. Such private-public partnerships jeopardize the integrity of public research by creating conflicts of interest between the scientist's public duty and his or her private proprietary interests. Will publicly funded research be reported to the public in a timely manner if it might have patentable potential on which the scientist wishes to capitalize? Will projects that promise to expand knowledge without any obvious profit potential be shelved? If the mild case of grant leveraging in search of the high-fat hog diet (Chapter 8) seems alarming, imagine how much more compromised the priorities of the university would have been if the scientist had had a profit motive as well as a grantsmanship motive for conducting such research.

Inasmuch as universities are constantly in search of ways to expand their budgets, a conflict of interest is also created between the institution's public purpose to expand knowledge, and its own need to profit from the sale of knowledge. This conflict not only jeopardizes the integrity of scientific inquiry, but moves the university to put a price on all information the university has to sell, whether it has product potential or not.

The Office of Technology Assessment (U.S. Congress 1986a)

notes a growing tendency to make new agricultural information from public and private sources available to farmers primarily through closed computer information systems requiring investment in computer technology and/or a user fee to access. Less and less information is made available in printed form, and more and more of that has to be paid for as well. Specialized information services proliferate, but only the bigger farming operations can afford them. At the same time, basic information services for the work-a-day farmer atrophy. Corporations can set up consortiums with profit-motivated, publicly paid scientists, while small commercial farmers who formerly relied on publicly generated information now have to buy computers and pay for access.

These policies should change. Instead of yielding to the private interests of scientists and the institutional needs of their universities, public policy should be more assertive in shaping agricultural technology. Public funds should be used to monitor technical development, to anticipate adverse environmental and economic consequences, to prepare people to make intelligent choices about the use of technologies, and to protect the public from irresponsible products. Most important, public funds should be used to find appropriate problem-solving applications of technology such as those advanced by the Small Farm Resources Project and other appropriate technology groups. The more spent by the private sector on agricultural research, the heavier the burden on public research funds to protect the public interest in agricultural technology.

To shoulder this burden, agricultural universities have to be made more accountable for their conduct. Their relationship to profit-motivated companies should be carefully regulated and extra emphasis placed on disclosure of both scientific findings and financial dealings. Even where legitimate proprietary interests are established in a research program, that interest should be subject to audit by public agencies commissioned to protect the integrity of publicly funded research. They should be legally authorized by law to confiscate knowledge benefiting the public when the public has a legitimate claim. After all, if knowledge is going to achieve the status of property, then the public sometimes will have a compelling need to take that property by a process similar to the taking of private land for roads, buildings, and parks. In the case of some research, the public has already paid for the knowledge and has a right to it. Only an independent public audit agency can responsibly determine when the knowledge at issue belongs to the public or ought to be protected as private property. And the burden of proof should fall on those who claim that publicly funded research has produced a private property interest. Publicly paid scientists should not be in the business of generating trade secrets for private companies.

Far more public research resources should also be spent developing and refining our capacity to shape technology to our values. More effort should be placed on preventive science. Instead of learning how to measure the deterioration of water quality, for example, we ought to learn how to predict it and prevent it. For every public dollar spent developing new technologies, two should be spent anticipating their consequences. Environmental assessment is not the only preventive research needed, either. Agricultural research projects should be required to anticipate economic impacts as well, and to do more than an aggregate cost-benefit analysis justifying research on the basis of increased productivity alone. The economic impact analysis should anticipate how the distribution of wealth and income in our society might be affected by research developments, identify the winners and losers, and describe how the losers would be compensated for their loss.

But guiding the use of research funds is only a small part of what is needed to regain control of technology. Ultimately, we need to become more reserved in introducing technologies whose impacts are unknown. That means not only more regulation, but more effective regulation.

But regulation has its dangers, too. It can be a convenient way for elites to impose control without facing the responsibilities of living in a democracy. In fact, regulation can be the tool of those with the most to gain from requiring the use of certain technologies. In the worthy cause of food safety, for instance, our nation established national health standards for meat packing plants that required most to make significant remodeling investments, replacing wood with stainless steel throughout the plant. Practices that ensured sanitation without costly renovations could have been required instead. After all, you can clean wood, and you can leave stainless steel filthy. But the renovations were mandated, and most small town slaughtering facilities were simply forced out of business, and the meat industry was even more rapidly centralized.

Regulation can also be misused to validate environmentally damaging practices by setting limits on them without correcting them. The government can set acceptable risk levels that control the immediate impact of a technology while ignoring its long-term, cumulative impact. The purest example is pesticide regulation. The federal government sets tolerable limits on the amount of cancer-causing pesticide residue on food we eat, but generally ignores the deterioration of our drinking water from farm chemical pollution. Industrial agribusinesses thrive on such regulation because it validates their practices.

Sometimes, regulation can actually usher in the use of environmentally dangerous farm practices. For example, some irrigators mix fertilizer and pesticides with water and apply it to their fields through sprinkler irrigation systems—a practice called chemigation. In Nebraska, they are required to register with the state and use the latest technology to prevent their water wells from malfunctioning, reversing the water flow and pumping chemicals directly into the groundwater. In return for registering and using these protective technologies, chemigators are granted immunity from lawsuits by anyone who might be damaged if the protective system fails. This kind of regulation only benefits industrial agribusiness by accommodating the dangerous technologies it uses.

Perhaps most serious, agricultural regulation has been zealous on the inconsequential and timid on the vital. A few years ago, the federal Occupational Safety and Health Administration tried to impose a bizarre array of safety standards on farms, including such earnest measures as requiring signs in barns warning that the manure on the floor might be slippery! Outrage and ridicule spewed forth, of course, and a big political fight ensued, which the bureaucrats generally lost. By contrast, the most basic worker safety and health measure in our society—coverage under workers' compensation laws—is not yet available to agricultural workers in most states (Higby 1984). Employees of most industrial agribusinesses aren't protected.

In short, regulation can be almost as dangerous to family farming as industrial technologies. Better regulation, not less regulation is needed. Here, public agricultural universities have a great contribution to make. Regulatory science should be part of the teaching curriculum at public agricultural universities, with emphasis on finding the best ways to ensure that those who use environmentally dangerous technologies pay the costs of the damage they do and of the regulation they require. Currently, government regulation is treated as a pariah in most agricultural classrooms. In general, it is portrayed as an obstacle to research and a nuisance to progressive farmers. In fact, regulatory policy should be elevated to an esteemed interdisciplinary field, drawing on science, law, and ethics.

Ultimately, however, only an informed and alert public can defend itself against the misuse of either technologies or regulations. Beyond regulation lies the greater challenge of education.

Unfortunately, the more technical our world becomes, the less we do to educate the general public about the implications of technical changes. Most public agricultural universities emulate private universities in focusing on programs and curricula that educate the best and the brightest to the limit of their capacity. Increasingly, they impose tougher entrance requirements, reduce their presence in rural areas, erect barriers to nontraditional students who are older or employed, are jealous of funding for community colleges, and rely more on telecommunications to centralize and standardize curricula. Critical thinking skills are ignored while technical training is accelerated. Training, not education, has become their business. This parallels the quest for private-public commercial partnerships.

Better to focus on the broader educational needs of society to understand technology than to train only the brightest to use it. Instead of private-public partnerships that corrupt the research process, why not public-public relationships between agricultural universities and local public schools in which the universities help students grasp the meaning of technologies and the alternative paths to technical development?

Finally, the research programs of agricultural universities themselves need to be reassessed. Some discoveries may not be worth making if they depend on the use of scarce public research funds. We don't need technologies that increase milk production by a third, though it might be commercially attractive to develop such technologies. Those scarce public research funds would be better spent finding ways to make dairy farming more profitable and less polluting by reducing the resources it consumes.

Agricultural research has largely unexplored potential for taking into account the needs of the whole farm, its people and its natural endowments. But to do so, it will have to consider sometimes competing social goals. If agricultural research could be forced to confront such conflicts, it could develop appropriate alternatives to the high technology that industrial agribusiness finds so appealing.

References

Ahearn, Mary. 1986. *Financial Well-Being of Farm Operators and Their Households.* National Economics Division, Economic Research Service, USDA, Agricultural Economic Report no. 563. Washington, D.C.

Akagi, Roy Hidemichi. 1963. *The Town Proprietors of the New England Colonies.* Gloucester, Mass.: Peter Smith.

American Agriculture. 1977. *Agricultural Strike* (flyer). Elwood, Nebr.: American Agriculture of Nebraska.

Anthan, George. 1982. "Packers May Control Own Feedlots." *Des Moines Register,* May 26, p. 1.

Anthan, George, and John Hyde. 1985. "Foreign, Corporate Farmland Buyers Vital, Knapp Says." *Des Moines Register,* June 24, p. 14A.

Aspelin, Arnold, and Gerald Engelman. 1966. *Packer Feeding of Cattle: Its Volume and Significance.* Packers and Stockyards Division, USDA, Marketing Research Report no. 776. Washington, D.C.

Associated Press. 1986a. "Big Operators Reaping Farm Subsidies." *Lincoln Star,* July 25, p. 1.

———. 1986b. "Diversified Farm Now Recommended." *Lincoln Star,* October 30.

———. 1986c. "Neighbors Fear Hog Project Near Pierre Would Raise Stink." *Omaha World Herald,* October 8.

Bailey, Elizabeth E., and Ann F. Friedlaender. 1982. "Market Structure and Multiproduct Industries." *Journal of Economic Literature* 20:1024–48.

Baker, Maurice, Michael Lundeen, Bruce Johnson, and J. David Aiken. 1986. *Land Ownership by Financial Institutions.* Corporate Farming in Nebraska, Report no. 7. Department of Agricultural Economics, University of Nebraska, Lincoln.

Banks, Vera J. 1984. *Farm Population Trends by Farm Characteristics, 1975–80.* Economic Development Division, Economic Research Service, USDA, Rural Development Research Report no. 40. Washington, D.C.

Baron, Donald. 1981. *Landownership Characteristics and Investment in Soil Conservation.* Economics and Statistics Service, USDA, Staff Report no. AGES 810911. Washington, D.C.

Barten, Amos, Jr. 1985. "Forced Off Land." Letter to the Editor, *Omaha World Herald,* exact date unknown.

Bidwell, Percy Wells, and John I. Falconer. 1925. History of Agriculture in the Northern United States, 1620–1860. Carnegie Institution. Washington, D.C.

Bitney, Larry L. et al. 1977. *Estimated Crop and Livestock Production Costs: Nebraska.* Cooperative Extension Service, Bulletin no. 72. University of Nebraska–Lincoln.

Blair, Aaron. 1982. "Cancer Risks Associated with Agriculture: Epidemiologic Evidence." In *Genetic Toxicology: An Agricultural Perspecive,* ed. by Raymond F. Fleck and Alexander Hollaender. New York: Plenum Publishing Corp.

Blaylock, James R., and David M. Smallwood. 1986. *U.S. Demand for Food: Household Expenditures, Demographics, and Projections.* Economic Research Service, USDA, Technical Bulletin no. 1713. Washington, D.C.

Bonnen, James T. 1968. "The Distribution of Benefits from Selected U.S. Farm Programs." In *Rural Poverty in the United States: A Report by the President's National Advisory Commission on Rural Poverty,* 461–505. Washington, D.C.

Brown, Lester R., with Erik P. Eckholm. 1974. *By Bread Alone.* Published for the Overseas Development Council. New York: Praeger Publishers.

Bullard, Charles. 1986. "Half of Cities' Water Tainted by Pesticides." *Des Moines Register,* exact date unknown.

Busch, Lawrence, William B. Lacey, and Carolyn Sachs. 1980. *Research Policy and Process in the Agricultural Sciences: Some Results from a National Study.* Agricultural Experiment Station, Department of Sociology, Research Study no. 66. University of Kentucky, Lexington.

292

Campbell, Bob. 1986. "Whiff of Trouble: Pig Farms Anger Neighbors." *Detroit Free Press,* September 1, p. 1.

Center for Rural Affairs. 1976. *Wheels of Fortune: A Report on the Impact of Center Pivot Irrigation on the Ownership of Land in Nebraska.* Walthill, Nebr.: Center for Rural Affairs.

———. 1979. "Bob Bergland Speaks Out . . . But What Does He Mean?" *New Land Review* (Spring): 6.

———. 1980. *Small Farm Energy Project: Final Report.* Walthill, Nebr.: Center for Rural Affairs.

———. 1982. "Reducing Tillage Operations: Successful No Chemical-Minimum Tillage Program." *Small Farm Energy,* Bulletin no. 35 (March–April).

———. 1985. "The Farm and Food Security Act." MS. Walthill, Nebr.

Cochrane, Willard W. 1979. *The Development of American Agriculture: A Historical Analysis.* Minneapolis: University of Minnesota Press.

Congressional Budget Office. 1985. *Diversity in Crop Farming: Its Meaning for Income-Support Policy.* Congress of the United States, Special Study. Washington, D.C.

Daugherty, Arthur B., and Robert C. Otte. 1983. *Farmland Ownership in the United States.* Economic Research Service, USDA, no. AGES 830311. Washington, D.C.

Dickens, Charles. 1983. "A Christmas Carol." In *The Complete Ghost Stories of Charles Dickens,* ed. by Peter Haining. New York: Franklin Watts.

Dorr, Robert. 1986. "Idled Center-Pivot Land Earning Top Dollar." *Omaha World Herald,* October 19, p. 1.

Dorr, Robert, and James Allen Flanery. 1985. "Big Loans, Zealous Lenders Blamed for PCA Failures." *Omaha World Herald,* November 24, p.1.

Eichers, Theodore R. 1980. *The Farm Pesticide Industry.* Economics, Statistics, and Cooperative Service, USDA, Agricultural Economic Report no. 461. Washington, D.C.

Emerson, Peter M. 1978. *Public Policy and the Changing Structure of American Agriculture.* Congressional Budget Office, Congress of the United States. Washington, D.C.

Ervin, David E. 1982. "Soil Erosion Control on Owner-Operated and Renter Cropland." *Journal of Soil and Water Conservation* 37 (5): 285–88.

Fiechter, Jonathan L. 1985. Statement before Committee on

Banking, Finance, and Urban Affairs, U.S. House of Representatives, by Jonathan L. Fiechter, Director for Economic and Policy Analysis, Office of the Comptroller of the Currency, March 20, 1985. MS.

Frost, Robert. 1962. *Complete Poems of Robert Frost.* New York: Holt, Rinehart, and Winston.

Fruhling, Larry. 1987. "Farm Managers Multiply as Farmers Fail." *Des Moines Sunday Register,* Feb. 1, p. 12V.

Gauger, Jeff. 1986. "Breeders Stress Natural Red Meat." *Omaha World Herald,* December 7.

General Accounting Office. 1982. *Tobacco Program's Production Rights and Effects on Competition.* Comptroller General of the United States, CED-82–70. Washington, D.C.

Gersten, Alan. 1986. "Report: 100 Nebraska Banks May Close." *Omaha World Herald,* June 5.

Gever, John, Robert Kaufmann, David Skole, and Charles Vörösmarty. 1986. *Beyond Oil: The Threat to Food and Fuel in the Coming Decades.* Complex Systems Research Center, University of New Hampshire. A Project of Carrying Capacity, Inc. Cambridge, Mass.: Ballinger Publishing.

Goldschmidt, Walter. 1978. *As You Sow: Three Studies in the Social Consequences of Agribusiness.* Montclair, N. J.: Allanheld, Osmun & Co.

Green, Constance McL. 1956. *Eli Whitney and the Birth of American Technology.* Boston: Little, Brown & Co.

Guither, Harold, ed. 1972. *Who Will Control U.S. Agriculture?* Cooperative Extension Service, North Central Regional Extension Publication 32, Special Publication no. 27. University of Illinois at Urbana–Champaign.

———. 1973. *Who Will Control U.S. Agriculture?* Cooperative Extension Service, North Central Regional Extension Publications 32–1 through 32–6, Special Publication no. 28. Cooperative Extension Service, University of Illinois at Urbana–Champaign.

Hall, B. F., and E. P. LeVeen. 1978. "Farm Size and Economic Efficiency: The Case of California." *American Journal of Agricultural Economics* 60:575–88.

Haney, Wava G., Margaret Krome, and G. W. Stevenson. 1986. *Sustainable Agriculture Research Sourcebook: A Compilation of Current Activities on Sustainable Agriculture at U.S. Universities.* Black Earth, Wis.: Wisconsin Rural Development Center.

Harrington, David H. and Jerome M. Stam. 1985. The Current Financial Condition of Farmers and Farm Lenders. Economic Research Service, USDA, Agriculture Information Bulletin no. 490. Washington, D.C.

Harrington, David H., Donn A. Reimund, Kenneth H. Baum, and R. Neal Peterson. 1983. *U.S. Farming in the Early 1980's: Production and Financial Structure*. Economic Research Service, USDA, Agricultural Economic Report no. 504. Washington, D.C.

Heid, Walter G., Jr. 1981. *The Young Solar Collector: An Evaluation of Its Multiple Farm Uses*. National Economics Division, Economics and Statistics Service, USDA, Agricultural Economic Report no. 466. Washington, D.C.

Heinlein, Gary. 1985. "Study Finds Growing Risks in Farming." *Des Moines Register,* June 14.

Higby, Annette. 1984. "Official (Un)Concern about Farm Health." In *It's Not All Sunshine and Fresh Air: Chronic Health Effects of Modern Farming Practices,* ed. by Marty Strange, 77–103. Walthill, Nebr.: Center for Rural Affairs.

Hightower, Jim. 1972. *Hard Tomatoes, Hard Times: The Failure of the Land Grant College Complex*. Washington, D.C.: Agribusiness Accountability Project.

Hofstadter, Richard. 1955. *The Age of Reform*. New York: Vintage.

Holland, David. n.d. *Production Efficiency and Economies of Size in Agriculture*. Department of Agricultural Economics, Scientific Paper no. 5266. Prepared for the National Rural Center. Washington State University, Pullman.

Huggett, Frank E. 1975. *The Land Question and European Society since 1650*. New York: Harcourt Brace Jovanovich.

Hughes, Dean, and Stephen Gabriel, Ronald Meekhof, Michael Boehlje, David Reinders, and George Amols. 1981. *National Agricultural Credit Study. Financing the Farm Sector in the 1980's: Aggregate Needs and the Roles of Public and Private Institutions*. Economics and Statistics Service, USDA, Staff Report no. AGES810413. Washington, D.C.

Hullinger, Ronald L. 1986. "Lifetime Land Leases: Why We Need a National Trust for Our Farmland." *Agri Finance* (May–June).

Johnson, Bruce B. 1983. "The Status of Family Farming in Nebraska." *Farm, Ranch, and Home Quarterly* (Spring/Summer): 23, 24. Institute of Agriculture and Natural Resources, University of Nebraska–Lincoln.

Johnson, Ralph D. 1972. *An Economic Evaluation of Alternative Mar-*

keting Methods for Fed Cattle. Nebraska Agricultural Experiment Station cooperating with Economic Research Service, USDA, Bulletin no. SB 520. University of Nebraska–Lincoln.

Johnston, Gene. 1984. "Mid-Cost Hog System Shows Most Profits." *Successful Farming* (November): H6–H7.

Johnston, W. E. 1972. "Economies of Size and the Spatial Distribution of Land in Farming Units." *American Journal of Agricultural Economics* 54:654–56.

Jose, H. Douglas et al. 1983. *Estimated Crop and Livestock Production Costs: Nebraska.* Cooperative Extension Service, Bulletin no. EC 83-872. University of Nebraska–Lincoln.

Knight–Ridder. 1986. "Farmers Dividing Up Land on Paper to Qualify for More Subsidies." *Omaha World Herald,* September 29, p. 11.

Krenz, R. D., W. G. Heid, and H. Sitler. 1974. *Economies of Large Scale Wheat Farms in the Great Plains.* Economic Research Service, USDA, Agricultural Economic Report no. 264. Washington, D.C.

Lappé, Marc. 1982. *Germs That Won't Die: Medical Consequences of the Misuse of Antibiotics.* Garden City, N.Y.: Anchor Press / Doubleday.

Leath, Mark N., Lynn H. Meyer, and Lowell D. Hill. 1982. *U.S. Corn Industry.* National Economics Division, Economic Research Service, USDA, Agricultural Economic Report no. 479. Washington, D.C.

Leibenluft, Robert F. 1981. *Competition in Farm Inputs: An Examination of Four Industries.* Federal Trade Commission, Policy Planning Issues Paper. Washington, D.C.

Lin, William, George Coffman, and J. B. Penn. 1980. *U.S. Farm Numbers, Sizes, and Related Structural Dimensions: Projections to Year 2000.* USDA, Technical Bulletin no. 1625. Washington, D.C.

Lins, David, and Peter Barry. 1980. "Availability of Financial Capital as a Factor of Structural Change in the U.S. Farm Production Sector." In *Farm Structure: A Historical Perspective on Changes in the Number and Size of Farms.* Committee on Agriculture, Nutrition, and Forestry, United States Senate. 96th Cong., 2d sess., Doc. no. 56-2140. Washington, D.C.

Locke, John. 1821. *Two Treatises on Government.* London.

Lockeridge, Kenneth A. 1970. *A New England Town: The First Hundred Years.* New York: W. W. Norton.

Looker, Dan. 1985. "Weeds Battle Eroding Winds on Abandoned Sandhills Fields." *Lincoln Star,* June 15, p. 1.

Lucas, R. E., J. B. Holtman, and L. J. Connor. 1977. "Soil Carbon Dynamics and Cropping Practices." In *Agriculture and Energy,* ed. by William Lockeretz. New York: Academic Press.

MacCannell, Dean. n.d. "Agribusiness and the Small Community." MS. University of California–Davis.

McGough, Robert. 1985. "A Modest Proposal." *Forbes* (September 23): 50.

Madden, J. Patrick. 1967. *Economies of Size in Farming.* Economic Research Service, USDA, Agricultural Economic Report no. 107. Washington, D.C.

Marshall, William E. 1986. "Objectives and Strategies, Profitability and Productivity." Speech to Minnesota Senate Counsel and Research Seminar on Minnesota's Rural Economic Crisis: Challenge for the Future, St. Paul, Minnesota, February 6, 1986.

Massachusetts Department of Food and Agriculture. 1985. *Massachusetts Agriculture: Annual Report.* Boston.

Miller, Steve, and Hal Harris. n.d. *Monopsony Power in Commodity Procurement: The Case of Slaughter Hogs.* Clemson University, South Carolina. MS.

Miller, Thomas A. 1974. *Estimating the Income Supplement in Farm Program Payments.* Economic Research Service, USDA, in cooperation with Colorado State University, Economic Research Service Technical Report no. 1492. Washington, D.C.

———. 1979. "Economies of Size and Other Growth Incentives." In *Structure Issues Of American Agriculture.* Economics and Statistics Service, USDA, Agricultural Economics Report no. 438:108–15. Washington, D.C.

Mobley, Earl. 1984. *Relating Capital and Production Management in Pork Production.* Paper for the American Pork Congress, March 6–9. Cooperative Extension Service, no. 10 (EDM) 1359. Iowa State University, Ames.

Moore, C. V. 1965. *Economies Associated with Size, Fresno County Cotton Farms.* Giannini Foundation Research Report no. 285. University of California–Davis.

Moser, Bobby, Dean Boyd, and Wayne R. Cast. 1978. "Piglet Survival." *Nebraska Swine Report.* E.C. 78–219, University of Nebraska–Lincoln.

Muhm, Don. 1987. "Massachusetts Works at Saving Farms." *Des Moines Sunday Register,* May 3, p. 2F.

Murray, Mary. 1985. "Nitrate Contamination Growing at Alarming Rate." *Des Moines Register,* October 14.

National Association of Conservation Districts. 1980. "Soil Degradation: Effects on Agricultural Productivity." In *National Agricultural Lands Study*. Interim Report no. 4. Washington, D.C.

National Research Council. 1972. *Report of the Committee on Research Advisory to the U.S. Department of Agriculture*. U.S. National Academy of Sciences. Washington, D.C.

Nebraska Department of Agriculture. 1972–82. *Nebraska Agricultural Statistics*. Nebraska Crop and Livestock Reporting Service, Annual Reports, Lincoln, Nebr.

Nebraska Department of Environmental Control. 1985. *Nebraska Ground Water Quality Protection Strategy: Final Report*. Lincoln, Nebr.

Nelson, Aaron G., and William G. Murray. 1967. *Agricultural Finance*, 5th ed. Ames: Iowa State University Press.

Northdurft, William E. 1986. *Going to Market: The New Aggressiveness in State Domestic Agricultural Marketing*. Council of State Policy and Planning Agencies. Washington, D.C.

Padover, Saul K. 1939. *Thomas Jefferson on Democracy*. New York: D. Appleton–Century.

Painter, Sidney. 1951. *Mediaeval Society*. Ithaca, N.Y.: Cornell University Press.

Panzar, John C., and Robert D. Willig. 1975. "Economies of Scale and Economies of Scope in Multi-Output Production." Econ. Discussion Paper 33, Bell Labs.

———. 1981. "Economies of Scope." *American Economic Review* 71(2): 268–72.

Plaxico, James S. 1984. "Farm Size, Production Costs, and Profits: A Survey of Current Knowledge." Agricultural Economics Paper no. AE 8494, Oklahoma State University, presented at the Texas Farm Forum, Austin, Texas, September 13–14.

Price, Charlene C., and Judy Brown. 1984. *Growth in the Health and Natural Foods Industry*. National Economics Division, USDA, Economic Research Service Staff Report no. AGES840501. Washington, D.C.

Quail, Gwen, Bruce Marion, Frederick Geithman, and Jeffrey Marquardt. 1986. *The Impact of Packer Buyer Concentration on Live Cattle Prices*. North Central Regional Extension Project 117, Working Paper no. 89. University of Wisconsin, Madison.

Ragsdale, Jim. 1986. "Pollution Report Cites Fertilizer Use." *St. Paul Pioneer Press Dispatch,* October 29, p. 1.

Reinsel, Robert D., and Ronald D. Krenz. 1972. *Capitalization of Farm Program Benefits into Land Values*. USDA, Economic Research Service Report no. 506. Washington, D.C.

Ricardo, David. 1817. *Principles of Political Economy and Taxation.* Homewood, Ill.: Richard D. Irwin. 1963.

Ruttan, Vernon W. 1982. *Agricultural Research Policy.* Minneapolis: University of Minnesota Press.

Salamon, Sonya. 1985. "Ethnic Communities and the Structure of Agriculture." *Rural Sociology* 50(3): 323–40.

Sampson, R. Neil. 1981. *Farmland or Wasteland: A Time to Choose.* Emmaus, Penn.: Rodale Press.

Schaefer, Ed. 1978. *Changing Character and Structure of American Agriculture: An Overview.* U.S. General Accounting Office, Community and Economic Development Division no. 78–178. Washington, D.C.

Schickele, Rainer. 1954. *Agricultural Policy: Farm Programs and National Welfare.* Lincoln: University of Nebraska Press.

Shaner, W. W., P. F. Philipp, and W. R. Schmehl. 1982. *Farming Systems Research and Development: Guidelines for Developing Countries.* Boulder, Colo.: Westview Press.

Sheffield, Leslie F. 1984. "Economic Impacts of Irrigation in Nebraska." Fortieth Annual Meeting of the Nebraska Water Resources Association, Lincoln, Nebraska, June 4–5.

Skolda, David. 1983. "America's Top 200,000: An Eye-Opener for Washington." *Farm Futures* (February): 32–34.

Sloggett, Gordon. 1981. *Prospects for Ground-Water Irrigation: Declining Levels and Rising Energy Costs.* Natural Resource Economics Division, Economic Research Service, USDA, Agricultural Economic Report no. 478. Washington, D.C.

Smith, Preston. 1987. "The 400 Largest Farms in the U.S." *Successful Farming* (March).

Stansberry, Jan. 1986. Interview with author, Nebraska Department of Health, November 25.

Stone, Larry. 1986. "Study: 25% of Iowans Drink Tainted Water." *Des Moines Register,* July 30.

Strange, Martin Douglas. 1982. *Structural Impacts of the Farm Program Payment Limitation.* Masters Thesis. Agricultural Economics Department, University of Missouri, Columbia.

Strange, Marty. 1983. "The Corn Glut." *Prairie Sentinel* 2(2). Walthill, Nebr.: Center for Rural Affairs.

Strange, Marty et al. 1982. *The Path Not Taken: A Case Study of Agricultural Research Decision-Making at the Animal Science Department of the University of Nebraska.* Walthill, Nebr.: Center for Rural Affairs.

Swanson, Larry D. 1980. "A Study in Socioeconomic Development: Changing Farm Structure and Rural Community Decline in the Context of the Technological Transformation of American Agriculture." Ph.D. diss. Economics Department, University of Nebraska–Lincoln.

Thomas, Fred. 1986. "Volatile Organic Compounds Show Up in Drinking Water of 45 Nebraska Towns." *Omaha World Herald,* April 4.

Thornton, Tamara Plankins. 1986. "Between Generations: Boston Agricultural Reform and the Aging of New England, 1815–1830." *The New England Quarterly,* 59(2): 189–211.

Tweeten, Luther. 1983. "The Economics of Small Farms." *Science* 219: 1037–41.

———. 1984. "Excess Farm Supply: Permanent or Transitory?" In *Farm Policy Perspectives: Setting the Stage for 1985 Agricultural Legislation.* Committee on Agriculture, Nutrition, and Forestry, U.S. Senate, 98th Cong., 2nd sess., Senate Print no. 98–174. Washington, D.C.

U.S. Bureau of the Census. 1982. *1979 Farm Finance Survey Census of Agriculture.* Vol. 5. Special Reports, Part 6, AC78-SR-6. Washington, D.C.

———. 1984. *1982 Census of Agriculture.* Washington, D.C.

U.S. Bureau of the Census, jointly with USDA. 1983. *Farm Population of the United States: 1982.* Current Population Reports, Series P-27, no. 56. Washington, D.C.

U.S. Central Intelligence Agency. 1976. *A Study of Climatological Research as It Pertains to Intelligence Problems.* Office of Research and Development. Washington, D.C.

U.S. Congress. 1986a. *Technology, Public Policy, and the Changing Structure of American Agriculture.* Office of Technology Assessment, OTA-F-285. Washington, D.C.

———. 1986b. *Technology, Public Policy, and the Changing Structure of Agriculture: Volume 2—Background Papers, Part D: Rural Communities.* Office of Technology Assessment, OTA-F-285. Washington, D.C.

U.S. Department of Agriculture. 1976–86. *Farm Real Estate Market Developments.* Economic Research Service. Washington, D.C.

———. 1979a. *Concentration in the Meat Packing Industry—National and Local Procurement Levels.* Agricultural Marketing Service, Packers and Stockyards Administration, Presented to Committee on Small Business, U.S. House of Representatives, 96th Cong., 1st sess., September 24. Washington, D.C.

―――. 1979b. *Structure Issues Of American Agriculture*. Economics, Statistics, and Cooperative Service, Agricultural Economic Report no. 438. Washington, D.C.

―――. 1981. *A Time to Choose: Summary Report on the Structure of Agriculture*. Washington, D.C.

―――. 1982–86. *Farm Labor*. Crop Reporting Board, Statistical Reporting Service. Washington, D.C.

―――. 1984a. *Background for 1985 Farm Legislation*. Economic Research Service, Agriculture Information Bulletin nos. 465–78 (separate reports for barley, corn, cotton, dairy, honey, peanuts, rice, oats, sorghum, soybeans, sugar, tobacco, wheat, wool, and mohair). Washington, D.C.

―――. 1984b. *World Indices of Agricultural and Food Production, 1974–83*. International Economics Division, Economic Research Service, Statistical Bulletin no. 710. Washington, D. C.

―――. 1986. *Agricultural Resources: Agricultural Land Values and Markets*. Economic Research Service, AR-2. Washington, D.C.

―――. 1987. *Economic Indicators of the Farm Sector: National Financial Summary, 1985*. National Economics Division, Economic Research Service, ECIFA 4-3. Washington, D.C.

U.S. National Academy of Sciences. 1972. *Genetic Vulnerability of Major Crops*. Washington, D.C.

U.S. Senate. 1984. *The Distribution of Benefits from the 1982 Federal Crop Programs*. Committee on the Budget, 98th Cong., 2d sess., Senate Print 98–238. Washington, D.C.

Wisner, Robert N., and Craig A. Chase. 1984. *World Food Trade and U.S. Agriculture, 1960–1983*. World Food Institute, Iowa State University, Ames.

Index

Accelerated depreciation, 149–50, 155, 161, 163–64
Agrarian myth, 239–44
Agricultural development: U.S. compared with other nations, 26, 212–15, 222
Agricultural policy. *See* Public policy
Agriculture: Bob Bergland's legacy to, 59–60; despair in, 233; development of, 26, 212–15, 222; dynamics of change in, 40–42, 75–76, 200; environmental threat from, 42; future of, 31; human values in, 16, 238–53; inequities in, 200, 245–47, 266–69; leadership in, 10, 238; macroeconomic effect on, 251; in Massachusetts, 232; pioneers in, 237; prevailing myths in, 5; reform of, 262–90; regulation of, 198–99; structure of, 56–77; sustainable, 209, 233–37; traditional values in, 231–37
American Agriculture Movement (AAM), 22, 58–60, 77, 138–39
Appropriate technology: abuse of, 230–31; cultural nature of, 228–29; debate over, 212; need for,

223; site specific, 225, 227; and Small Farm Energy Project, 225–29; technical criteria for, 229
Attrition, policy of, 5, 166–67, 176, 242, 243

Bergland, Bob, 59–60, 77
Bigness: myth surrounding, 6, 78–103, 109–10, 122–23, 127, 166, 211–12, 236; and promotion of capital investment, 262; public bias for, 85. *See also* Large farms
Borrowers, interests of, 256–57
Broiler and egg production, 52, 281–82
Butz, Earl, 18

Capital, 37, 107–9, 125–26, 262–64
Capital gain: lure of nonfarm investors by, 259; taxation of, 21, 48, 149, 155, 197, 275
Capital investment, 90, 92, 147, 249, 263
Capitalization of farm-program benefits, 133–34
Cash accounting, 148–49, 152–54, 163–64

IBP, 281

Income: and commodity prices, 176–77; considerations for farm programs, 134, 271; distribution of, 57, 62–63, 189–91, 191–92; farmers' use of, 46–47, 190, 191–93; impact of energy conservation practices on, 226; impact of technology on, 179–80; as residual return, 191; supplementation of, 66, 130; variability of by farm size, 116; versus cheap food, 166

Incorporation, 150–52

Industrial agribusiness, 36–39; and rural communities, 86–87; effectiveness of sales-size criteria in, 69; efficiency of, 77–80, 121; farm ownership in, 126; farm policy and, 262; food production by, 40–41; furthered by commodity price supports, 200; influence on research priorities of, 216–20; management options in, 112; myth of, 36, 121–22; politics of, 4–5, 52–55; promoters and apologists for, 39, 123; risk in, 115–16; role of technology in, 7, 89, 202–6; and stewardship of natural resources, 42; tax features fostering, 148–50; types of capital investment made by, 204; vision of, 29–30, 80, 208, 252; values of, 244. *See also* Large farms; Efficiency; Bigness

Inheritance, 50–51; taxes, 54–55, 274–75

Input: industries, 180, 181–82, 279–85; prices, 177–80, 182–83; borrowed money as, 112, 178–80

Inputs to farming: changing with industrialization, 177–78; conservation of, 223; in the efficiency equation, 91–92, 94; purchased, 37, 178–80; in quota system, 265;

and technological development, 213

Interest rates, 19, 25, 26, 119–20, 188, 257

Inverted bidding system, 284

Investment tax credit, 149, 156, 157–58

Investors, nonfarm, 49, 152–53, 259, 276

Iowa, 97–99, 203

Irrigation development, 117–21, 160–61, 263

Jefferson, Thomas, 35, 135, 240–41, 274

Johnson, Bruce B., 72

Kalter, Robert, 223–24

Labor: "freeing" of agricultural, 47; imputed cost of, 89–90, 190; in an industrial agribusiness system, 37, 41; need for in agriculture, 125–26, 221; in structure of agriculture analysis, 72; and technological development, 213–14

Land: accessibility of, 135–37, 213–14; competition for, 132–34; critical questions surrounding, 5; farmer's cost of, 109–10, 185, 187–88; foreclosure policies, 256–59; in the historical development of agriculture, 43–51, 169; lender inventory of, 258; as an investment, 48, 49; paying for by farming, 275; as a production input, 47; redistribution of, 261; as residual claimant, 185–89; right to development of, 277; rising equity in (1970s), 197; stewardship of, 9, 42, 160–61, 248

Land boom. *See* Economic boom

Land ethic, 249

Land market, 48, 198–99, 273–79